NATIONAL GEOGRAPHIC
KIDS™

THE ULTIMATE DINO-PEDIA

NATIONAL GEOGRAPHIC

NATIONAL GEOGRAPHIC
KIDS

THE ULTIMATE

DINO-PEDIA

THE MOST COMPLETE DINOSAUR REFERENCE EVER

BY "DINO" DON LESSEM
ILLUSTRATED BY FRANCO TEMPESTA
WITH A FOREWORD BY DR. RODOLFO CORIA

NATIONAL GEOGRAPHIC

Washington, D.C.

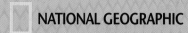

TABLE OF CONTENTS

ARGENTINE PALEONTOLOGIST DR. RODOLFO CORIA
WITH THE BACKBONES HE EXCAVATED OF ARGENTINO-
SAURUS, THE WORLD'S LARGEST DINOSAUR.

No other group of animals has triggered the curiosity and interest of as many people as dinosaurs have.

No matter the age, gender, or nationality of the reader, the evolution and diversity of these kings of the Mesozoic era evoke wonder and fascination.

Dinosaurs have been brought back to life in our dreams, schools, museums, and theaters. The last decades have witnessed a virtual tsunami of new discoveries all over the world, and currently, no continent exists without at least one example of these ancient inhabitants.

Welcome to *The Ultimate Dinopedia*. I hope that by learning about dinosaurs, you will be led to a fresh appreciation of your own existence. After all, just like dinosaurs more than 65 million years ago, we all are on board the same, gigantic spaceship called Earth.

Rodolfo Coria, paleontologist
Plaza Huincul, Argentina

Welcome to the wonderful world of dinosaurs. Some of what you read here will be news to you, even if you know a lot about dinosaurs. That's because we are lucky to live in the best time ever for dinosaur discovery.

Just in the last few years we've learned about so many strange new kinds of dinosaurs: dinosaurs that lived in holes, dinosaurs that climbed trees, dinosaurs smaller than robins, and lots more.

We've found dinosaurs in places we had never found them before, from the Arctic to the jungle. And we've even found answers to questions we never thought could be answered, such as what color some dinosaurs were. We know much more about how dinosaurs behaved, how they evolved, and how they are related.

"DINO" DON HOLDS A LIVE RAPTOR, A GOLDEN EAGLE IN MONGOLIA.

We've put the coolest dinosaur discoveries we could find in *The Ultimate Dinopedia* and profiled many of the ones you know best and least, complete with beautiful paintings by dinosaur artist Franco Tempesta. This is the most complete encyclopedia yet of dinosaurs, including what they ate, where they lived, what fossils of them we've found, and where. So, please, keep digging dinosaurs!

"Dino" Don Lessem

Philadelphia, Pennsylvania

HOW TO USE
THIS BOOK

This book is full of information about dinosaurs. Here you will learn about all of the elements that make up each page and how they help you learn about these amazing animals.

This book is divided into four sections: Discovering Dinosaurs, a collection of spreads that gives general information about dinosaurs; Meat Eaters and Plant Eaters, sections that contain profiles of all the best-known dinosaurs; and the Dinosaur Dictionary, a section that lists a fact box for almost every dinosaur ever discovered.

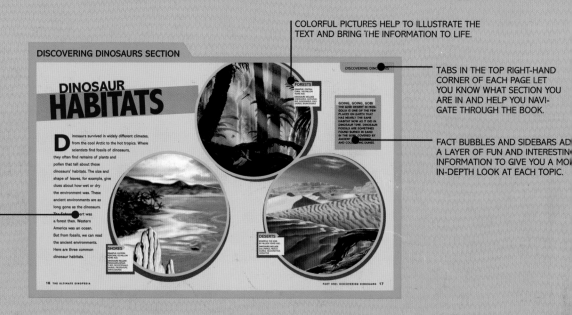

COLORFUL PICTURES HELP TO ILLUSTRATE THE TEXT AND BRING THE INFORMATION TO LIFE.

DISCOVERING DINOSAURS SECTION

DISCOVERING DINOSAURS

TABS IN THE TOP RIGHT-HAND CORNER OF EACH PAGE LET YOU KNOW WHAT SECTION YOU ARE IN AND HELP YOU NAVIGATE THROUGH THE BOOK.

FACT BUBBLES AND SIDEBARS ADD A LAYER OF FUN AND INTERESTING INFORMATION TO GIVE YOU A MORE IN-DEPTH LOOK AT EACH TOPIC.

THE TEXT PROVIDES THE BASIC INFORMATION YOU NEED TO UNDERSTAND THE TOPIC BEING DISCUSSED.

THE NAME OF EACH DINOSAUR APPEARS CLEARLY AT THE TOP OF EACH PAGE, AND A PRONUNCIATION GUIDE HELPS YOU SOUND OUT EACH DINOSAUR NAME.

THE TABS IN THE TOP RIGHT-HAND CORNER OF EACH PROFILE PAGE HELP YOU NAVIGATE THROUGH THE BOOK. THE TAB ON THE LEFT TELLS YOU WHICH FAMILY GROUP A DINOSAUR BELONGS TO. THE TAB ON THE RIGHT TELLS YOU WHICH SECTION YOU ARE IN.

FACT BOXES PROVIDE AT-A-GLANCE INFORMATION ABOUT EACH DINOSAUR. EACH BOX INCLUDES THE DINOSAUR'S NAME AND ITS MEANING, WHEN IT LIVED (PERIOD), WHERE IT WAS FOUND, FOSSILS THAT HAVE BEEN DISCOVERED, AND ITS SIZE, MEASURED IN LENGTH.

THE DINOSAUR COMPARISON KEY SHOWS YOU HOW BIG DINOSAURS WERE COMPARED TO A KID 4 FEET, 6 INCHES (1.4 M) TALL.

AN INTRODUCTION TO EACH DINOSAUR APPEARS IN THE MAIN TEXT. HERE YOU WILL READ ABOUT EVERYTHING FROM HOW A DINOSAUR WAS FOUND TO WHO ITS WORST ENEMIES WERE.

FACT BUBBLES ADD A LAYER OF INFORMATION THAT GIVES YOU A CLOSER LOOK AT EACH DINOSAUR. SOMETIMES PICTURES ARE INCLUDED TO ILLUSTRATE THE FACT.

COLORFUL ILLUSTRATIONS GIVE YOU AN IDEA OF WHAT EACH PROFILED DINOSAUR MIGHT HAVE LOOKED LIKE.

CAPTIONS DESCRIBE EACH ILLUSTRATION AND PROVIDE AN EXTRA LAYER OF INFORMATION ABOUT HABITAT, EATING HABITS, BODY ARMOR, AND MORE.

THE TABS IN THE TOP LEFT-HAND CORNER OF EACH PAGE LET YOU KNOW WHAT SECTION YOU ARE IN.

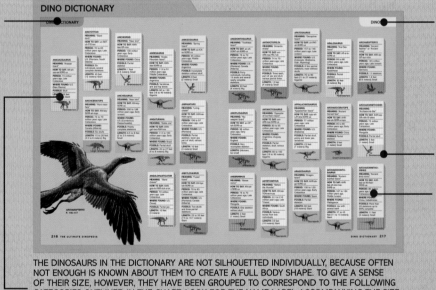

THE DINOSAUR DICTIONARY IS ARRANGED ALPHABETICALLY TO MAKE IT EASY FOR YOU TO QUICKLY FIND THE DINOSAUR YOU ARE LOOKING FOR. THE TABS IN THE TOP RIGHT-HAND CORNER OF EACH PAGE IDENTIFY THE LETTER RANGE.

THE COLOR CODING, DINOSAUR PICTURE, AND NAME AT THE BOTTOM OF THE FACT BOX SHOW THE DINOSAUR FAMILY GROUP. FOR A COMPLETE KEY, SEE PAGE 212. FOR MORE INFORMATION, SEE THE DINOSAUR FAMILY TREE ON PAGES 22–23.

FACT BOXES IN THE DINOSAUR DICTIONARY PROVIDE AT-A-GLANCE INFORMATION ABOUT EACH DINOSAUR, JUST AS FACT BOXES ON THE PROFILE PAGES DO.

THE DINOSAURS IN THE DICTIONARY ARE NOT SILHOUETTED INDIVIDUALLY, BECAUSE OFTEN NOT ENOUGH IS KNOWN ABOUT THEM TO CREATE A FULL BODY SHAPE. TO GIVE A SENSE OF THEIR SIZE, HOWEVER, THEY HAVE BEEN GROUPED TO CORRESPOND TO THE FOLLOWING CATEGORIES OUTLINED IN THE CHART. LOOK FOR THE NAME LABEL ACCOMPANYING THE SIZE DATA, THEN REFER TO THE CHART BELOW FOR A SENSE OF HOW YOU MIGHT HAVE MEASURED UP TO THE DIFFERENT KINDS OF DINOS.

DINOSAUR DICTIONARY SIZE CATEGORIES

SMALL UP TO 15 FEET (5 M) LONG

BIG 15 TO 30 FEET (5 TO 10 M) LONG

GIANT 30 TO 65 FEET (10 TO 25 M) LONG

GIGANTIC MORE THAN 65 FEET (25 M) LONG

DISCOVER DINOSAURS

DINOSAURS AND MANY OTHER ANIMALS roamed the shores of an ancient seaway in western North America more than 65 million years ago.

ING

WHAT IS A DINOSAUR?

What exactly is a dinosaur? That's not a simple question to answer. Dinosaurs were scaly descendants of reptiles. Dinosaurs laid hard eggs and stood with their legs held directly under their bodies—not bowed out like crocodile legs. And at least some dinosaurs had feathers.

Some of these same facts are true of birds. In fact, by some definitions birds can be considered dinosaurs. Something—probably an asteriod impact—killed off the land-living dinosaurs 65 million years ago, but birds lived on, as did many reptiles and mammals.

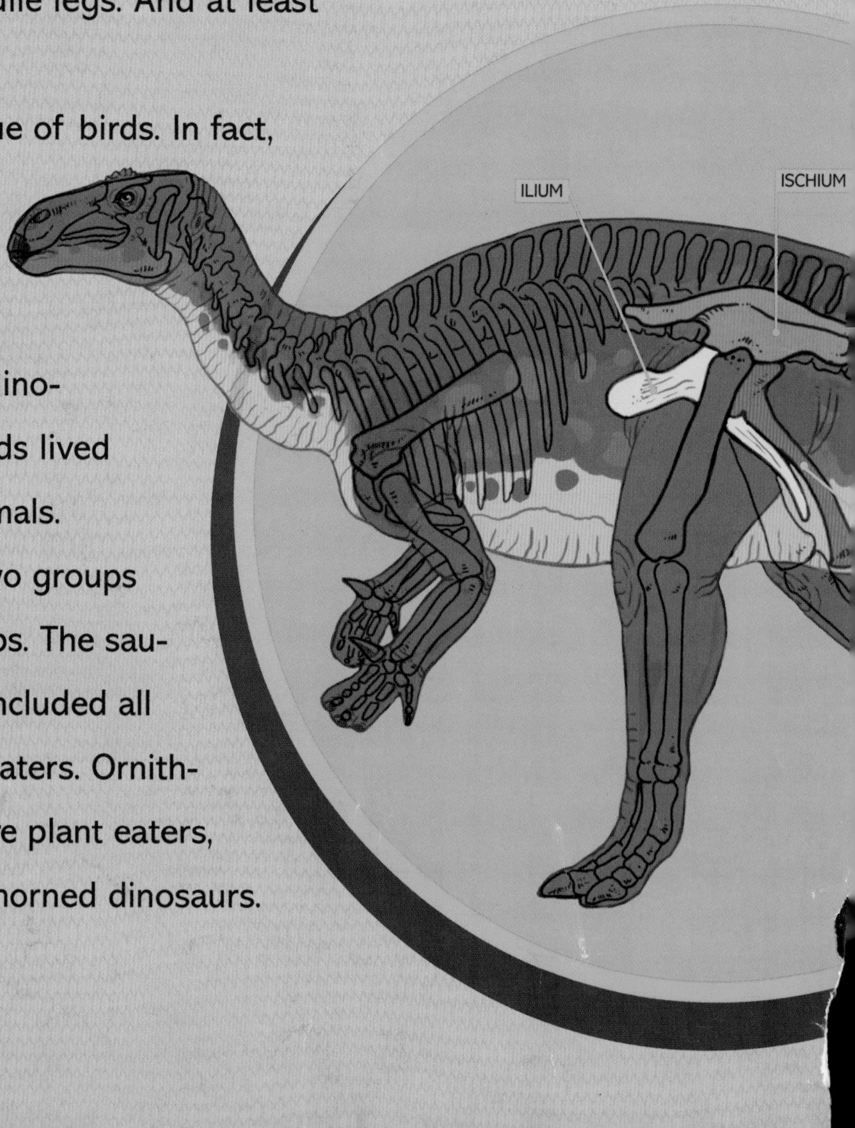

Dinosaurs belonged to one of two groups according to the design of their hips. The saurischian (lizard-hipped) dinosaurs included all meat eaters and the largest plant eaters. Ornithischian (bird-hipped) dinosaurs were plant eaters, such as stegosaurs, duckbills, and horned dinosaurs.

ILIUM

ISCHIUM

ILIUM

ISCHIUM

PUBIS

LIZARD-HIPPED DINOSAURS, CALLED SAURISCHIANS, HAD ONE HIP BONE POINTING FORWARD AND SHAPED LIKE A BOOT AT THE BOTTOM. BOTH MEAT-EATING DINOSAURS AND GIANT PLANT EATERS WERE LIZARD-HIPPED.

PUBIS

BIRD-HIPPED DINOSAURS, CALLED ORNITHISCHIANS, HAD HIP BONES SHAPED LIKE THOSE OF A BIRD. TWO BONES POINTED DOWN AND BACK.

SIGNS
OF DINOSAUR
SUCCESS

THEY RULED THE LAND FOR ALMOST 165 MILLION YEARS.

THEY LIVED ON EVERY CONTINENT.

THEY RANGED IN SIZE FROM SPARROW TO HOUSE.

THEY INCLUDED THE BIGGEST-BRAINED, FASTEST, AND LARGEST ANIMALS OF THEIR TIME.

DINOSAUR WORLDS

The world changed enormously over dinosaur time. The weather grew more extreme: colder in winter, hotter in summer. The dinosaurs, other animals, and plants changed. Mountains rose up, and rivers changed course. All of this happened as the continents themselves moved across the Earth.

THE WONDER DOWN UNDER

ONE HUNDRED MILLION YEARS AGO AUSTRALIA WAS SO FAR SOUTH THAT IT WAS DARK HALF THE YEAR. ONE AUSTRALIAN RESEARCHER THINKS AUSTRALIAN DINOSAURS FROM THAT TIME HAD EXTRA-LARGE EYES FOR SEEING IN WINTER DARKNESS.

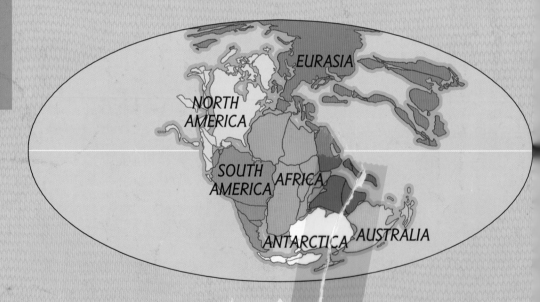

EURASIA

NORTH AMERICA

SOUTH AMERICA

AFRICA

ANTARCTICA

AUSTRALIA

THE TRIASSIC PERIOD
250 million to 200 million years ago

The Earth was a single warm and wet land called Pangaea.

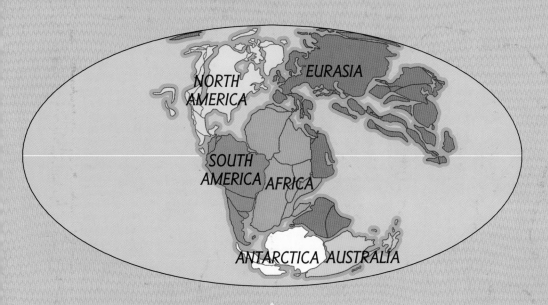

THE JURASSIC PERIOD
200 million to 145 million years ago

The land split into a northern super-continent called Laurasia and a southern super-continent called Gondwana.

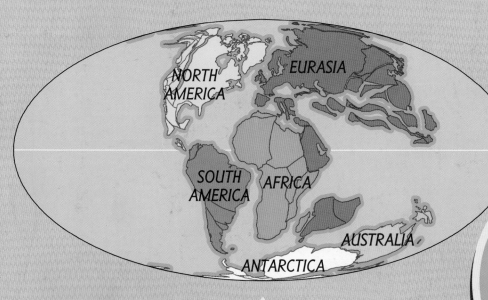

THE CRETACEOUS PERIOD
145 million to 65 million years ago

The continents moved to nearly their current positions. India had broken away from Africa and was moving slowly towards Asia.

IN DINOSAUR TIMES, **ANTARCTICA** HAD NOT YET DRIFTED TO THE SOUTH POLE. DURING THE TRIASSIC, IT WAS LINKED TO **AFRICA** AND **AUSTRALIA**. THESE LANDS DIVIDED, AND ANTARCTICA SLOWLY DRIFTED SOUTH IN THE JURASSIC AND CRETACEOUS.

DINOSAUR HABITATS

Dinosaurs survived in widely different climates, from the cool Arctic to the hot tropics. Where scientists find fossils of dinosaurs, they often find remains of plants and pollen that tell about those dinosaurs' habitats. The size and shape of leaves, for example, give clues about how wet or dry the environment was. These ancient environments are as long gone as the dinosaurs. The Sahara desert was a forest then. Western America was an ocean. But from fossils, we can read the ancient environments. Here are three common dinosaur habitats.

SHORES

EXAMPLE: EASTERN MONTANA, 65 MILLION YEARS AGO.

DINOSAURS INCLUDE PARASAUROLOPHUS, T. REX, PACHYCEPHALO-SAURUS, TRICERATOPS, ANKYLOSAURUS

FORESTS

EXAMPLE: CENTRAL CHINA, 160 MILLION YEARS AGO.

DINOSAURS INCLUDE *OMEISAURUS, DATOUSAURUS, GASOSAURUS, XIAOSAURUS, SHUNOSAURUS*

GOING, GOING, GOBI

THE GOBI DESERT IN MONGOLIA IS ONE OF THE FEW PLACES ON EARTH THAT HAS NEARLY THE SAME HABITAT NOW AS IT DID IN DINOSAUR TIME. DINOSAUR FOSSILS ARE SOMETIMES FOUND BURIED IN SAND IN THE GOBI, COVERED BY ANCIENT SANDSTORMS AND COLLAPSING DUNES.

DESERTS

EXAMPLE: THE GOBI, 80 MILLION YEARS AGO.

DINOSAURS INCLUDE *GALLIMIMUS, PINACOSAURUS, VELOCIRAPTOR, OVIRAPTOR*

HOW FOSSILS FORM

MILLIONS OF YEARS AFTER FOSSILS FORM IN THE GROUND, SHIFTS IN THE EARTH'S GREAT PLATES OF LAND—THE SAME MOVEMENT THAT CAUSES EARTHQUAKES AND VOLCANOES—CAN BRING THEM TO THE SURFACE.

AMATEURS DISCOVER MORE THAN 80 PERCENT OF ALL FOSSILS BY ACCIDENT. CLAY DIGGERS IN NEW JERSEY FOUND THE FIRST NEARLY COMPLETE DINOSAUR SKELETON, AND CHILDREN ALSO HAVE DISCOVERED MANY NEW KINDS OF DINOSAURS.

Usually when an animal dies, its flesh decays or gets eaten. Over time, the skeleton turns to dust. But not always. Only rarely do dead creatures become fossils. Fossils are the tracks or traces of parts of plants and animals. Without them, we would never know about all the amazing animals of the past.

For a dinosaur to become a fossil it needed to die in the right place—a place where it was covered over soon after dying so that its skeleton wouldn't be broken down by air, wind, and rain. If a dinosaur died near a river or lake, sand or mud may have covered it. In a desert, sand can quickly cover over a dead animal. Over thousands of years, minerals enter the tiny holes in spongy bones. Those minerals help turn the bone into fossil as the ground around the bones hardens into rock.

LIFE OF A FOSSIL

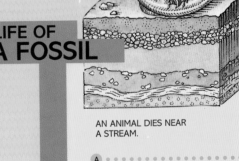

AN ANIMAL DIES NEAR A STREAM.

A

CREATURES FROM VANISHED ANCIENT SEAS ARE OFTEN PRESERVED IN ROCK THAT IS NOW ON LAND. THE CRINOID FOSSILS ARE FROM RELATIVES OF THE SEA STAR AND SEA URCHIN.

BURIAL IN SAND PRESERVES FOSSILS WELL. SAND BURIED A PROTOCERATOPS WHILE IT WAS BITING DOWN ON A VELOCIRAPTOR'S HAND, IN THIS IMAGE OF THE FAMOUS "FIGHTING DINOSAURS" FOSSIL.

SANDSTONE CAN PRESERVE FOSSILS IN GREAT DETAIL. HERE IS A FISH FOSSIL FROM DINOSAUR TIME, MORE THAN 65 MILLION YEARS AGO.

AMMONITES WERE SHELLED SEA CREATURES THAT LIVED IN THE AGE OF DINOSAURS, AND BEFORE. THEIR FOSSILS CAN BE SPOTTED EASILY ON MONMOUTH BEACH IN THE UNITED KINGDOM.

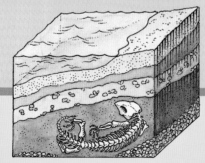

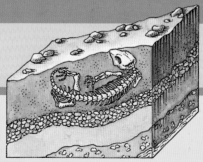

THE ANIMAL IS BURIED, COVERED WITH DIRT CARRIED BY THE STREAM.

THE STRATA FORM AS ROCK LAYERS ON TOP OF ROCK OVER TIME.

THE FOSSIL PUSHES UP TO THE SURFACE AS THE GROUND SHIFTS—READY TO BE DISCOVERED!

B   C   D

LIFE ON EARTH

Creatures lived on Earth for more than 3 billion years before dinosaurs evolved, so more than nine-tenths of Earth's history had gone by when dinosaurs appeared. Geologic time, as the history of the Earth is called, is so long that it's hard to hold in your head.

So try this. Imagine that you are a human timeline. The planet formed at the bottom of your shoes, and today is at the top of your head. The first life on Earth—one-celled organisms in the ocean—shows up at your knees. The first ocean animals to grow more than an inch (2.5 cm) long appear near your armpit. The first animals came up on land when the age of the Earth reaches as high as your chin. The first little dinosaurs evolved from more primitive reptiles at the time marked off by the tip of your nose. The last dinosaurs, including *Tyrannosaurus rex* (p. 91), became extinct somewhere around the middle of your forehead. And where did humans appear? Not until the ends of your hair.

PERIODS OF GEOLOGIC TIME IN EARTH'S HISTORY

1. CAMBRIAN
545–505 MILLION YEARS AGO (MYA)
HARD-BODIED SEA CREATURES

2. ORDOVICIAN
505–438 MYA
FIRST FISH

3. SILURIAN
438–410 MYA
MILLIPEDES ON LAND

4. DEVONIAN
410–355 MYA
FIRST SHARKS, INSECTS

5. CARBONIFEROUS
355–280 MYA
AMPHIBIANS

6. PERMIAN
280–250 MYA
REPTILES, FLYING INSECTS

7. TRIASSIC
250–200 MYA
CROCODILES, PTEROSAURS,
DINOSAURS, MAMMALS

8. JURASSIC
200–145 MYA
DINOSAUR GIANTS

9. CRETACEOUS
145–65 MYA
FLOWERS, BIRDS

10. PALEOCENE
65–23 MYA
WHALES, RATS, MONKEYS

11. NEOGENE
23 MYA–PRESENT
PARROTS, CHIMPANZEES,
HORSES, HUMANS

TODAY

200,000 YEARS AGO
Modern humans appear

65 MILLION YEARS AGO
Dinosaurs become extinct

230 MILLION YEARS AGO
Dinosaurs appear

300 MILLION YEARS AGO
Amphibians appear

500 MILLION YEARS AGO
Opabinia rules oceans

3.8 BILLION YEARS AGO
Microscopic blue-green algae appear, the first life on Earth

4.5 BILLION YEARS AGO
Earth forms

START HERE

21

DINOSAUR FAMILY TREE

DINOSAURS evolved 230 ▶ million years ago from small, two-legged, meat-eating reptiles. The earliest dinosaurs soon branched off into two groups, ornithischia and saurischia. The groups are based on dinosaurs' hip bones (see pp. 12–13). These groups kept branching as dinosaurs developed and changed to live in almost every environment on Earth.

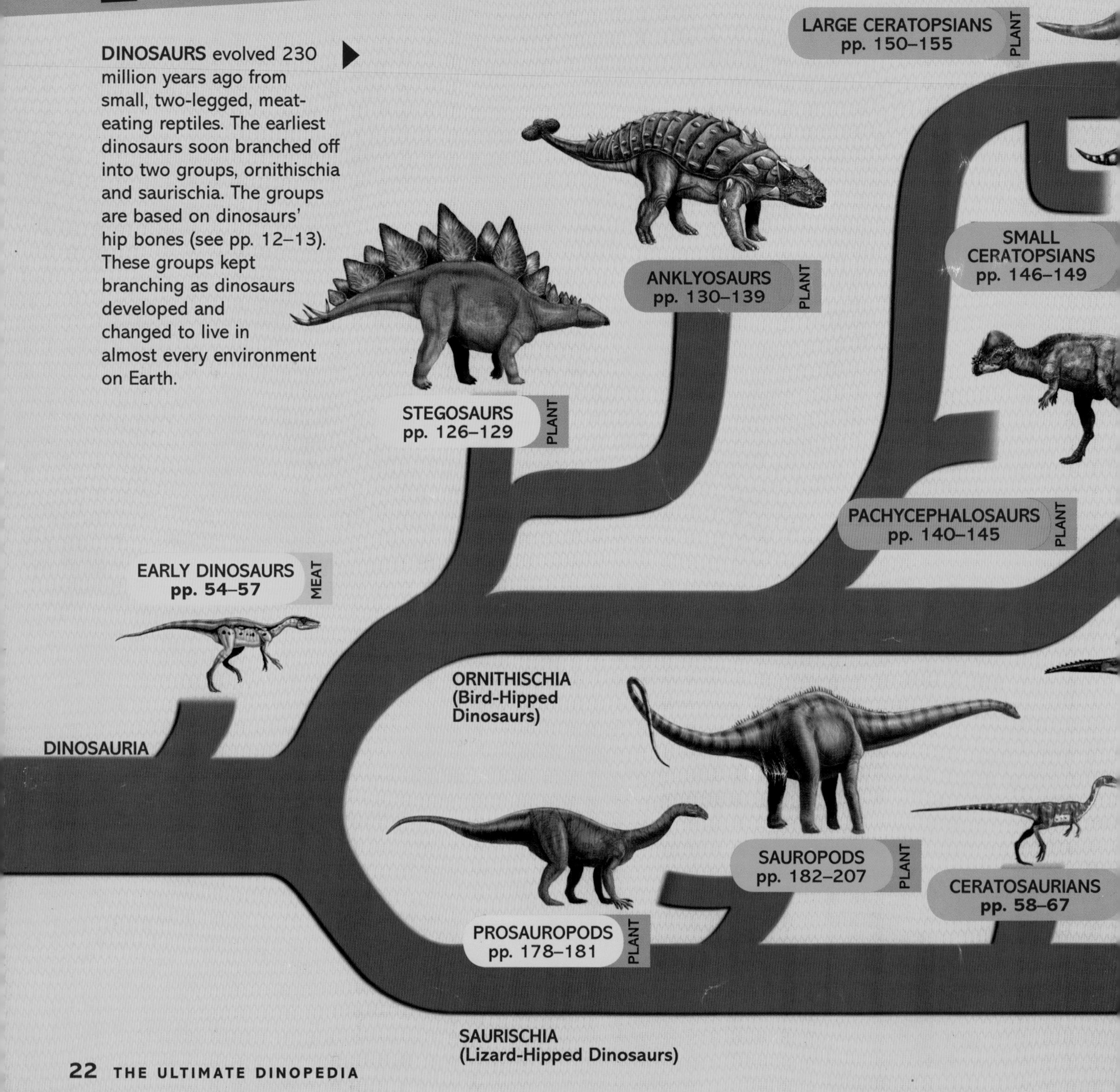

LARGE CERATOPSIANS pp. 150–155 — PLANT

ANKLYOSAURS pp. 130–139 — PLANT

SMALL CERATOPSIANS pp. 146–149

STEGOSAURS pp. 126–129 — PLANT

PACHYCEPHALOSAURS pp. 140–145 — PLANT

EARLY DINOSAURS pp. 54–57 — MEAT

ORNITHISCHIA (Bird-Hipped Dinosaurs)

DINOSAURIA

SAUROPODS pp. 182–207 — PLANT

CERATOSAURIANS pp. 58–67

PROSAUROPODS pp. 178–181 — PLANT

SAURISCHIA (Lizard-Hipped Dinosaurs)

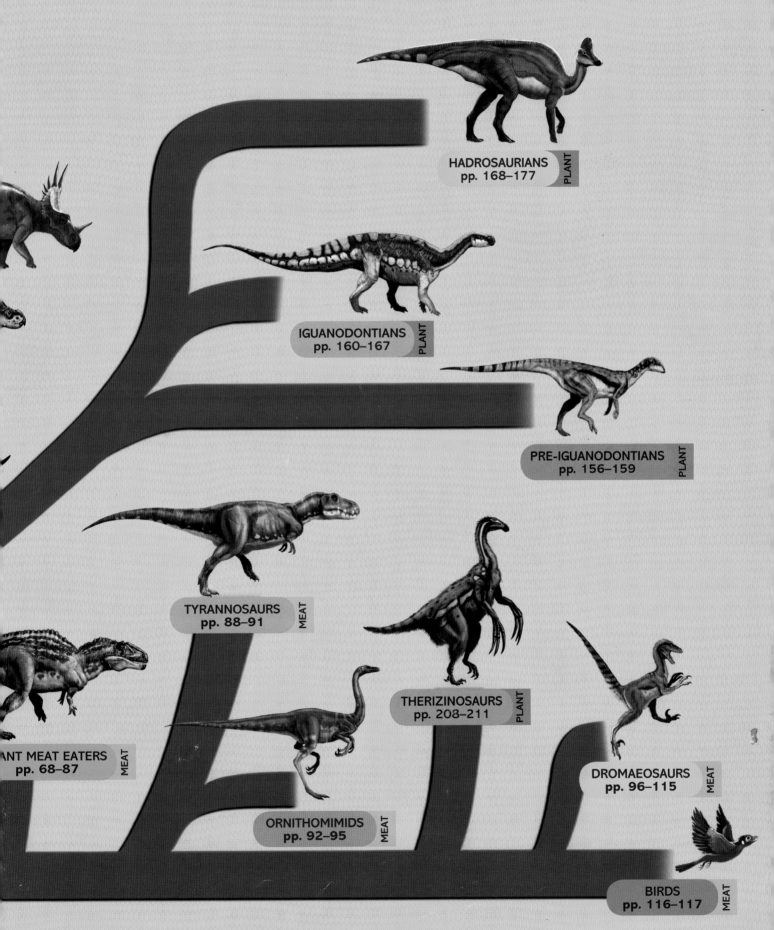

HADROSAURIANS
pp. 168–177
PLANT

IGUANODONTIANS
pp. 160–167
PLANT

PRE-IGUANODONTIANS
pp. 156–159
PLANT

TYRANNOSAURS
pp. 88–91
MEAT

THERIZINOSAURS
pp. 208–211
PLANT

ANT MEAT EATERS
pp. 68–87
MEAT

ORNITHOMIMIDS
pp. 92–95
MEAT

DROMAEOSAURS
pp. 96–115
MEAT

BIRDS
pp. 116–117
MEAT

HATCHING

THE SKELETON OF *AUCASAURUS* (P. 59) WAS FOUND AT A SITE WITH THOUSANDS OF DINOSAUR NESTS AND EGGS OF LARGE PLANT-EATING DINOSAURS. PERHAPS THE *AUCASAURUS* FED UPON THE YOUNGSTERS.

THE LARGEST **DINOSAUR EGG** COULD HOLD ABOUT **6 GALLONS (22 L)** OF FLUID, WHILE THE LARGEST BIRD EGG, FROM THE 10 FOOT TALL EXTINCT AEPYORNIS HELD MORE THAN **10 GALLONS (38 L),** OR THE EQUIVALENT OF **180 CHICKEN EGGS.**

Dinosaurs laid hard-shelled eggs in nests, just as birds do today. Other than being thicker, dinosaur eggshells look a lot like the ones you peel off hard-boiled eggs. Big dinosaurs couldn't have sat on their eggs without scrambling them, so they probably piled plants on top to keep the eggs warm.

Some dinosaurs laid just a few eggs. Others filled nests with more than two dozen. Often, the eggs were arranged in a spiral design, but eggs from the biggest dinosaurs may not have been laid in very organized nests at all. It is likely that larger dinosaurs laid eggs more than once a year.

Meat-eating dinosaurs' eggs were mostly long and thin, and plant eaters' eggs were more rounded. The biggest found look like double-sized flattened footballs. The smallest are less than one inch (2.5 cm) long.

AN *OVIRAPTOR* watches over its newly hatched young in the Gobi Desert of Mongolia. Fossils of *Oviraptor* (p. 99) were found still seated upon a nest of unhatched eggs. The parent dinosaur probably died in a sandstorm or in the collapse of a sand dune.

BRINGING UP
BABY

THIS FOSSIL FERN SHOWS THAT FERNS WERE AN AVAILABLE SOURCE OF BABY FOOD FOR DINOSAURS. IT IS POSSILBE THAT DINOSAUR PARENTS GROUND UP PLANTS TO FEED TO THEIR YOUNG IN THE NEST.

LEARNING TO KILL
YOUNG PREDATORS NEEDED PRACTICE TO BECOME GOOD HUNTERS. PLAYING WITH OTHER YOUNG DINOSAURS AND GROUP HUNTS WITH ADULTS WOULD HAVE HELPED THEM LEARN TO CATCH THEIR PREY.

Like many birds today, some dinosaurs probably needed to be fed by their parents while they grew. One scientist suggested that a duckbill more than 20 feet (6 m) long took care of its young.

Paleontologist Jack Horner named *Maiasaura* (p. 240) the "good mother reptile" after finding many tiny fossils with nests and eggs. He also found fossil plant matter that he thought the mother *Maiasaura* might have chewed for her babies. Dr. Horner thought the babies' bones had soft ends, so the hatchlings could not walk. They needed a parent's care.

Many scientists agree with Dr. Horner. Some think the plant material he found was not baby food but part of the nest. And they question whether the babies' fossil bones really show they were helpless. We do know that young dinosaurs grew very fast.

We can't tell much about the family life of dinosaurs from fossils. But several finds of adult and young dinosaurs together suggest that even the biggest meat eaters traveled in groups of adults and young.

THE *MAIASAURA* duckbill ▶ didn't have the boney head-gear of some of its relatives, but it may have had fleshy lumps or other decorations on its head. We can't tell anything about these decorations from fossil bones, so many dinosaurs may have had features we know nothing about.

MIGRATION AND HERDING

EVERY YEAR, MILLIONS OF BIG PLANT-EATING DINO-SAURS MARCHED NORTH AND SOUTH IN THE NORTH AMERICAN WEST. WHY DO WE THINK SO? MILLIONS OF FOOTPRINTS IN COLORADO SHOW THE ROUTE THAT IS NOW CALLED THE DINOSAUR TRAIL.

4 REASONS FOR DINOSAUR MIGRATION

1. TO FIND NEW SOURCES OF FOOD
2. TO FIND WATER SOURCES IN THE DRY SEASON
3. TO FIND SAFE NESTING SITES TO LAY EGGS
4. FOR WARMER WEATHER

Many dinosaurs lived in herds. Duck-billed dinosaurs and horned dinosaurs traveled in groups of hundreds, perhaps thousands. Giant plant eaters also roamed in groups.

Why? Big plant eaters consumed a lot of food. By staying on the move, these dinosaurs could find food in new locations. Otherwise they might have used up all of the food in their habitat.

Just as birds and many herding animals migrate seasonally today, dinosaur herds may have traveled thousands of miles each year, following the changing daylight hours. In summer months, plants grew more rapidly close to the poles. In winter, better food could be found close to the Equator.

Traveling in herds kept plant-eating dinosaurs safer from predators. They could protect their young by keeping them in the middle of the big groups.

A HUGE HERD OF *Edmontosaurus* (p. 141) marches north in Alaska on a long summer Arctic night. Dinosaur fossils and footprints have been found in the far north, and scientists believe this is evidence of their migration.

COURTSHIP AND MATING

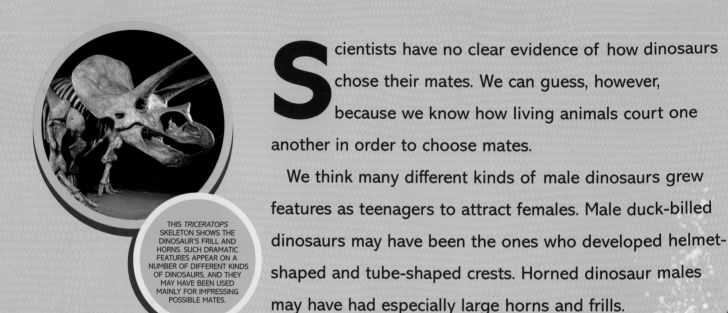

S cientists have no clear evidence of how dinosaurs chose their mates. We can guess, however, because we know how living animals court one another in order to choose mates.

We think many different kinds of male dinosaurs grew features as teenagers to attract females. Male duck-billed dinosaurs may have been the ones who developed helmet-shaped and tube-shaped crests. Horned dinosaur males may have had especially large horns and frills.

THIS *TRICERATOPS* SKELETON SHOWS THE DINOSAUR'S FRILL AND HORNS. SUCH DRAMATIC FEATURES APPEAR ON A NUMBER OF DIFFERENT KINDS OF DINOSAURS, AND THEY MAY HAVE BEEN USED MAINLY FOR IMPRESSING POSSIBLE MATES.

TWO *CORYTHOSAURUS*
(p. 173) duckbills slap their necks against each other in a contest for a mate. Many modern grazing animals, including giraffes, do this. We have no direct evidence of this behavior in dinosaurs, but it is a possibility. We do know that some adult corythosaurs had big crests and others had smaller crests. Perhaps the tall-crested duckbills were males battling for a female.

GREAT DINOSAUR HUNTERS

People have been finding dinosaur bones for thousands of years, but only in the last 200 years have scientists identified dinosaurs.

GIDEON MANTELL
English country doctor who in 1822 first identified a dinosaur from *Iguanodon* (p. 167) teeth dug up by local miners

RICHARD OWEN
British scientist who created the word "dinosaur," meaning "terrible lizard," in 1842

O. C. MARSH AND EDWARD DRINKER COPE
Rival dinosaur scientists of the late 19th century who named more dinosaurs than anyone in history, including the giants *Apatosaurus* (p. 191) and *Brachiosaurus* (p. 189)

BARNUM BROWN
Wild West dinosaur hunter of the early 1900s, "Mr. Dinosaur" was the man who found *Tyrannosaurus rex* (p. 91).

ROY CHAPMAN ANDREWS
Explorer of the Gobi Desert whose team found the first dinosaur nests and *Velociraptor* (p. 115) in the 1920s. With his gun, hat, and fear of snakes, he was the model for Indiana Jones.

JOSE BONAPARTE

Argentine paleontologist of the late 20th century who named the biggest dinosaur of all, *Argentinosaurus* (p. 199)

JOHN R. "JACK" HORNER

Montana dinosaur explorer whose discoveries include duckbill *Maiasaura* (p. 240) and nests and babies of the little meat eater *Troodon* (p. 113)

Xu Xing

Chinese scientist who named more dinosaurs than any living scientist. His discoveries include many feathered dinosaurs, such as tiny *Microraptor* (p. 103).

PAUL SERENO

Chicago dinosaur scientist who named one of the earliest dinosaurs, *Eoraptor* (p. 55), and found *Jobaria* (p. 235) and other African dinosaurs in the Sahara

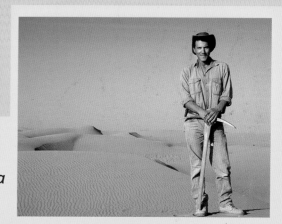

PHILIP CURRIE

Canadian expert on meat-eating dinosaurs who has explored the Gobi Desert, Argentina, and western Canada. He discovered group life among *Albertosaurus*.

RODOLFO CORIA

Argentine paleontologist who named the two biggest meat eaters, *Giganotosaurus* (p. 81) and *Mapusaurus* (p. 83)

DINOSAUR
FINDS

D inosaurs adapted to a wide range of land environments, so it is not surprising that they have been found on every continent. Some of the most exciting dinosaur finds are highlighted on this map.

NORTH AMERICA

Hell Creek, Montana
Several *Tyrannosaurus rex* specimens, *Triceratops* and many other Late Cretaceous dinosaurs

Dinosaur National Monument, Utah
Several large plant eaters including *Apatosaurus* and *Barosaurus*, and meat eaters such as *Allosaurus*

Red Deer River, Alberta, Can
The richest source of dinosaur specie in the world, including *Albertosaurus*

Como Bluff, Wyoming
Stegosaurus, Camarasaurus, Allosaurus and other large Late Jurassic dinosaur

Paluxy River, Texas
Trackways showing encounter betwe large plant eater and large meat eate in Early Cretaceous

SOUTH AMERIC

Ischigualasto, Argentina
Two of the oldest dinosaurs known, the meat eaters *Eoraptor* and *Herrerasaurus*

Plaza Huincul, Argentina
The largest meat-eating and plant-eating dinosaurs in the world, *Argentinosaurus, Giganotosaurus* and *Mapusaurus* and many other species

• Dinosaur fossil location

COUNTRIES
WITH THE MOST
KINDS OF DINOSAURS
- UNITED STATES
- CANADA
- CHINA
- ARGENTINA
- MONGOLIA
- ENGLAND
- AUSTRALIA
- NIGER
- SOUTH AFRICA

Isle of Wight, England
Many Early Cretaceous
dinosaurs including
Hypsilophodon, *Neovenator*,
Iguanodon and 12 other species

EUROPE

Bernissart, Belgium
Many well-preserved
Iguanodon dinosaurs

Solnhofen, Germany
Compsognathus, *Archaeopteryx*
and many Late Jurassic plants,
fish and other animals

Gobi Desert, Mongolia
Source of many of the best preserved
dinosaur skeletons including the
fighting *Velociraptor* and *Protoceratops*

ASIA

Liaoning, China
Beautifully preserved fossils
of many Early Cretaceous animals
including feathered dinosaurs such
as *Mei* and *Microraptor*

Zigong, China
A very well preserved collection of
meat eaters and giant plant eaters
from the Middle Jurassic Period,
including Gasosaurus

Sahara Desert, Niger
Suchomimus, *Deltadromeus*
and other Cretaceous
dinosaurs

AFRICA

Tendaguru, Tanzania
Brachiosaurus, *Allosaurus*,
Kentrosaurus, *Barosaurus*,
Ceratosaurus and others

Madagascar
The oldest known dinosaur fossils and
large early meat eaters and plant eaters
including *Majungatholus* and *Rapetosaurus*

Karoo Basin, South Africa
Many early dinosaur plant eaters and
meat eaters such as *Heterodontosaurus*,
Fabrosaurus and *Massospondylus*

Lark Quarry, Australia
Thousands of dinosaur footprints
and fossils of *Diamantinasaurus*
and *Wintonotitan*

AUSTRALIA

Dinosaur Cove, Australia
Leaellynasaura, *Timimus* and other
small Antarctic dinosaurs

ANTARCTICA

OUT
ON A DIG
& IN THE LAB

EQUIPMENT
- SHOVEL
- PICK
- BRUSH
- AWL
- TENT OR TEEPEE
- SLEEPING BAG
- NOTEBOOK
- TOILET PAPER OR BURLAP
- PLASTER OF PARIS

PRESERVING FOSSILS
WHEN FOSSIL BONES ARE FULLY UNCOVERED, A PLATFORM IS DUG AROUND THEM, AND THE FOSSIL AND SURROUNDING ROCK ARE CUT AWAY. THE BONES ARE THEN COVERED WITH BURLAP OR ALUMINUM FOIL OR EVEN TOILET PAPER. THIS METHOD HELPS TO SEPARATE THE FOSSIL FROM A QUICK-DRYING PLASTER COATING THAT THE DIG TEAM APPLIES TO PROTECT THEIR NEW FIND.

During summers all over the world, teams of experts and volunteers dig up dinosaur fossils. In the best finds, a small part of the dinosaur is exposed, and the rest of the skeleton is preserved beneath the ground. More often, however, only a small piece of the dinosaur is ever found.

Researchers carefully map a fossil site. As bones are removed, researchers take detailed notes. This information can help paleontologists determine how the animal was killed and buried. Then they remove layers of rock, called overburden, using jackhammers, chisels, and shovels.

When they have dug close to the fossil layer, the explorers switch to hand tools, such as awls and screwdrivers, to scrape rock away from the bone. Then each bone is coated with hardening chemicals. Fossils are taken out of the ground and covered in protective plaster. They are then sent to the lab to be cleaned and studied.

BUILDING SUE, THE MO

T. REX "SUE" IS BEING EXCAVATED IN SOUTH DAKOTA BY A TEAM OF DIGGERS THIS DINOSAUR WAS NAMED FOR SUE HENDRICKSON, THE SCIENTIST WHO DISCOVERED IT.

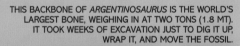

RECREATING THE COMPLETE SKELETON OF *ARGENTINOSAURUS*, THE WORLD'S LARGEST DINOSAUR, WAS THE END OF A LONG PROCESS THAT INCLUDED EXPLORATION, EXCAVATION, PREPARATION, MOLDING, CASTING, SCULPTING, AND MOUNTING THE ENORMOUS DINOSAUR.

ARGENTINOSAURUS WAS EXCAVATED AT THIS SITE IN THE DESERT OF WESTERN ARGENTINA. A CHANCE DISCOVERY OF A GIANT SHINBONE BY A FARMER LED SCIENTISTS TO BEGIN DIGGING UP THIS GIANT DINOSAUR.

THIS BACKBONE OF *ARGENTINOSAURUS* IS THE WORLD'S LARGEST BONE, WEIGHING IN AT TWO TONS (1.8 MT). IT TOOK WEEKS OF EXCAVATION JUST TO DIG IT UP, WRAP IT, AND MOVE THE FOSSIL.

COMPLETE *T. REX* EVER FOUND

AFTER "SUE" WAS EXCAVATED, ALL HER BONES WERE CAREFULLY PACKED IN CRATES AND SENT TO THE FIELD MUSEUM IN CHICAGO. HERE SCIENTISTS ARE UNPACKING SUE'S LEFT HIPBONE.

CLEANING AND PREPARING FOSSILS IS HARD WORK. TECHNICIANS SPENT MORE THAN 25,000 HOURS PREPARING SUE'S BONES.

SILICONE RUBBER IS POURED OVER ONE OF SUE'S LEG BONES. THE RUBBER WILL SOLIDIFY AND FORM A MOLD OF THE BONE.

T. REX SUE STANDS 42 FEET (13 M) LONG FROM HEAD TO TAIL. MORE THAN 200 OF HER FOSSILIZED BONES ARE HELD TOGETHER BY A FRAME MADE OF STEEL.

GREAT DINOSAUR MISTAKES

O ver the years, scientists have often been wrong about dinosaurs. The constant process of scientific questioning shows us how much there will always be to learn!

ANIMALS THAT ARE NOT DINOSAURS

DIMETRODONS: SAIL-BACKED MAMMAL-LIKE REPTILES

PTEROSAURS: FLYING REPTILES

PLESIOSAURS: MARINE REPTILES

CROCODILES: DEVELOPED BEFORE DINOSAURS

ALL DINOSAURS WERE HUGE

On average, dinosaurs were smaller than a large car. *Fruitadens* (p. 230), weighed less than 2 pounds (0.9 kg).

ALL DINOSAURS WERE STUPID

Giant dinosaurs were dumb with brains the size of ping-pong balls, but little dinosaurs like *Troodon* (p. 113) had pretty big brains for their size, so they were likely smarter than any animal of their time.

APATOSAURUS BOO-BOO

For many years, the American Museum of Natural History in New York showed an *Apatosaurus* (p. 191) that had the head of a *Camarasaurus* (p. 222) instead.

STEGOSAURUS HAD TWO BRAINS

Long ago, some researchers thought that *Stegosaurus* had a second brain in its back

FOR MANY YEARS, NEW YORK'S NATURAL HISTORY MUSEUM HAD THE WRONG HEAD ON ITS *APATOSAURUS* (THEN CALLED *BRONTOSAURUS*).

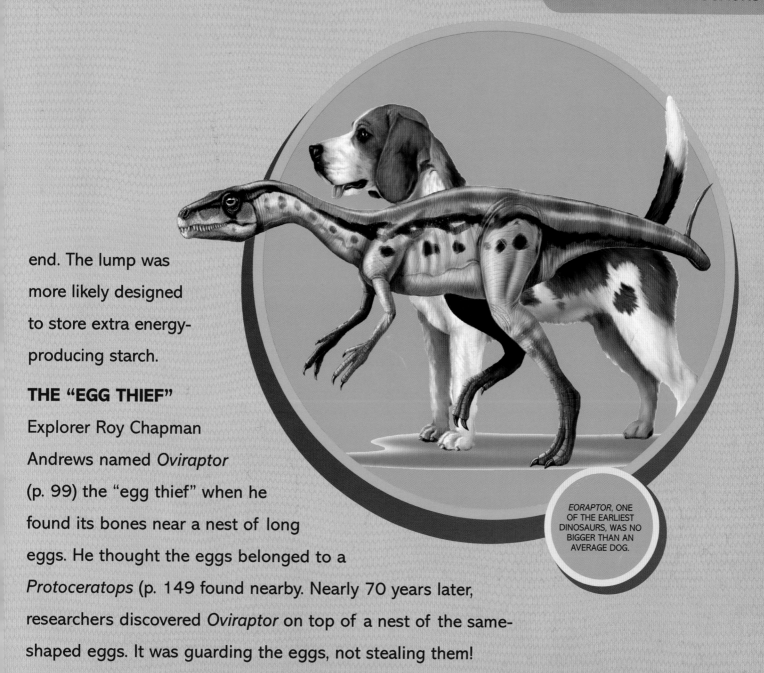

EORAPTOR, ONE OF THE EARLIEST DINOSAURS, WAS NO BIGGER THAN AN AVERAGE DOG.

end. The lump was more likely designed to store extra energy-producing starch.

THE "EGG THIEF"

Explorer Roy Chapman Andrews named *Oviraptor* (p. 99) the "egg thief" when he found its bones near a nest of long eggs. He thought the eggs belonged to a *Protoceratops* (p. 149 found nearby. Nearly 70 years later, researchers discovered *Oviraptor* on top of a nest of the same-shaped eggs. It was guarding the eggs, not stealing them!

THE EARLIEST ILLUSTRATION OF *IGUANODON* SHOWED A LIZARD-LIKE CREATURE WITH A LARGE NOSE HORN.

◀ IGUANODON'S HEAD SPIKE

Gideon Mantell identified the first dinosaur, *Iguanodon* (p. 167). But he goofed when he suggested that its thumb spike was a nose horn.

WHAT KILLED THE DINOSAURS? WRONG IDEAS

SCIENTISTS HAVE SUGGESTED OVER 100 CAUSES INCLUDING

CONSTIPATION

GAS FROM DIGESTING PLANTS

POISONOUS PLANTS

OVER-EATING

AN ICE AGE

NEW DINO DISCOVERIES

On average, a new kind of dinosaur is found every two weeks. While we know nearly 1,000 kinds so far, there are probably thousands more dinosaur species yet unknown. Here are some of the most recent exciting discoveries.

AUSTRORAPTOR awst-ro-RAP-tor
MEANING "Southern thief"
SIZE 16 feet (5 meters) long, Big
PERIOD 70 million years ago, Late Cretaceous
WHERE FOUND Argentina
FOSSILS Partial skeleton with fragmentary skull
GROUP Dromaeosaurid

AUSTRORAPTOR **IS THE** largest of the dromaeosaurid dinosaurs from South America. Unlike other raptors around the world, its teeth were cone-shaped and its arms were short.

AUSTRALOVENATOR awst-ra-LO-ven-ate-or
MEANING "Southern hunter"
SIZE 20 feet (6 meters) long, Big
PERIOD 100 million years ago, Early Cretaceous
WHERE FOUND Australia
FOSSILS Partial skeleton with fragmentary skull
GROUP Dromaeosaurid

THE LARGEST MEAT EATER known from Australia, it was a close relative of the North American *Allosaurus* (p. 75).

RAPTORREX rap-TOR-ex
MEANING "Robber king"
SIZE 10 feet (3 meters) long, Big
PERIOD 125 million years ago, Early Cretaceous
WHERE FOUND China
FOSSILS One individual
GROUP Tyrannosaurid

A RAPTOR-SIZED early ancestor of *Tyrannosaurus rex*.

BARROSASAURUS BARR-o-sa-SORE-us
MEANING Lizard from Barrosa Hill
SIZE 95 feet (30 meters) long, Gigantic
PERIOD 80 million years ago, Late Cretaceous
WHERE FOUND Argentina
FOSSILS Three incomplete vertebrae
GROUP Sauropod
DISCOVERED TEN YEARS AGO but only lately named, *Barrosasaurus* was one of the largest of all plant-eating dinosaurs.

FRUITADENS froo-TA-dens
MEANING "Fruita tooth"
SIZE 26 to 30 inches (65 to 75 cm) long, Small
PERIOD 150 million years ago, Late Jurassic
WHERE FOUND U.S. (Colorado)
FOSSILS Partial skulls and skeletons
GROUP Pre-iguanodontian
THE SMALLEST known bird-hipped dinosaur. Discovered 30 years ago, *Fruitadens* was only recently found to be a new kind of dinosaur.

HESPERONYCHUS HESS-per-oh-NY-cuss
MEANING "West claw"
SIZE under 3 feet (1 meter) long, Small
PERIOD 75 million years ago, Late Cretaceous
WHERE FOUND Canada (Alberta)
FOSSILS Partial skeleton
GROUP Dromaeosaurid
THIS TINY DINOSAUR is the smallest meat eater known from North America.

DIAMANTINASAURUS dye-ah-man-tin-ah-SAWR-us
MEANING Diamantina River lizard
SIZE 50 feet (15 meters) long, Giant
PERIOD 100 million years ago, Early Cretaceous
WHERE FOUND Australia
FOSSILS Front and hind legs, hips, and some ribs
GROUP Sauropod
THIS HEAVY-BUILT GIANT plant eater is the largest dinosaur ever found in Australia.

WHAT COLORS WERE DINOSAURS?

Fossils generally give no information about the outer appearance of animals. So until very recently, scientists had no idea what color dinosaurs might have been. But a fossil of *Anchiornis* (p. 216), a newly discovered chicken-sized meat eater from China, contained a surprise. *Anchiornis*'s fossils were very well preserved, so its feathers survived. They showed black and white wings and a reddish head. Many feathers were studied to reveal the animal's color pattern. The picture to the left shows what this meat eater might have looked like.

OTHER ANIMALS FROM DINOSAUR TIME

Dinosaurs of many shapes and sizes ruled the land for more than 150 million years, but they were not the only amazing animals roaming the land, skies, and sea.

Sharks and fish swam the seas just as they do today. The largest sea creatures included turtles 12 feet (4 m) wide, and deadly ocean reptiles. Small mammals shared the land with dinosaurs. And while birds flew, the skies were ruled by flying reptiles as large as fighter planes.

ON LAND, MAMMALS LIVED IN THE SHADOW OF DINOSAURS. MOST—LIKE THE ONE PICTURED—WERE AS SMALL AS MICE. BUT ONE RECENTLY FOUND REPENOMAMUS WAS AS BIG AS A BEAVER AND ATE DINOSAURS!

THE BIGGEST OF THEIR KIND

FLYING REPTILE *(QUETZALCOATLUS)*
45 FOOT (14 M) WINGSPAN

MARINE REPTILE *(SHONISAURUS)*
70 FEET (21 M) LONG

TURTLE *(ARCHELON)*
12 FEET (4 M) WIDE

CROCODILE *(DEINOSUCHUS)*
40 FEET (12 M) LONG

FISH *(LEEDSICTHYS)*
66 FEET (20 M) LONG

THE SKIES WERE DOMINATED BY FLYING REPTILES CALLED PTEROSAURS. PTEROSAURS APPEARED BEFORE DINOSAURS AND GREW FIVE TIMES AS WIDE AS CONDORS.

REPTILES RULED THE SEAS AS WELL. ICHTHYOSAURS (PICTURED) WERE SHAPED LIKE HUGE DOLPHINS. LONG-NECK PLESIOSAURS FISHED IN THE OCEAN. FIERCE TYLOSAURS GREW AS LONG AS *T. REX*. GIANT TURTLES AND BIG SHARKS ALSO SWAM IN THE SEAS.

THE EXTINCTION MYSTERY

Dinosaurs survived more than 500 times longer than humans have been on the Earth. But every kind of animal that ever lives eventually disappears. Dinosaurs disappeared 65 million years ago. But what could have killed off the most successful of all land animals? Here are three theories:

Asteroid impact—Huge rocks from space may have crashed into the Earth, producing clouds of dust and smoke that changed weather patterns. Dinosaurs may not have been able to adjust. Evidence of this collision includes high levels of the mineral iridium in rocks from the time. Iridium is found in asteroids but rarely on Earth.

Volcanic activity—Huge lava fields in India are proof that many volcanoes erupted at the end of dinosaur time. This activity may have caused climate changes that the dinosaurs could not tolerate.

Slow climate change—Winters were growing colder and summers hotter near the end of dinosaur time. For several million years before the final extinction, the numbers and varieties of dinosaurs in at least some places were decreasing.

A COMBINATION OF EVENTS?

SCIENTISTS HAVE SUGGESTED MORE THAN 100 CAUSES OF DINOSAUR EXTINCTION, AND IT IS POSSIBLE THAT ONE EVENT TRIGGERED ANOTHER. FOR EXAMPLE, AN EARTHQUAKE OR ASTEROID IMPACT MAY HAVE TRIGGERD HUGE TSUNAMI TIDAL WAVES STRONG ENOUGH TO WIPE OUT LIVING CREATURES.

**DUCK-BILLED DINO-
SAURS FLEE IN TERROR**
as a huge asteroid strikes the
Gulf of Mexico 65 million
years ago. This disaster may
have ended all dinosaur life.

THE MEAT EATERS

THE GREATEST ANIMAL BATTLE IN HISTORY took place on a 100-million-year-old Argentine shore. Two adult *Mapusaurus*, the largest predators known, tear at the body of the largest land animal of all time, *Argentinosaurus*. Two young *Mapusaurus* feed on the giant's neck. Pterosaurs and wading birds fly over the scene, and crocodiles lurk nearby in the water.

FAMILIES

Throughout dinosaur time, large and small dinosaurs roamed the Earth. The theropods—meat-eating dinosaurs—arose early in dinosaur time and lasted until the end of dinosaur time and beyond. Modern birds are the closest living relatives of theropods!

EARLY DINOSAURS   MEAT

Small, two-legged meat eaters
pp. 54–57

GIANT MEAT EATERS

Even bigger than *T. rex*, these largest of the meat eaters lived in North Africa and South America 100 million years ago. They all had three or more fingers.
pp. 68–87

CERATOSAURIANS   MEAT

Early small and large theropods with four fingers
pp. 58–67

DINOSAURIA

**SAURISCHIA
(Lizard-Hipped Dinosaurs)**

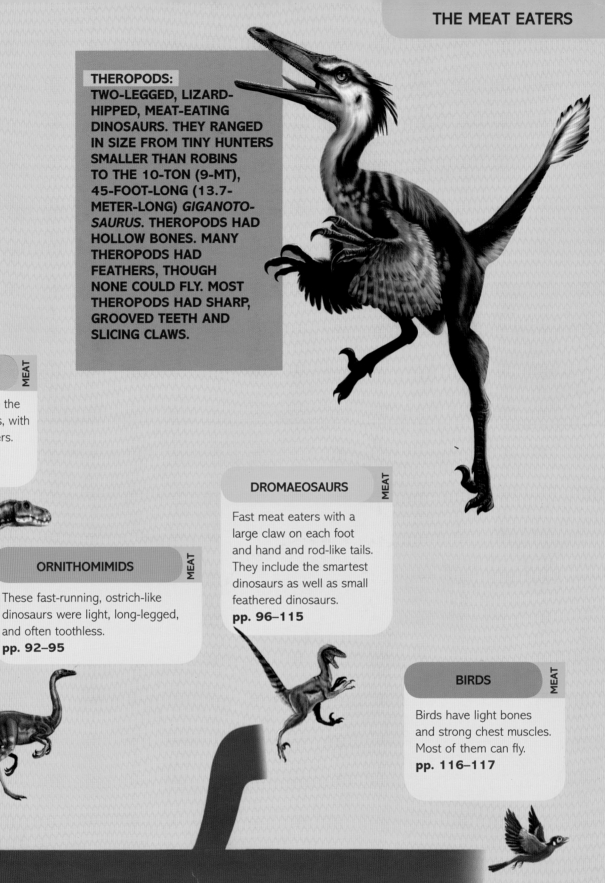

THEROPODS:
TWO-LEGGED, LIZARD-HIPPED, MEAT-EATING DINOSAURS. THEY RANGED IN SIZE FROM TINY HUNTERS SMALLER THAN ROBINS TO THE 10-TON (9-MT), 45-FOOT-LONG (13.7-METER-LONG) *GIGANOTO-SAURUS*. THEROPODS HAD HOLLOW BONES. MANY THEROPODS HAD FEATHERS, THOUGH NONE COULD FLY. MOST THEROPODS HAD SHARP, GROOVED TEETH AND SLICING CLAWS.

TYRANNOSAURS MEAT

hese fierce predators were the
st of the giant meat eaters, with
owerful jaws and two fingers.
p. 88–91

ORNITHOMIMIDS MEAT

These fast-running, ostrich-like dinosaurs were light, long-legged, and often toothless.
pp. 92–95

DROMAEOSAURS MEAT

Fast meat eaters with a large claw on each foot and hand and rod-like tails. They include the smartest dinosaurs as well as small feathered dinosaurs.
pp. 96–115

BIRDS MEAT

Birds have light bones and strong chest muscles. Most of them can fly.
pp. 116–117

WEAPONS

TOP 10 POSSIBLE DINOSAUR BATTLES

1. *MAPUSAURUS VS. ARGENTINOSAURUS*
2. *T. REX VS. TRICERATOPS*
3. *ALLOSAURUS VS. STEGOSAURUS*
4. *UTAHRAPTOR VS. GASTONIA*
5. *YANGCHUANOSAURUS VS. SHUNOSAURUS*
6. *CARCHARODONTOSAURUS VS. OURANOSAURUS*
7. *DEINONYCHUS VS. TENONTOSAURUS*
8. *DASPLETOSAURUS VS. EDMONTOSAURUS*
9. *ACROCANTHOSAURUS VS. PALUXYSAURUS*
10. *TARBOSAURUS VS. SAUROLOPHUS*

Killer dinosaurs had two main weapons for attacking prey—claws and teeth.

CLAWS: Meat eaters had sharp, slicing claws up to one foot (0.3 m) long. The nastiest of these blades belonged to the Argentine predator Megaraptor. Some claws were retractable, like cats' claws. They were made of hard bone but covered with a thick layer of keratin—the same material that makes up your fingernails.

TEETH: Most meat eaters had sharp-edged teeth with grooves for slicing. The biggest teeth were the size of bananas, set in jaws strong enough to dent metal. *Tyrannosaurus rex*'s teeth were the largest of any dinosaur's.

A PACK OF ATTACKING *Velociraptors* surround two ornithomimid dinosaurs in Mongolia's Gobi Desert. Without teeth or strong claws, the ornithomimid's only defense would be its superior speed. But once cornered, the larger dinosaur might have fallen to the sharp teeth and claws of the little raptors.

PREDATORS OR SCAVENGERS?

Meat-eating dinosaurs had two dining styles. Either they could kill what they wanted, or they could eat animals already dead. *Tyrannosaurus rex* and other large meat eaters could have killed most big animals in their world. They had bigger brains and better vision, and they could run faster than plant eaters.

But dinosaurs may not have needed to do much hunting. For meat eaters, it was safer and less tiring to scavenge for already-dead dinosaurs. Old age, injury, and disease among the plant-eater herds may have provided meat eaters with most of their food.

MODERN PREDATORS, SUCH AS WOLVES, USE MANY OF THE SAME HUNTING TECHNIQUES AS DINOSAUR PREDATORS LIKELY USED. THEY TARGET OLD AND SICK PREY ANIMALS, AND THEN USE THEIR TEETH AND CLAWS TO BRING THEM DOWN.

TOP 10 DINOSAUR PREDATORS

1. *TYRANNOSAURUS REX*
2. *GIGANOTOSAURUS*
3. *DESPLETOSAURUS*
4. *ACROCANTHOSAURUS*
5. *ALLOSAURUS*
6. *LOURINHANOSAURUS*
7. *MEGALOSAURUS*
8. *YANGCHUANOSAURUS*
9. *ALBERTOSAURUS*
10. *UTAHRAPTOR*

BY ATTACKING IN PACKS, meat-eating dinosaurs could have increased their success rate. Even human-sized raptor dinosaurs could have taken down a large sauropod many times their size by hunting in packs. *Velociraptor, Troodon,* and *Deinonychus* dinosaurs might have hunted in this way to kill prey larger than themselves.

A PAIR OF ▶
ALLOSAURUS
close in on a fleeing *Camarasaurus*. If the *Camarasaurus* doesn't appear to be running, perhaps that's because it couldn't. With their enormous weight, the giant sauropods may not have been able to move at more than a slow walk.

EORAPTOR

EE-oh-RAP-tore

NAME *Eoraptor*

MEANING "Dawn raptor"

PERIOD 225 million years ago, Late Triassic

FOUND Argentina

FOSSILS Skull, leg bones

LENGTH 5 feet (1.5 meters) long

EORAPTOR, SHOWN HERE with a dicynodont, a mammal-like reptile plant eater, may have been too small to hunt any other dinosaurs, but it was among the faster and smarter killers of its time. It could have hunted little lizards or our tiny mammal ancestors. The first mammals were not much bigger than mice—a little snack for *Eoraptor*.

HONORED ANCESTOR

What was the first dinosaur? It is almost impossible to know what the very first of any kind of animal is. There may always be something older waiting to be discovered. At the moment, the oldest known dinosaur fossils are bits and pieces of not-yet-named dinosaurs recently found in Madagascar.

We didn't know much about that *Eoraptor* when it was first found in 1991 either. But later finds—including a skull—helped us picture *Eoraptor*. We now know that *Eoraptor* was a very early dinosaur with features unlike later dinosaurs. It had a fifth finger, where other dinosaurs had four or fewer, and it didn't have the split in the middle of its jawbone that other meat eaters had.

PALEONTOLOGIST PAUL SERENO SAYS THAT WHEN HE DISCOVERED THE BEAUTIFULLY PRESERVED, SHARP-TOOTHED SKULL OF *EORAPTOR*, HE CRIED WITH JOY.

HERRERA-SAURUS

Huh-RARE-ah-SORE-us

NAME *Herrerasaurus*

MEANING "Herrera's lizard," for discoverer Don Victorino Herrera

PERIOD 225 million years ago, Late Triassic

FOUND Argentina

FOSSILS Skull

LENGTH 16.5 feet (5 meters) long

BIG MOUTH, BIG MEAL

You're looking at the earliest big killer dinosaur that has been found. With its hinged jaws, *Herrerasaurus* could open its mouth wide to gobble up big chunks of meat. Cutting the meat was the job of its notched teeth, which had grooves like a steak knife.

Herrerasaurus had short arm bones but long hands. It wasn't the biggest meat eater of its time, but the other giants were not dinosaurs—they were four-legged crocodilians. Unlike those big killers, *Herrerasaurus* stood on its hind legs. Its hips had features of both later kinds of dinosaurs—bird-hipped and lizard-hipped.

THE SKULL OF HERRERASAURUS was long and narrow like the heads of later meat-eating dinosaurs. But *Herrerasaurus*'s lower jaw had a joint it could flex to strengthen its bite for chomping on prey, as shown here. Some lizards have this jaw structure, but not many dinosaurs did.

FOSSILS OF *HERRERASAURUS* HAVE BEEN FOUND IN A SOUTH AMERICAN DESERT CALLED THE VALLEY OF THE MOON. IN THE TIME OF *HERRE-RASAURUS*, THE ARID TERRAIN WAS INSTEAD A WARM FOREST.

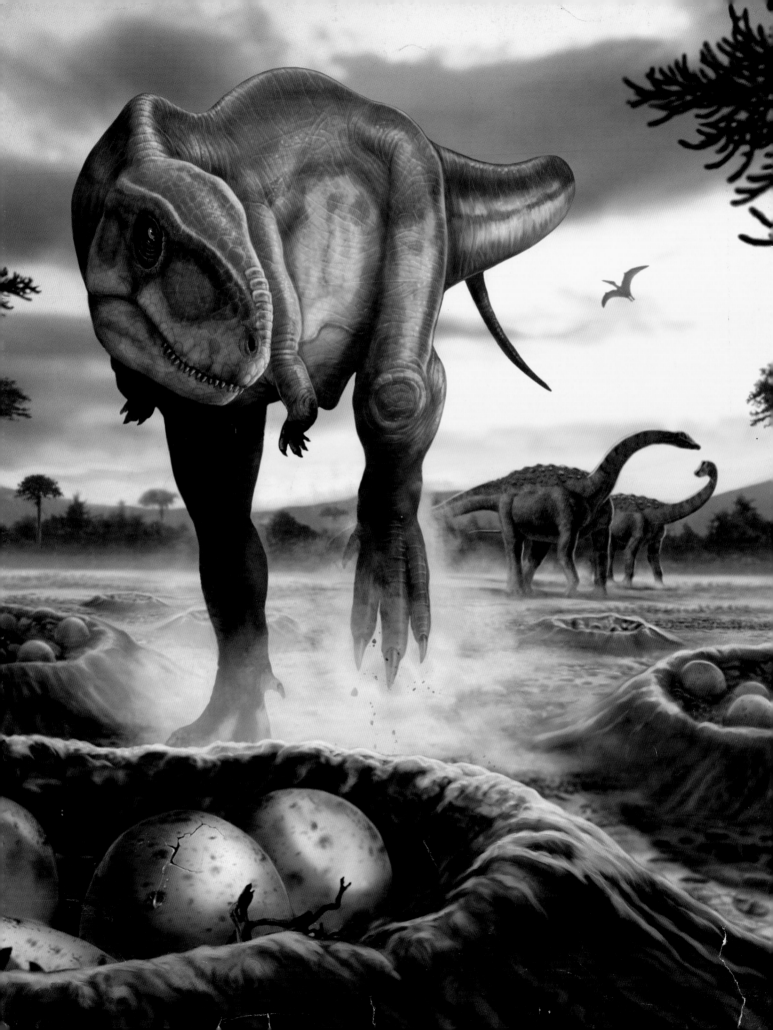

AUCA-SAURUS

AW-kuh-SORE-us

NAME *Aucasaurus*

MEANING "Reptile from Auca (in Patagonia)"

PERIOD 84 million years ago, Late Cretaceous

FOUND Argentina

FOSSILS One nearly complete skeleton

LENGTH 14 feet (4.3 meters) long

NEST RAIDER?

Aucasaurus was one of many mid-sized South American meat eaters, the best known of which is *Carnotaurus* (p. 61). *Aucasaurus* had longer arms than *Carnotaurus* and no horns on its head. Its strong jaws and teeth were its weapons. Its legs were long and light, suggesting that it might have run down its prey.

A complete skeleton of *Aucasaurus* was found on top of the fossil nest of hundreds of sauropod eggs. So *Aucasaurus* may have had an appetite for baby dinosaurs and eggs.

AUCASAURUS WAS A FIERCE HUNTER and crafty egg raider, just as you see here. But it was also the victim of other predators—although probably only those at least as big as itself!

AUCASAURUS WAS FOUND WITH A BROKEN SKULL IN A SHALLOW LAKE. **SCIENTISTS THINK** PERHAPS IT WAS BITTEN OR HIT WITH A **POWERFUL BLOW** FROM ANOTHER DINOSAUR.

CARNO-TAURUS

KAR-no-TORE-us

NAME *Carnotaurus*

MEANING "Meat-eating bull lizard"

PERIOD 80 million years ago, Late Cretaceous

FOUND Argentina

FOSSILS Nearly complete skeleton with skin impressions

LENGTH 25 feet (7.6 meters) long

CARNOTAURUS WAS A peculiar-looking dinosaur. Its head was squarish for a big dinosaur, but its lower jaw was thin. Its eyes faced forward unlike those of most dinosaurs. That may have given it particularly strong vision. Only animals whose eyes face the same direction have depth perception.

BULL-HEADED PREDATOR

Carnotaurus was one of the strangest of the South American dinosaurs. Its mid-sized meat-eater relatives lived across the Southern Hemisphere, in Africa and India as well as South America. (The Indian subcontinent was then located south of the Equator.)

Carnotaurus was named "bull" for its horns, which were large for a meat eater. *Carnotaurus*'s neck was unusually long, too. But perhaps strangest of all were its tiny arms, even shorter than *T. rex*'s. Very clear impressions of its skin were found next to its skeleton. *Carnotaurus* had many small bumps in a repeating pattern on its hide.

CARNOTAURUS WAS THE BAD GUY IN THE ANIMATED DISNEY MOVIE DINOSAUR. IT WAS MADE BIGGER, MEANER, AND FASTER THAN IT REALLY WAS, A SORT OF EXAGGERATION COMMON IN MOVIES.

COELO-PHYSIS

SEE-low-FIE-sis

NAME *Coelophysis*

MEANING "Hollow form"

PERIOD 200 million years ago, Late Triassic

FOUND U.S. (Arizona, New Mexico)

FOSSILS Many complete skeletons

LENGTH Less than 9 feet (3 meters) long

SMALL BUT QUICK LIZARD EATER

Coelophysis was a light little meat eater and probably a fast hunter. Like many other Triassic dinosaurs, *Coelophysis* had four fingers, but only three functioned, showing that dinosaur hands were already changing. The last meat eaters, the tyrannosaurs, had only two fingers.

Coelophysis's claim to fame is that it is the oldest dinosaur known from multiple complete skeletons. A jumble of fossils from more than one hundred *Coelophysis* skeletons were found at the Ghost Ranch Quarry in New Mexico in 1947. They are among the earliest small dinosaurs known.

THE NECK OF THIS *COELOPHYSIS* WAS NOT TWISTED BACK IN LIFE. SOON AFTER DEATH, ANIMAL MUSCLES CONTRACT, PULLING THE HEAD AND NECK BACKWARD.

A LIZARD-EATING *COELOPHYSIS* brings food to its young. A bone of a young *Coelophysis* was found in the stomach region of an adult. But later research indicated that the bone belonged to a young dinosaur skeleton underneath the adult. Other bones found in the stomach of adult *Coelophysis* belong to small reptiles.

CRYOLOPHO-SAURUS

CRY-oh-LOW-fo-SORE-us

NAME *Cryolophosaurus*

MEANING "Frozen-crested reptile"

PERIOD 195 million years ago, Early Jurassic

FOUND Antarctica

FOSSILS Partial skeleton with skull

LENGTH 20 feet (6.1 meters) long

SOUTH POLE FIND

Cryolophosaurus was discovered about one hundred miles from the South Pole. Geologist William Hammer found the well-preserved skull by chance on the icy slopes of a mountain.

Dr. Hammer jokes that *Cryolophosaurus* should be called "Elvisaurus" for its strange head crest. That bone looks a bit like the hairstyle of rock-and-roll singer Elvis Presley. *Cryolophosaurus*'s bony crest is unlike any other early meat-eating dinosaur's head decoration. Perhaps this crest was a design to attract mates or to make the dinosaur seem more frightening to rivals. Another oddly crested dinosaur, *Dilophosaurus*, lived at nearly the same time and grew to the same size. You can meet it on the next page.

CRYOLOPHOSAURUS IS THE FIRST DINOSAUR DISCOVERED IN ANTARCTICA.

CRYOLOPHOSAURUS LIVED for many months in long hours of little light. Though Antarctica was not as far south as it is today, winters were dark. But here southern lights fill the night skies. We don't know how good *Cryolophosaurus*'s eyesight was, but keen vision would certainly have helped it hunt in the long twilight of winter.

DILOPHO-SAURUS

DIE-low-fo-SORE-us

NAME *Dilophosaurus*

MEANING "Double-crested reptile"

PERIOD 195 million years ago, Early Jurassic

FOUND U.S. (Arizona); China

FOSSILS Several nearly complete skeletons

LENGTH 20 feet (6.1 meters) long

DILOPHOSAURUS HUNTS a big prosauropod plant eater. In China, *Dilophosaurus* bones were found near those of *Yunnanosaurus*, one of the first large plant-eating dinosaurs. But could *Dilophosaurus* have killed a big *Yunnanosaurus* like this one? Some scientists think its bite wasn't powerful enough to hunt.

DOUBLE CRESTED CARNIVORE

Dilophosaurus takes its name from its most unusual feature—its rounded double crest. But it had other odd features. Its jawbones were not strongly connected. There was a gap behind its forward teeth. And its teeth had a narrow base. So they might have broken off more easily in feeding than the teeth of other big meat eaters.

Some scientists think that with all of these features, *Dilophosaurus* could only have eaten fish or already dead animals. Others disagree and believe that *Dilophosaurus* was a capable hunter, able to take on the biggest plant eaters of its time—the prosauropods.

IN THE MOVIE *JURASSIC PARK*, *DILOPHOSAURUS* WAS A LITTLE POISON "SPITTER" WITH A NECK THAT FANNED OUT. IN TRUTH, IT WAS BIG, WITHOUT A NECK FRILL OR DEADLY VENOM.

YANGCHUANO-SAURUS

YANG-chew-an-oh-SORE-us

NAME
Yangchuanosaurus

MEANING "Reptile from Yangchuan"

PERIOD 163 million years ago, Late Jurassic

FOUND China

FOSSILS Several nearly complete skeletons

LENGTH 36 feet (8.2 meters) long

YANGCHUANOSAURUS COMING at you! Not a view you'd want to see if you were a plant eater in its time. The powerful teeth and claws of *Yangchuanosaurus* made it a formidable hunter.

JURASSIC TERROR

Yangchuanosaurus may have been the biggest Asian predator of all in the Jurassic Period. *Yangchuanosaurus* dominated Asia as *Allosaurus* (p. 75) later terrorized Jurassic North America.

China was home to many giant plant eaters when *Yangchuanosaurus* roamed, including 100-foot-long (30-m-long) *Mamenchisaurus* (p. 205). But these giants had no weapons to match the arsenal of *Yangchuano-saurus*. Using its teeth and claws, *Yangchuanosaurus* could kill and tear up animals much bigger than itself or rip up creatures it found already dead.

THE FIRST SKELETON OF YANGCHUANOSAURUS WAS FOUND BY A CONSTRUCTION WORKER DIGGING A DAM IN CHINA'S YELLOW RIVER VALLEY IN 1977.

MEGALO-SAURUS

MEG-ah-low-SORE-us

NAME *Megalosaurus*

MEANING "Great reptile"

PERIOD 166 million years ago, Middle Jurassic

FOUND England, France, Portugal

FOSSILS Many bones, but no complete skeletons

LENGTH 27 feet (8.5 meters) long

A *MEGALOSAURUS* IN SEARCH of prey was a frightening sight. *Megalosaurus* wasn't a fast meat eater, but it was faster than the slow-moving stegosaurs of its time, which may have been its prey. *Megalosaurus* could have used its strong jaws to tear at its victims.

MEGA MEAT EATER

When people first discovered *Megalosaurus* bones in England in 1677, they believed the huge bones belonged to an ancient giant or dragon. It wasn't until William Buckland, a British reverend and professor, named *Megalosaurus* that it was identified as a dinosaur.

Megalosaurus was the first dinosaur to have a scientific description published, even though Gideon Mantell had examined the teeth of *Iguanodon* shortly before.

The first illustrations of this bulky meat eater made it look like a Chinese paper dragon—a huge-headed, square, four-legged beast. But *Megalosaurus* was two-legged with short arms that were probably of little use.

MEGALO-SAURUS IS THE FIRST DINOSAUR MENTIONED IN POPULAR BOOKS. IT APPEARS IN *CHARLES DICKENS'S* 1852 NOVEL *BLEAK HOUSE.*

LOURINHANO-SAURUS

Lew-reen-ha-no-SORE-us

NAME
Lourinhanosaurus

MEANING "Reptile from Lourinha"

PERIOD 145 million years ago, Late Jurassic

FOUND Portugal

FOSSILS Partial skeleton, no skull

LENGTH 26 feet (8 meters) long

FLESH EATER WITH BELLY ROCKS

Just what kind of meat eater *Lourinhanosaurus* was is not clear to scientists. Some think it was a cousin of *Allosaurus* (p. 75), while others think it may have been more closely related to the older *Megalosaurus* (p. 71). The fossil bones found in Portugal belong to a "teenaged" dinosaur—not fully grown, but already nearly 14 feet (4.5 m) long.

Part of the find was a number of gastroliths, or polished stones. *Lourinhanosaurus* would have swallowed stones to help grind up the food in its gut. Some animals do this today—chickens, for example, aid their digestion by swallowing little bits of grit.

HOW CAN WE PICTURE *LOURINHANOSAURUS*, shown here eating a large plant eater, when we don't have his skull? Answer: By creating a head like its closest-known relative, *Allosaurus*, but reduced to *Lourinhanosaurus*'s size.

LOURINHANOSAURUS AND OTHER DINOSAURS FROM ITS LOCATION IN PORTUGAL WERE DISCOVERED BY OCTAVIO MATEUS, A YOUNG PALEONTOLOGY STUDENT FROM A NEARBY TOWN. OCTAVIO'S MOTHER WORKED TO CREATE A DINOSAUR MUSEUM NEAR THE DISCOVERY SITE.

ALLO-SAURUS

AL-oh-SORE-us

NAME *Allosaurus*

MEANING "Strange reptile"

PERIOD 145 million years ago, Late Jurassic

FOUND U.S. (Colorado, Utah, Wyoming, Montana)

FOSSILS Many skeletons

LENGTH 28 feet (8.5 meters) long

IT IS POSSIBLE that *Allosaurus* hunted in a group like this, though there is no direct evidence. Hundreds of bones from many allosaurs were found together in Price, Utah. But scientists think these fossils built up over time. Perhaps one *Allosaurus* after another fell into a pit that was a long-time danger to dinosaurs.

DEADLY JURASSIC HUNTER

Allosaurus was the king of the Jurassic predators in North America. Even the giant plant eaters, such as *Apatosaurus* (p. 191) and *Diplodocus* (p. 193), might not have been safe from *Allosaurus*. Powerful jaws held nearly 70 sharp, thick teeth. The claws on its three-fingered hands measured up to 8 inches (20 cm) long.

Allosaurus did not have a very large skull or teeth for an animal of its size, but the bones of its skull were flexible. The lower jawbones could bend outward, making a large space in its mouth for holding meat.

ALLOSAURUS FROM NORTH AMERICA WAS CLOSELY RELATED TO GIANT MEAT EATERS OF ITS TIME IN AFRICA, EUROPE, AND AUSTRALIA.

ACROCANTHO-SAURUS

ACK-row-CAN-tho-SORE-us

NAME
Acrocanthosaurus

MEANING "High-spined lizard"

PERIOD 121 million years ago, Early Cretaceous

FOUND U.S. (Oklahoma, Texas, Arizona)

FOSSILS Two nearly complete skeletons

SIZE 40 feet (12.5 meters) long

ACROCANTHOSAURUS WAS a fierce-looking killer. Its upper jaws held 38 sharp teeth of varying sizes. *Acrocanthosaurus* had bony ridges over its eyes, as did the earlier *Allosaurus*. Later big meat eaters in South America also had similar bony ridges over their eyes.

SLOW-RUNNING ATTACKER

Acrocanthosaurus was one of the biggest of all killer dinosaurs. It is THE biggest ever found in the southern United States. Spines up to 2 feet (0.6 m) long on its neck and back supported a muscled ridge of unknown purpose. But it was not the most terrifying of all killers. It had long thigh bones compared to its shinbones, a sign of a slow runner. *Acrocanthosaurus*'s thick tail could not have helped it get around quickly either.

Still, it was probably capable of killing any plant eater in its world. Its most likely prey would have included *Paluxysaurus* (p. 245), *Tenontosaurus* (p. 257), and even the tallest dinosaur of all, *Sauroposeidon*.

SPECTACULAR FOSSIL FOOTPRINTS SHOW A MEAT EATER ATTACKING A GIANT PLANT EATER. THIS FOOTPRINT MIGHT BE THE TRACK OF AN ATTACKING *ACROCANTHOSAURUS*.

CARCHARODONTO-SAURUS

CAR-care-oh-DON-toe-SORE-us

NAME
Carcharodontosaurus

MEANING "Shark-toothed reptile"

PERIOD 110 million years ago, Late Cretaceous

FOUND Algeria, Egypt, Morocco, Niger

FOSSILS Two skeletons and several other fossils

LENGTH 40 feet (12.2 meters) long

CARCHARODONTOSAU-RUS MAY have hunted in packs like its close cousin, *Mapusaurus*. But even alone, as shown here up against a *Rebbachisaurus* (p. 201), *Carcharodontosaurus* was a terrifying hunter. It was nearly as large as the biggest plant eaters we know from its world. *Carcharodontosaurus*'s strong sense of smell and sight would have given it a big advantage in hunting the plant eaters of its day.

TERRIBLE TEETH

Carcharodontosaurus was a giant predator the size of *Tyrannosaurus rex*. It lived at the same time as its even larger close relatives *Giganotosaurus* (p. 81) and *Mapusaurus* (p. 83). All had three-fingered hands and long, narrow skulls and teeth. Parts of *Carcharodontosaurus* were found by German scientists nearly a century ago, but the animal became well known only in the 1990s, when two good skeletons were discovered in Africa.

Carcharodontosaurus's teeth are jagged on the edges and sharp. Those features reminded the scientist who named it of shark teeth, though the teeth of sharks are both wider and shorter.

LIKE THE FIRST FOSSILS OF *SPINOSAURUS* (P. 87), THE FIRST BONES FOUND OF *CARCHARODONTOSAURUS* WERE ACCIDENTALLY BLOWN UP BY BRITISH BOMBERS IN WORLD WAR II.

GIGANOTO-SAURUS

JYE-ga-NO-toe-SORE-us

NAME *Giganotosaurus*

MEANING "Giant reptile of the south"

PERIOD 100 million years ago, Early Cretaceous

FOUND Argentina

FOSSILS One nearly complete skeleton and jawbone

LENGTH 45 feet (13 meters) long

GIGANOTOSAURUS had teeth that were razor sharp on two edges. *Giganotosaurus* was even more solidly built than *Mapusaurus* (p. 83), another South American meat eater, and so *Giganotosaurus* was perhaps an even deadlier killer.

SOUTHERN DINO CZAR

Is *Giganotosaurus* the deadliest killer dinosaur? It was 5 feet longer and as much as 3 tons (2.7 MT) heavier than "Sue," the biggest *Tyrannosaurus rex*. It was almost the same length as *Mapusaurus* (p. 83) but more sturdily built. And while *Spinosaurus* (p. 87) may have been longer, it was far lighter.

Giganotosaurus was discovered in the Argentine desert by a garage mechanic riding on a dune buggy. The skeleton, more than 80 percent complete, was excavated by paleontologist Rodolfo Coria. That skeleton is the only evidence we have of *Giganotosaurus*, except for one other piece of a jawbone.

GIGANOTOSAURUS PROBABLY TRAVELED IN GROUPS OF MANY AGES, JUST AS LIONS DO TODAY. LIONESSES TAKE THE LEAD IN HUNTING ON THE SAVANNA, BUT IN THE CRETACEOUS, *GIGANOTOSAURUS* PROBABLY MADE HUNTING MORE OF A FAMILY AFFAIR. A PACK OF HUNGRY *GIGANOTOSAURUS* WOULD HAVE BEEN A MATCH FOR ANY ANCIENT ANIMAL.

MAPU-SAURUS

MAP-oo-SORE-us

NAME *Mapusaurus*

MEANING "Lizard of the Mapuche Indians," after Indians of South America

PERIOD 100 million years ago, Late Cretaceous

FOUND Argentina

FOSSILS Seven partial skeletons

LENGTH 46 feet (14 meters) long

A *MAPUSAURUS* BABY COULD TEAR meat from a dead plant eater just as its parents did. From fossil finds, it appears *Mapusaurus* young, "teenagers," and adults sometimes traveled together. They may have hunted together as well. Eating, hunting, and playing as a group would have helped young *Mapusaurus* learn survival skills.

DINOSAUR SMACKDOWN!

The greatest battle of all time had to be the largest meat eater versus the large plant eater: *Mapusaurus* versus *Argentinosaurus* (p. 199). They lived at the same time. But how could the biggest meat eater take down a 100-foot-long (30-m-long) plant eater ten times its weight?

By hunting in a pack, that's how. Paleontologist Rodolfo Coria found the bones of seven different *Mapusaurus* in one hillside. The bones belonged to two adults and several 20-foot-long (6-m-long) "teenagers" and 9-foot-long (2.7-m-long) "babies." Together, they would have made a terrifying fighting force.

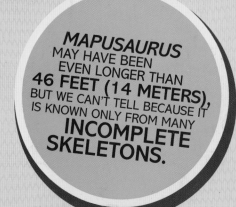

MAPUSAURUS MAY HAVE BEEN EVEN LONGER THAN 46 FEET (14 METERS), BUT WE CAN'T TELL BECAUSE IT IS KNOWN ONLY FROM MANY INCOMPLETE SKELETONS.

BARY-ONYX

BARE-ee-ON-icks

NAME
Baryonyx

MEANING "Heavy claw"

PERIOD 125 million years ago, Early Cretaceous

FOUND England, Niger, Spain

FOSSILS One nearly complete skeleton, claws, and part of a skull

LENGTH 28 feet (8.5 meters) long

SCIENTISTS HAVE SUG-GESTED THAT Baryonyx's strange claws were used to spear fish while it sat on a river bank, as bears do today. Baryonyx's narrow jaw, like a crocodile's, was well-suited to catching fish. Its snout was also angled like the tip of a crocodile's head. Perhaps that design helped Baryonyx hold flopping fish in its mouth.

DINO FISHERMAN

Baryonyx is named for its unusual thumb claw, which was more than a foot (0.3 m) long. But that was not its only strange feature. Its skull was positioned at a much sharper angle to its neck than other meat eaters. Its long, narrow jaw held nearly 100 teeth, most of them in its lower jaw. A smaller, narrow-jawed dinosaur, Suchomimus (p. 255), was found in 2004 in Africa. But Baryonyx appears to have also lived across northern Africa and southern Europe.

Scientists are confident that Baryonyx was a fish eater. They found the best clue of all to support that diet hypothesis—fish scales in the fossil's stomach area.

BARYONYX WAS FOUND BY AN AMATEUR FOSSIL HUNTER, WILLIAM WALKER, WHO SAW ONE OF ITS CLAWS STICKING OUT OF THE SIDE OF A CLAY PIT.

SPINO-SAURUS

SPINE-oh-SORE-us

NAME *Spinosaurus*

MEANING "Spiny lizard"

PERIOD 97.5 million years ago, Late Cretaceous

FOUND Egypt, Morocco

FOSSILS Several partial skeletons

LENGTH 45 feet (13.7 meters) long

WAS *SPINOSAURUS* A FISHING dinosaur, like *Baryonyx* (p. 85)? Its jaws were long like those of *Baryonyx* and crocodiles. And its teeth were cone-shaped like a crocodile's. Its nostrils were raised like a crocodile's, too. High nostrils are good for breathing if your head is in the water.

LONGEST MEAT EATER

Spinosaurus was not the heaviest of meat eaters, but some scientists think it may have been one of the longest, at 40 to 50 feet (12 to 15 m) long.

Spinosaurus is best known for its tall, thin back spines. These spikes reached up to 7 feet (2 m) high. Perhaps they were connected with skin in the shape of a sail. Why? That's also a mystery. But maybe the sail helped it cool off in the hot sun near the Equator. Or it may have helped to impress *Spinosaurus*'s mates. *Spinosaurus* was not the only dinosaur with a sail roaming North Africa at that time. *Ouranosaurus* (p. 245), a big plant eater, had one also.

THE FIRST BONES FOUND OF *SPINOSAURUS* WERE BLOWN UP IN A GERMAN MUSEUM DURING **WORLD WAR II.**

ALBERTO-SAURUS

al-BUR-toh-SORE-us

NAME *Albertosaurus*

MEANING "Reptile from Alberta"

PERIOD 70 million years ago, Late Cretaceous

FOUND Canada (Alberta)

FOSSILS Many skeletons

LENGTH 25 feet (7.6 meters) long

TWO *ALBERTOSAURUS* THREATEN EACH OTHER. Why would they be fighting? Perhaps over food. Or water. Or territory. Or access to a mate. And did these big meat eaters have feathers like small meat eaters did? For now, we have no evidence.

FIERCE PACK HUNTER

Albertosaurus was a large tyrannosaur that lived five million years before *Tyrannosaurus rex*. Like its much bigger cousin, *Albertosaurus* was a strong-jawed meat eater with thick, sharp, grooved teeth. Though *Albertosaurus*'s skull was little more than half as long as *T. rex*'s, it had 60 teeth— several more than *T. rex*. And like all tyrannosaurs, *Alberto-saurus* had only two fingers on small arms.

Albertosaurus spent at least some of its time traveling in a pack. For many years we had no idea that big meat eaters lived in groups. Instead we imagined them as solitary animals like tigers. All that changed when Canadian paleontologist Philip Currie discovered bones from 22 *Albertosaurus* in a single location.

THOUGH *ALBERTOSAURUS* WEIGHED NEARLY **TWO TONS,** SOME SCIENTISTS SUGGEST IT MAY HAVE RUN ALMOST **30 MPH** (48 KPH).

TYRANNOSAURUS REX

tye-RAN-oh-SORE-us

NAME
Tyrannosaurus rex

MEANING "Tyrant lizard king"

PERIOD 65 million years ago, Late Cretaceous

FOUND U.S. (Colorado, Montana, New Mexico, South Dakota, Wyoming); Canada (Alberta, Saskatchewan)

FOSSILS More than 20 skeletons up to 90 percent complete

LENGTH 40 feet (12 meters) long

NATURE HAS NEVER PRODUCED a weapon as powerful as the jaws of *T. rex*. With its thick, sharp teeth, it could smash bones and rip off hundreds of pounds of meat in a single bite. If cars had been around in *T. rex*'s day, its bite could have dented the metal.

THE DINO KING

Everybody knows *Tyrannosaurus rex,* and it's the most popular of all dinosaurs. It was not the largest meat eater, but it was one of the scariest. Its brain was twice the size of other giant meat eaters like *Giganotosaurus* (p. 81), and it was faster and had better vision. Though its arms were tiny and nearly useless, its jaws were strong enough to crush any animal.

T. rex was named more than one hundred years ago, but the most complete *T. rex*, "Sue," was discovered in South Dakota twenty years ago. The first juvenile *T. rex* was found even more recently by a dig crew from the Los Angeles County Museum. The half-grown youngster will go on display in 2011.

T. REX HAS A NEARLY IDENTICAL COUSIN IN ASIA NAMED *TARBOSAURUS.*

ARCHAEORNI THOMIMUS

AHR-kee-or-NI-thoh-MIME-us

NAME
Archaeornithomimus

MEANING "Ancient bird mimic"

PERIOD 80 million years ago, Late Cretaceous

FOUND China, Uzbekhistan

FOSSILS More than 20 skeletons up to 90 percent complete

LENGTH 11 feet (3 meters) long

ARCHAEORNITHOMI-MUS WERE FAST runners, which would have helped them get away from predators. Perhaps they also traveled in packs, which would have provided some protection. And they may have had feathers that would have acted as insulation on cold nights in what is now the Gobi Desert.

MEAT EATER OR NOT?

Archaeornithomimus looked much like *Struthiomimus* (p. 95) and other big ornithomimids, even though it lived several million years before. *Archaeornithomimus* only weighed about 100 pounds (40 kg). Its long legs and light build helped it run quickly.

Archaeornithomimus is known from incomplete fossils discovered in northern China, and foot bones recently found in Maryland have also been identified as *Archaeornithomimus*. It's unclear whether *Archaeornithomimus* ate meat. It had a sharp beak but not powerful teeth. Perhaps it was omnivorous, eating both plants and meat, including fruit, insects, small mammals and lizards.

ARCHAEORNITHOMIMUS HAD SMALLER HANDS AND A MUCH SHORTER **THIRD FINGER** THAN LATER ORNITHOMIMIDS. **WHY?** WE DON'T KNOW.

STRUTHIO-MIMUS

Strooth-ee-oh-MY-muss

NAME *Struthiomimus*

MEANING "Ostrich mimic"

PERIOD 76 million years ago, Late Cretaceous

FOUND U.S. (Wyoming, Utah); Canada (Alberta)

FOSSILS Several skeletons

LENGTH 14 feet (4.3 meters) long

PERHAPS THE FASTEST OF ALL DINOSAURS was *Struthiomimus*. We may never know for sure how fast, but fossilized footprints suggest that the light, long-legged, ostrich-like dinosaur ran more than 30 miles an hour. That's as fast as a horse can run and faster than any human.

LONG-TAILED RUNNER

Struthiomimus was a meat-eating dinosaur without teeth. It may have lived on small reptiles and mammals, even insects and fruit. Its neck, arms, hands, and legs were all long and thin. Many of *Struthiomimus*'s relatives had feathers, and so it probably did as well. Other ostrich dinosaurs grew even larger. The family of ornithomimids ("bird mimics") is known from both western North America and central Asia.

Despite growing to 14 feet (4 m) long, *Struthiomimus* is estimated to have weighed less than 330 pounds (150 kg). Its long, stiff tail may have helped it balance as it ran.

RECENT FOSSIL FINDS SHOW THAT STRUTHIOMIMUS HAD A LARGE, HARD BEAK.

UTAH-RAPTOR

YOO-tah-RAP-tore

NAME *Utahraptor*

MEANING "Utah thief"

PERIOD 125 million years ago, Early Cretaceous

FOUND U.S. (Utah)

FOSSILS One half-complete skeleton

LENGTH 19.5 feet (5.9 meters) long

ARMED AND DANGEROUS

What was the scariest of all dinosaurs? If not *Tyrannosaurus rex* then perhaps this one-ton killer. Yes, *T. rex* was twice as big, but *Utahraptor* was pretty huge, too—the size of an ice-cream truck. And it was probably faster than *T. rex. Utahraptor* had strong jaws full of sharp teeth and powerful legs to jump high and kick hard with the enormous, sharp claws on both its hands and its legs.

Utahraptor was an early raptor dinosaur. It was also the largest raptor we know. That is unusual. Usually within a group of dinosaurs, the different kinds grow bigger through time, but the dromaeosaurid raptors started big and got smaller.

UTAHRAPTOR'S MOST TERRIFYING WEAPONS were its eight-inch-long (20-cm-long) claws. One deadly claw on each limb gave a leaping *Utahraptor* the tool it needed to slice its opponent.

PALEONTOLOGIST JIM KIRKLAND DUG UP *UTAHRAPTOR* ON A TIP FROM A CUSTOMER IN A PANCAKE SHOP!

OVIRAPTOR

OH-vih-RAP-tore

NAME *Oviraptor*

MEANING "Egg thief"

PERIOD 70 million years ago, Late Cretaceous

FOUND Mongolia, China

FOSSILS Several complete skeletons

LENGTH 8 feet (2.4 meters) long

THOUGH IT WAS NAMED THE "EGG THIEF," *Oviraptor* was a good dinosaur parent. The proof was the discovery twenty years ago of a fossil *Oviraptor* STILL on top of its nest of eggs. A sandstorm or collapsing sand dune probably buried the *Oviraptor* as it sat on its eggs.

DESERT NESTERS

Oviraptor is a dinosaur with a reputation it never deserved. It got its name, "egg thief," when it was mistakenly thought to have stolen eggs from the nest of a plant eater. (See "Great Dinosaur Mistakes," p. 39, for more of the story.)

Oviraptor was the first known member of a group of Asian meat eaters with no teeth. How could a meat eater have no teeth? They may have eaten reptiles and even nuts or fruits instead of chewing flesh.

Oviraptor was discovered with its fossilized eggs. Its position atop its nest suggests it may have had feathered wings that sheltered its young. It laid a dozen eggs or more in a spiral design within the nest. The eggs were oval in shape, unlike the rounded eggs of many plant eaters. They were only 7 inches (17 cm) long.

AN *OVIRAPTOR* EGG WAS SOLD TO COLGATE UNIVERSITY IN THE 1920s FOR $5,000 BY THE LEGENDARY ROY CHAPMAN ANDREWS (SEE PAGE 32).

CONCHO-RAPTOR

CONK-oh-RAP-tore

NAME *Conchoraptor*

MEANING "Conch thief"

PERIOD 80 million years ago, Late Cretaceous

FOUND Mongolia, China

FOSSILS Many skeletons

SIZE 6 feet (2 meters) long

SEASHORE SCAVENGER

Conchoraptor was toothless and small like its close cousin, *Oviraptor* (p. 99). Other members of their group grew to more than 20 feet (6.5 m) long, but *Conchoraptor* was less than a third that length. But *Conchoraptor* was not just like *Oviraptor*. It had no head crest, and its hands were more primitive than *Oviraptor*'s.

The bones of *Conchoraptor* were first discovered more than thirty years ago in the Gobi desert. At that time they were thought to be from a young *Oviraptor*. Scientists later realized that the fossils belonged to a full-grown member of a brand new species.

SNAILS AND OTHER ANIMALS TODAY USE SHELLS AS PROTECTION FROM BIRD BEAKS. CREATURES IN DINOSAUR TIME USED SHELLS FOR PROTECTION TOO.

ONE OF *CONCHORAP-TOR'S* DISTINCTIVE features was a powerful beak. It was named for this beak and for scientists' theories that the beak could have been used to crack open conchs, snails, or other shelled animals, such as the crabs in the picture. *Conchoraptor* lived near the shores of lakes where some of these creatures were common.

MICRO-RAPTOR

MY-crow-RAP-tore

NAME *Microraptor*

MEANING "Small thief"

PERIOD 124 million years ago, Early Cretaceous

FOUND China

FOSSILS More than 20 nearly complete skeletons

LENGTH 22 inches (55.9 cm) long

LITTLE GLIDER

Microraptor was one of the smallest of all meat-eating dinosaurs. It weighed less than a pound. Its long upper arm bones were similar to those of *Troodon* and birds. *Microraptor* was discovered in an area of northeastern China famous for its many discoveries of remarkably well-preserved dinosaurs. The fine-grained rocks containing the fossils even show the impressions of feathers. Scientists have reconstructed *Microraptor* to learn if this dinosaur could fly. They concluded that *Microraptor* could glide and perhaps climb trees to launch itself into the air, but it wouldn't have been able to achieve fully powered flight.

LITTLE *MICRORAPTOR* HAD SHARP claws and four feathered limbs. It couldn't fly. But maybe it could climb trees and glide to the ground. At the end of its tail, it had a fan of feathers that may have helped keep it balanced in the air.

A CHINESE FOSSIL SELLER GLUED TOGETHER THE **TAIL END** OF **MICRORAPTOR** AND THE TOP HALF OF AN ANCIENT BIRD TO CREATE WHAT SOME SCIENTISTS BRIEFLY THOUGHT WAS A NEW EARLY LINK BETWEEN BIRDS AND **DINOSAURS.**

COMPSOG- NATHUS

KOMP-sog-NAH-thus

NAME *Compsognathus*

MEANING "Delicate jaw"

PERIOD 145 million years ago, Late Jurassic

FOUND Germany, France

FOSSILS Several complete skeletons

LENGTH 3 feet (0.9 meters) long

COMPSOGNATHUS was a fast, strong-eyed hunter. Insects, lizards, and small mammals may have been its favorite prey. And we have proof. The remains of a lizard were found in the chest area of a *Compsognathus*. The lizard fossil was a whole skeleton. So *Compsognathus* may have swallowed its prey whole.

FEISTY LIZARD SLURPER

Compsognathus has produced a lot of confusion. It was discovered in the same limestone quarries that produced *Archaeopteryx* (p. 117). At first scientists thought the fossils were from the same dinosaur. Then for many years, scientists didn't recognize the third finger on *Compsognathus*'s hands, so they thought it was related to the much later, two-fingered *Tyrannosaurus rex* (p. 91).

And, scientists also thought that *Compsognathus* was one of the smallest dinosaurs. But then they figured out that the fossil they were measuring was a half-sized "teenager."

COMPSOGNATHUS WAS NO BIGGER THAN A TURKEY. FOSSIL IMPRESSIONS FOUND IN 2006 SHOW THAT COMPSOGNATHUS HAD BUMPY SKIN. DID IT HAVE FEATHERS TOO? WE'RE NOT SURE.

BUITRE-RAPTOR

BWEE-tre-RAP-tore

NAME *Buitreraptor*

MEANING "Thief from La Buitrera"

PERIOD 90 million years ago, Late Cretaceous

FOUND Argentina

FOSSILS Complete Skeleton

LENGTH 3 feet (1 meter) long

RAPTOR FROM THE SOUTH

Raptor dinosaurs have long been known from North America, Europe, and Asia. But only recently have the hook-clawed creatures been found in the Southern Hemisphere. *Buitreraptor* had the long, straight tail and long, sharp claws that are typical of dromaeosaurid dinosaurs. But in other ways, *Buitreraptor* was unique.

For example, it had teeth with no grooves, which may have made it unable to hunt other dinosaurs. But just like other small raptors, *Buitreraptor* may have had feathers. The feathers would have conserved energy and kept little meat-eating dinosaurs warm.

WITHOUT GROOVED TEETH for slicing meat, *Buitreraptor* might not have been able to hunt other dinosaurs. Instead the fast, small *Buitreraptor* may have hunted small mammals and reptiles—or even insects, as shown here. Its best weapons were its sharp claws, not its smooth-sided teeth.

LITTLE **BUITRERAPTOR** WAS FOUND NEAR THE SITE IN **ARGENTINA** WHERE *GIGANOTOSAURUS* (P. 81), ONE OF THE **LARGEST MEAT EATERS**, WAS DISCOVERED.

SCANSORI-OPTERYX

SCAN-sore-ee-OP-tore-icks

NAME *Scansoriopteryx*

MEANING "Climbing wing"

PERIOD 113 million years ago, Early Cretaceous

FOUND China

FOSSILS One skeleton of a hatchling

LENGTH hatchling: 1 foot (30 centimeters) long

A YOUNG *SCANSORI-OPTERYX*—the only kind we know—climbs a tree with the help of its long and claw-tipped third finger. Its backward-pointing toes are a feature of climbing birds as well. Despite its long feathers, *Scansoriopteryx* could not fly, but perhaps it was able to glide from trees.

TREETOP HUNTER

Scansoriopteryx has some odd features for a little meat eater—and they all suggest it climbed trees. It has long front limbs. Its third finger is twice the size of its second finger (in meat eaters the second finger is usually the biggest). And it had especially strong toe claws.

Why would a dinosaur want to live in trees? Treetops would be a safe hideaway from bigger animals. And *Scansoriopteryx* could find insects in the trees. Although *Scansoriopteryx* couldn't fly, it was feathered like many other small dinosaurs of its time.

SCANSORIOPTERYX MAY HAVE FED ON INSECTS LIVING IN TREE BARK, MUCH AS WOODPECKERS DO TODAY, EXCEPT IT WOULD HAVE USED ITS LONG FINGERS TO GET THE BUGS.

DEINO-NYCHUS

die-NON-e-cuss

NAME *Deinonychus*

MEANING "Terrible claw"

PERIOD 119 million years ago, Early Cretaceous

FOUND U.S. (Montana, Oklahoma, Wyoming, Utah)

FOSSILS Several complete skeletons

LENGTH 10 feet (3 meters) long

A PACK OF *DEINONY-CHUS* feasts on a big plant-eating *Tenontosaurus*. This scene is based on fossil evidence. The bones of several *Deinonychus* were found around the body of a *Tenontosaurus* (p. 257). Probably some of the attacking pack of *Deinonychus* were killed by the big plant eater before the rest of the pack took it down.

SWITCHBLADE CLAWS

Deinonychus was a human-sized raptor dinosaur. Compared to other raptors, it had shorter, thicker legs, so while it was not as fast, it was more powerful. Its most dangerous weapons were its slicing claws. The claws on the second toes of each foot were more than five inches (12.7 cm) long. They could be retracted like a cat's claws when the dinosaur ran. Then they could be snapped out to slice at prey.

Deinonychus skeletons were found with a *Tenontosaurus* (p. 257) plant eater fossil in Montana. The discovery led to scientific speculation that *Deinonychus* was a pack hunter.

THE DISCOVERY IN 1954 OF *DEINONYCHUS* WITH ITS MANY BIRDLIKE FEATURES INDICATED TO MANY SCIENTISTS THAT BIRDS WERE DESCENDED FROM DINOSAURS.

TROODON

TRO-oh-don

NAME *Troodon*

MEANING "Wound tooth"

PERIOD 76 million years ago, Late Cretaceous

FOUND U.S. (Montana, Wyoming, Alaska); Canada (Alberta)

FOSSILS 20 skeletons, many teeth and eggs

LENGTH 6.5 feet (2 meters) long

***TROODON* WAS SMARTER THAN** your mousey mammal ancestors. Its big brain meant it enjoyed good eyesight and sense of smell. With its raptor-style claws and speed, it was likely a good hunter. Perhaps it even hunted in twilight to take advantage of its strong eyesight.

DINO BRAINIAC

Troodon was a slender little meat eater. How did it survive among so many bigger dinosaurs? Well, it helped that *Troodon* was the smartest of all dinosaurs. Scientists estimate its intelligence by the size of its brain compared to its body. On that scale, *Troodon* was about as smart as an ostrich today.

Troodon is also special because of its teeth. It had several different shapes of teeth, which probably allowed it to eat different types of food. Little mammals and lizards were likely among its favorite dinners. But its long claws suggest it may have killed large prey such as young duck-billed dinosaurs, particularly if *Troodon* hunted in packs.

TROODON'S BRAIN WAS AS BIG AS A GOLF BALL ON AN ANIMAL NO BIGGER THAN A FIFTH-GRADER. A FIFTH-GRADER'S BRAIN IS BIGGER THAN A BASEBALL.

VELOCI-RAPTOR

veh-LOSS-ih-RAP-tore

NAME *Velociraptor*

MEANING "Speed thief"

PERIOD 80 million years ago, Late Cretaceous

FOUND Mongolia

FOSSILS Skeletons

LENGTH 6.5 feet (2 meters) long

A *VELOCIRAPTOR* RAIDS another *Velociraptor*'s nest to kill its babies. There is a good chance such a scene actually took place. A baby *Velociraptor* skull was found with two little holes on the top. The teeth of an adult *Velociraptor* fit perfectly into those holes.

VICIOUS CANNIBAL?

Like *Troodon* (p. 113), *Velociraptor* was smart for a dinosaur. Although its brain was comparatively large (though not as big as *Troodon*'s), the poodle-sized *Velociraptor* was one of the smallest raptor dinosaurs. Like all raptors, it had a long, stiff tail. The tail could not be raised, but it could be moved from side to side. Perhaps it functioned like a rudder to help balance a running *Velociraptor*. Also, like other raptors, *Velociraptor* had one large, hooked claw on each hand and foot. Its claws were only two inches (5 cm) long, but it was a fast killer with sharp little teeth. It hunted in packs and probably fed mostly on small lizards, mammals, and even baby dinosaurs and eggs.

VELOCIRAPTOR WAS FOUND IN THE GOBI DESERT IN 1924 BY A TEAM LED BY THE REAL-LIFE INDIANA JONES, PALEONTOLOGIST ROY CHAPMAN ANDREWS.

ARCHAE-OPTERYX

ARK-ee-OP-turr-icks

NAME *Archaeopteryx*

MEANING "Ancient feather" or "Ancient wing"

PERIOD 145 million years ago, Late Jurassic

FOUND Germany

FOSSILS 11 skeletons

LENGTH 1.6 feet (0.5 meters) long

THE FIRST BIRD?

Archaeopteryx is among the most famous of all fossils. After it was discovered in 1861, impressions of feathers were seen on the smooth limestone in which it was found. But until those feather impressions were noticed, that fossil was thought to be *Compsognathus* (p. 105), a little dinosaur.

Archaeopteryx was a bird, though a very primitive one with much in common with raptor dinosaurs. Like those dinosaurs, *Archaeopteryx* had sharp teeth, three fingers with claws, and a long, bony tail. Very few birds today have any of those features. *Archaeopteryx* is considered the closest link we have yet found between dinosaurs and birds.

MAYBE ARCHAEOP-TERYX COULD FLY. That's what its feathers, much like those of modern birds, suggest. Or maybe it couldn't fly. It lacked strong chest bones, so it probably didn't have strong muscles to flap its wings. But it could probably glide through the forest. And with its strong claws, it might have climbed trees to launch itself into the air.

ONE OF THE **11 KNOWN SKELETONS** OF THIS FAMOUS DINOSAUR **WAS STOLEN MORE THAN 20 YEARS AGO.** IT HAS NEVER BEEN FOUND.

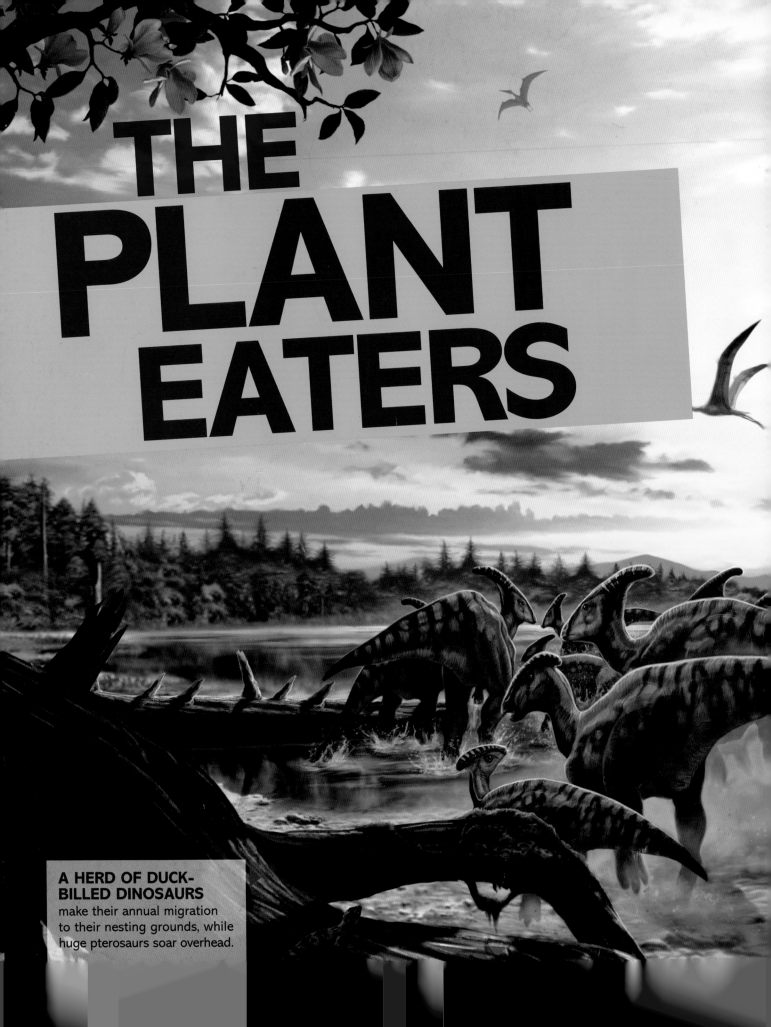

THE PLANT EATERS

A HERD OF DUCK-BILLED DINOSAURS make their annual migration to their nesting grounds, while huge pterosaurs soar overhead.

FAMILIES

SMALL & LARGE CERATOPSIANS
PLANT

Armored dinosaurs nearly covered in bony plates. Some had clubs at the end of their tails.
pp. 146–155

ANKLYOSAURS
PLANT

Armored dinosaurs nearly covered in bony plates. Some had clubs at the end of their tails.
pp. 130–139

STEGOSAURS
PLANT

Plate-backed dinosaurs of the Jurassic Period
pp. 126–129

PACHYCEPHALOSAURS
PLANT

Thick-headed dinosaurs— Small, two-legged dinosaurs with domed or spiky flat heads
pp. 140–145

ORNITHISCHIA (Bird-Hipped Dinosaurs)

DINOSAURIA

PROSAUROPODS
PLANT

Early large plant eaters with tiny heads that walked on all fours or on two hind legs.
pp. 178–181

SAUROPODS
PLANT

Large plant eaters with tiny heads that walked on all fours or on two hind legs.
pp. 182–207

THERIZINOSAURS

Sharp-clawed plant eaters
pp. 208–211

SAURISCHIA (Lizard-Hipped Dinosaurs)

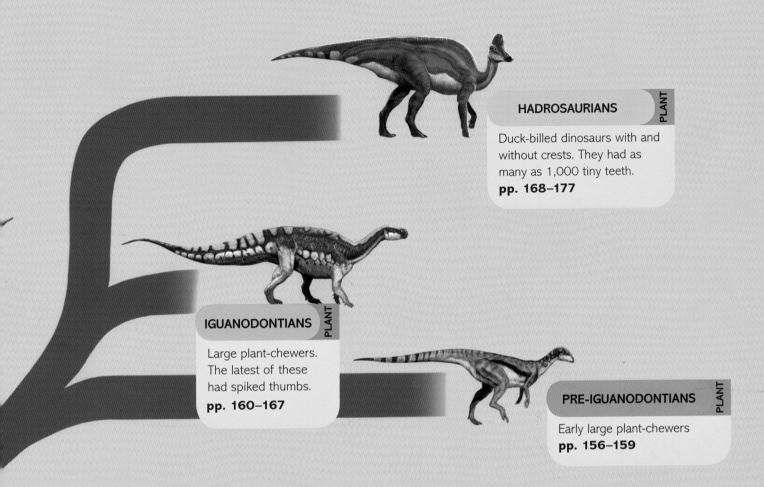

HADROSAURIANS PLANT

Duck-billed dinosaurs with and without crests. They had as many as 1,000 tiny teeth.
pp. 168–177

IGUANODONTIANS PLANT

Large plant-chewers. The latest of these had spiked thumbs.
pp. 160–167

PRE-IGUANODONTIANS PLANT

Early large plant-chewers
pp. 156–159

Very early in dinosaur time the plant eaters split into their ornithischian (bird-hipped) and saurischian (lizard-hipped) lines. The saurischians soon became four-legged prosauropods nearly 30 feet (10 m) long. Then, in the Jurassic Period—the middle of dinosaur time—they evolved into truly gigantic sauropods, as much as ten times bigger than the biggest meat eaters or bird-hipped plant eaters. The sauropods were joined by only one other group of plant eaters, the mysterious therizinosaurs. These appeared in the Cretaceous Period—late dinosaur time—from meat-eating ancestors. Meanwhile the ornithischians spread into many spectacular forms, including armored, dome-headed, duck-billed, and plate-backed dinosaurs.

DEFENSES

GASTONIA MAY HAVE BEEN THE MOST HEAVILY ARMORED OF ALL DINOSAURS. IT COULD HAVE USED THAT ARMOR TO PROTECT ITSELF FROM *UTAHRAPTOR*, THE BIGGEST OF ALL THE RAPTOR KILLERS.

Plant-eating dinosaurs had much to fear from the meat eaters in their world. And they didn't have big powerful teeth or claws like the predators did, so it wasn't easy to fight back.

As in all animal environments, there were many more plant eaters than meat eaters in dinosaur time. So perhaps their best defense was to stay in huge groups, hiding their young in the middle to keep them from being snatched.

Their huge size allowed the biggest plant eaters to throw off meat eaters and even kill them with a kick of their thick legs or a swipe of their huge tails.

Some plant eaters relied on heavy armor to protect themselves from the strong bites of meat eaters. Some even had armor over their eyelids! Duck-billed plant eaters could call out warnings with their nose-horn trumpets. And perhaps some of the largest plant eaters could snap their long tails like bullwhips to produce a frighteningly loud boom to scare predators away.

COOLEST DINOSAUR DEFENSES*

1. *ANKYLOSAURUS*: TAIL CLUB
2. *GASTONIA*: BODY ARMOR
3. *DIPLODOCUS*: WHIP TAIL
4. *IGUANODON*: THUMB SPIKE
5. *PARASAUROLOPHUS*: TRUMPET SOUND
6. *TRICERATOPS*: HORNS
7. *KENTROSAURUS*: SPIKES

*Scientists have no proof that any of these dinosaurs used these defenses in battle.

TYRANNOSAURUS REX (p. 91) rises to attack an *Ankylosaurus* (p. 139). Were the plant eaters' many scales, plates, and a club tail enough protection from *T. rex*'s powerful bite? Surely, it would have been difficult for *T. rex* to flip over the heavy, low-to-the-ground *Ankylosaurus* to get at its underbelly.

PLANT EATER
DIET

THE SAUROPOD GIANTS HAD TINY HEADS, AND THEIR FEW PENCIL-SHAPED TEETH ACTED LIKE RAKES TO RIP OFF BRANCHES FROM EVERGREEN TREES. ENORMOUS QUANTITIES OF PLANTS THEN SLID DOWN THEIR LONG NECKS INTO AN ENORMOUS VAT OF A GUT FOR DIGESTION.

Dinosaur planteaters evolved a wide variety of different teeth for their different diets and habitats. Small planteaters often had snipping teeth to snap off leaves. Big but low to the ground dinosaurs like ankylosaurs had little leaf-shaped teeth for grinding. But the most elaborate teeth and jaws ever seen in nature belonged to the duckbilled dinosaurs. These big animals had more than 1,000 tiny diamond-shaped teeth in their mouths. Big arrays of these teeth were worked like an accordion to grind tough evergreen plants. Unlike any other animals before or since, duckbills could chew in three directions: not just up and down and forward and back, but flexing in and out at the sides.

These dinosaurs liked to eat different types plants, and new studies indicate that some of the most nutritious dinosaur foods were horsetail plants and the seeds of Araucarian trees. Both of these plants still grow on Earth today.

10 KINDS
OF PLANT EATER
TEETH

1. *DIPLODOCUS:* SPOON-SHAPED TEETH
2. *BRACHIOSAURUS:* PENCIL-SHAPED TEETH
3. *TRICERATOPS:* LEAF-SHAPED TEETH
4. *STEGOSAURUS:* SCISSOR-SHAPED TEETH
5. *HETERODONTOSAURUS:* TALL CHEWING TEETH, SMALL CHOPPING FRONT TEETH, AND TWO LARGE TUSKS
6. *EDMONTOSAURUS:* TINY, DIAMOND-SHAPED TEETH
7. *HYPSILOPHODONT:* ROWS OF CUTTING TEETH AND CHOPPING FRONT TEETH
8. *IGUANODON:* CURVED AND GROOVED GRINDING TEETH
9. *ANKYLOSAURUS:* LEAF-SHAPED TEETH
10. *LUFENGOSAURUS:* SHARP, WIDELY SPACED CUTTING TEETH

TWO *BRACHIOSAURUS* grab at evergreen needles high in the Jurassic treetops of the North American West. A little pterosaur flies by. *Brachiosaurus* (p. 189) was built to reach far higher in the treetops than other giant dinosaurs in its world. So it had a good private source of food for its enormous appetite.

HUAYANGO-SAURUS

hwah-YANG-oh-SORE-us

NAME *Huayangosaurus*

MEANING "Lizard from Huayang"

PERIOD 170 million years ago, Middle Jurassic

FOUND China

FOSSILS Twelve mostly complete skeletons

LENGTH 13 feet (4 meters) long

HUAYANGOSAURUS had two big spikes over its hips. Perhaps those spikes prevented meat eaters from attacking it from above.

SPIKY STEGOSAUR

Huayangosaurus was an early stegosaur, just half the size of the later *Stegosaurus* (p. 129), with a double row of plates that were shaped like spikes. *Huayangosaurus* had teeth in the front of its mouth. Later stegosaurs had none.

We have many fossils that tell us a lot about *Huayangosaurus*'s world. It fed on low-growing plants along the riverbanks of central China. Above it, giant plant eaters, including *Shunosaurus* (p. 187), fed on trees with their long necks. Tiny *Xiaosaurus* (p. 260) ran by, stopping to nibble at plants close to the ground. And all of these plant eaters would have feared *Yangchuanosaurus* (p. 69), a sizeable and nasty meat eater.

TWELVE *HUAYANGOSAURUS* SKELETONS WERE FOUND IN THE SAME RICH QUARRY IN CENTRAL CHINA THAT PRODUCED COMPLETE *SHUNOSAURUS* (P. 187) AND OTHER OUTSTANDING SKELETONS.

STEGO-SAURUS

STEG-oh-SORE-us

NAME *Stegosaurus*

MEANING "Roof lizard"

PERIOD 200 million years ago, Late Jurassic

FOUND U.S. (Colorado, Utah, Wyoming)

FOSSILS Many partial and complete skeletons, various skulls

LENGTH 26 to 30 feet (8 to 9 meters) long

STEGOSAURUS **COULD SWING ITS** large tail from side to side with great force. *Stegosaurus* tail fossils show lots of damage, which might have come from fighting.

BEWARE THE TAIL!

Stegosaurus was the largest of the plate-backed plant eaters, and it has stumped scientists for many years. When found more than a century ago, it was thought to have walked on two legs. And scientists once thought the bundle of nerves near its tail was a second brain. One scientist suggested that its plates could flap. Others thought the plates were used in defense—but they are too thin. Maybe they were used to cool or warm the animal or to attract mates.

    Stegosaurus's spiked tail, however, could have been a weapon. A tailbone of *Allosaurus* (p. 75) has a hole in it the size of a *Stegosaurus* tail spike.

FOOTPRINT FINDS SUGGEST THAT *STEGOSAURUS* MIGHT HAVE TRAVELED IN FAMILY GROUPS.

SCUTELLO SAURUS

skoo-TELL-oh-SORE-us

NAME *Scutellosaurus*

MEANING "Little shield lizard"

PERIOD 200 to 195 million years ago, Late Jurassic

FOUND U.S. (Arizona)

FOSSILS Two incomplete skeletons, hundreds of armor plates

LENGTH 4 feet (1.2 meters) long

A LIGHT SUIT OF ARMOR

Little *Scutellosaurus* was a very early ancestor of the huge tank-like ankylosaurs. It is the smallest and the oldest armored dinosaur known. More than 300 armored plates sat atop its skin from neck to tail. The shape of these armored patches varied from flat to grooved. *Scutellosaurus*'s close relative, *Scelidosaurus* (p. 251), from England, was even more heavily armored.

Scutellosaurus ran on its hind legs but also may have walked on all fours. It was among the smartest and fastest dinosaurs. That speed would have helped, more than its light armor, to protect *Scutellosaurus* from predators.

SCUTELLOSAURUS HAD AN UNUSUALLY long tail. Why? With many armored plates, *Scutellosaurus* may have been heavier than its small size suggests, and a long tail might have helped it balance the weight of its body in front of its hips.

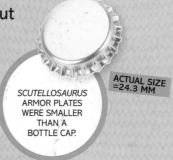

SCUTELLOSAURUS ARMOR PLATES WERE SMALLER THAN A BOTTLE CAP.

ACTUAL SIZE =24.3 MM

GASTONIA

gas-TONE-ee-ah

NAME *Gastonia*

MEANING Named after its discoverer, artist Robert Gaston

PERIOD 125 million years ago, Early Cretaceous

FOUND U.S. (Utah)

FOSSILS Four or five individuals

LENGTH 13 to 16 feet (4 to 5 meters) long

GASTONIA **NEEDED THICK ARMOR** to defend itself from one of the nastiest of all killer dinosaurs—*Utahraptor* (p. 97). The largest of all raptors was 20 feet (6 m) long and weighed one ton. It had huge, sharp claws and sharp teeth.

THE GREAT DEFENDER

Gastonia was one of the most heavily armored of all dinosaurs. A jumble of more than a thousand of *Gastonia*'s bones and bits of armor were discovered together. The remains belonged to several *Gastonia,* so it's difficult to be sure how many spikes and plates each *Gastonia* had. But it certainly had a lot! Thick layers of bone shielded its brain. A smooth plate under the skin across its hips protected its lower spine. Its tail featured double rows of spikes sticking up on each side. Swinging its tail, *Gastonia* could have used those sharp edges like scissors to cut an attacker.

BONES OF *UTAHRAPTOR* (P. 97) WERE DISCOVERED ALONGSIDE THOSE OF *GASTONIA.* PERHAPS THE LOCATION WAS AN **ANCIENT BATTLE SITE.**

MINMI

MIN-mee

NAME *Minmi*

MEANING Named after Minmi Crossing, Australia, where it was found

PERIOD 119 to 113 million years ago, Early Cretaceous

FOUND Australia

FOSSILS Mostly complete skeleton and some fragments

LENGTH 6.6 feet (2 meters) long

MINMI **ATE FERNS, SEEDS, FRUITS,** and leaves of plants. It nibbled and probably chewed this vegetation with its small, sharp teeth. It swallowed the seeds of plants whole.

SLOW AND SMALL

Minmi was unusually small for an armored dinosaur. Because we have discovered its footprints and the contents of its stomach, we know more about the life of *Minmi* than we do about most dinosaurs. For instance, we know it was slow-moving and not very brainy.

It had many kinds of armor. It had large armor patches on its nose. On its neck and shoulders were big plates with ridges. Spikes protruded from its hips, and triangular plates decorated its tail.

This dinosaur lived in what is now Australia. In *Minmi*'s day, Australia was dark in winter, but in the summer months, days were long and sunshine was plentiful. Vegetation grew all around, and *Minmi* had plenty of food to eat.

MINMI HAD STOMACH ARMOR THAT GREW UNDERNEATH **ITS SKIN.**

TARCHIA

TAHR-key-ah

NAME *Tarchia*

MEANING "Brainy one"

PERIOD 78 to 69 million years ago, Late Cretaceous

FOUND Mongolia

FOSSILS One nearly complete skeleton without skull, two complete skulls

LENGTH 26 to 28 feet (8 to 8.5 meters) long

***TARCHIA* HAD AN ODDLY SHAPED HEAD** with triangular spikes that stuck out sideways from its skull and curved horns that pushed out of the rear of its skull.

THE SMART TANK

Tarchia is the last and one of the largest known Asian club-tailed armored dinosaurs. It lived in what is now the Gobi Desert and weighed nearly 10,000 pounds (4,536 kg).

In *Tarchia*'s time, the area of the Gobi Desert was dry, but it was not entirely desert. There were small streams and lakes as well as sand dunes. In this environment, *Tarchia* would have grazed on low-growing plants, which it ground down with its small, leaf-shaped teeth.

Tarchia's big skull was wider than it was long, and it was covered in bony lumps of many shapes and sizes. As strange as that skull sounds, it was similar to the bumpy skulls of armored dinosaurs of its time from North America.

TARCHIA GOT ITS "BRAINY" NAME BECAUSE ITS BRAIN IS **TWICE** THE SIZE OF THE BRAIN OF *SAICHANIA* (P. 251), THE OTHER ARMORED DINOSAUR DISCOVERED NEARBY, EVEN THOUGH *TARCHIA*'S HEAD IS ONLY **HALF AS BIG.**

ANKYLO-SAURUS

AN-kye-loh-SORE-us

NAME *Ankylosaurus*

MEANING "Fused lizard"

PERIOD 70 to 65 million years ago, Late Cretaceous

FOUND U.S. (Montana); Canada (Alberta)

FOSSILS Two skulls and three partial skeletons

LENGTH 25 to 35 feet (7.5 to 10.7 meters) long

ANKYLOSAURUS HAD A TAIL CLUB made of seven bones fused together into a hard and heavy mass. Scientists believe that if swung accurately, *Ankylosaurus*'s tail could have broken the bones of attackers such as this giant crocodile.

CLUB-TAIL DEFENDER

Ankylosaurs were as large as tanks and nearly as hard to attack, even though they were slow moving, and their tail clubs would not have been much defense against a *Tyrannosaurus rex*. But their extremely tough armor might have foiled the 8-inch-long (20-cm-long) teeth of the king of the dinosaurs.

Ankylosaurus roamed across the North American West, snipping plants with its little leaf-shaped teeth. It had few teeth compared to the duckbills and horned dinosaurs that were also feeding in its world. But on the warm plains that bordered a huge seaway, *Ankylosaurus* had plenty to eat.

THE FANCY HORNS OF MALE DEER AND MOOSE ARE MOSTLY USED IN ATTRACTING MATES AND THREATENING RIVALS. THE TAIL CLUB OF AN *ANKYLOSAUR* MAY HAVE SERVED THE SAME PURPOSE.

PACHYCEPHALO-SAURUS

pack-ih-SEF-ah-low-SORE-us

NAME *Pachycephalo-saurus*

MEANING "Thick-headed lizard"

PERIOD 76 to 65 million years ago, Late Cretaceous

FOUND U.S. (Montana, South Dakota, Wyoming)

FOSSILS One nearly complete skull, some tops of skulls

LENGTH 15 feet (4.6 meters) long

PACHYCEPHALOSAU-RUS IS OFTEN shown butting heads with its rivals, like bighorn sheep do today. But scientists believe that it could not have survived banging heads. Instead, they suggest that these dinosaurs may have whacked each other in the sides with their thick heads. Why? Maybe it was competition for territory or mates.

THICKHEADED AND FAST MOVING

Pachycephalosaurus was by far the biggest member of the group of thickheaded dinosaurs that are together called pachycephalosaurs. Some lived in Asia, but *Pachycephalo-saurus* roamed the North American West. Like all of its cousins, it was a plant eater that walked on its hind legs. *Pachycephalo-saurus* was not as quick as its smaller relatives, but compared to the giant duckbills and horned dinosaurs in its world, it was quite speedy.

And its eyes were set forward in its skull, giving pachycephalosaurs good 3-D vision.

THE SKULL OF *PACHYCEPHALOSAURUS* WAS NEARLY NINE INCHES (22.9 CM) THICK!

DRACOREX

DRAY-co-rex

NAME *Dracorex*

MEANING "Dragon king"

PERIOD 70 to 65 million years ago, Late Cretaceous

FOUND U.S. (South Dakota)

FOSSILS Nearly complete skull, four backbones

LENGTH 10 feet (3 meters) long

DRACOREX'S HEAD WAS COVERED WITH nasty-looking spikes, horns, and bubble-shaped lumps of bone. But its head lacked the thick dome known from other North American pachycephalosaurs. Perhaps that was because *Dracorex* was not yet fully grown.

HARRY POTTER'S DRAGON KING

Dracorex was a medium-sized pachycephalosaur. It had many strange knobs on its head, as most of these thick-headed dinosaurs did. Its head was flatter than the domes on many of its relatives.

But *Dracorex* and another fancy-horned little plant eater named *Stygimoloch* (p. 255) might not be different kinds of dinosaurs at all. Paleontologists have recently suggested that they are just young *Pachycephalosaurus* (p. 141) and that as they grew, their headgear would have changed, like antlers on a deer.

Dracorex's scary head inspired the paleontologists to name it after Draco Malfoy, the evil character in the Harry Potter books.

DRACOREX IS NOT THE ONLY DINOSAUR NAMED FOR FANTASY FICTION. *BOROGOVIA* (P. 221), A LITTLE MEAT EATER, WAS NAMED FOR THE BOROGOVES, MONSTERS IN THE POEM *JABBERWOCKY* BY ALICE IN WONDERLAND AUTHOR LEWIS CARROLL.

MICRO-PACHYCEPHALO-SAURUS

MY-cro-PACK-ee-SEF-ah-lo-SORE-us

NAME *Micropachycephalosaurus*

MEANING "Tiny thick-headed lizard"

PERIOD 83 to 73 million years ago, Late Cretaceous

FOUND China

FOSSILS Very incomplete skeleton

LENGTH 1.5 to 3 feet (0.5 to 1 meter) long

LITTLE DINO: BIG NAME

Most thickheaded pachycephalosaurs were small dinosaurs, but mysterious little *Micropachycephalosaurus* was the smallest of them all. It may not have even been a pachycephalosaur. It was named by a Chinese scientist on the basis of its thick skull. Later researchers could not find the skull, and the other bones discovered had no features in common with the pachycephalosaurs. So what was *Micropachycephalosaurus*? For now, all that can be said is that it was a small, bird-hipped plant eater.

HOW COULD A DINOSAUR as small as *Micropachycephalosaurus* have survived in a world of much larger hunters? By hiding or climbing onto branches to escape predators. Perhaps it searched for food in twilight when it might not be seen so easily by predators.

THOUGH IT IS ONE OF THE SMALLEST DINOSAURS, *MICROPACHYCEPHALOSAURUS* HAS THE LONGEST DINOSAUR NAME.

PSITTACO-SAURUS

SIT-ah-co-SORE-us

NAME *Psittacosaurus*

MEANING "Parrot lizard"

PERIOD 119 to 97.5 million years ago, Early Cretaceous

FOUND Mongolia, China, Thailand

FOSSILS Many complete skeletons from over 400 individuals

LENGTH 5.6 feet (2 meters) long

AT LEAST SOME PSITTACOSAURUS had what appear to be quills on their backs and tails. Many small dinosaurs have recently been found with feathers or quills on all or part of their bodies. None of these were designed for flight, but they may have helped to keep the little animals warm.

POWERFUL PARROT BEAK

Though it doesn't look it, *Psittacosaurus* was an early relative of *Triceratops* (p. 153). But it was a swift little plant eater that ran on two legs, not all fours. *Psittacosaurus* and *Triceratops* did share the curved parrot-style beak that gives *Psittacosaurus* its name. That sharp beak carried a powerful bite. And it may have been covered in keratin—the same material that makes up your fingernails. *Psittacosaurus* may have snipped off the low branches of very tough plants. It lived in a dry environment and may have wandered to the shores of lakes to find enough plant life to feed itself.

UNLIKE ALL OTHER HORNED DINOSAURS, *PSITTACOSAURUS* HAD JUST FOUR FRONT TOES, NOT FIVE.

PROTOCERA TOPS

PRO-toh-SERR-ah-tops

NAME *Protoceratops*

MEANING "First horned face"

PERIOD 86 to 71 million years ago, Late Cretaceous

FOUND Mongolia

FOSSILS Dozens of skeletons and eggs

LENGTH 6 feet (1.8 meters) long

PROTOCERATOPS VERSUS VELOCIRAPTOR! This is one dinosaur battle we can be sure actually took place. Two female Polish paleontologists discovered the fossils left from this deadly encounter.

DESERT BATTLER

Protoceratops was a sheep-sized plant eater common in the Gobi Desert of ancient Mongolia. Still a desert today, the Gobi preserves *Protoceratops* fossils in near-perfect condition. The most famous of these discoveries is one of the greatest of all fossil finds—a *Protoceratops* locked in battle with a *Velociraptor* (p. 115). A collapsing sand dune probably killed them during their struggle.

The first nest of dinosaur eggs ever found was discovered in 1924 near a *Protoceratops*, so *Protoceratops* became famous as a parent. But later discoveries showed that *Oviraptor* was the true parent of the babies in that nest. *Protoceratops*'s eggs have not yet been definitely identified.

WHEN DISCOVERED IN 1924, **PROTOCERATOPS** WAS THOUGHT TO BE THE ANCESTOR OF NORTH AMERICAN HORNED DINOSAURS, SUCH AS **TRICERATOPS** (P. 153). **IT IS NOT.**

STYRACO-SAURUS

sty-RACK-oh-SORE-us

NAME *Styracosaurus*

MEANING "Spike lizard"

PERIOD 77 to 73 million years ago, Late Cretaceous

FOUND U.S. (Montana); Canada (Alberta)

FOSSILS Many complete skeletons

LENGTH 18 feet (5.25 meters) long

STYRACOSAURUS COULD GRASP branches and low-growing plants with its big beak. It had a wide menu of plants to choose from in its forested world. Flowering plants as well as evergreens were among its diet choices.

FANCY HEADGEAR

Styracosaurus had one of the most elaborately decorated heads of any horned dinosaur. And its skull came in many different styles. Styraco-saurs had a big nose horn and four or more long spikes on their frills. And some had knobs and hooks of bone, too. The first *Styracosaurus* found had overlapping spikes on one side of its face. But that turned out to be from an injury that healed strangely.

Styracosaurus probably traveled in groups. We know because they died in great numbers in at least one location in Canada. Perhaps they were gathering around a watering hole at a time of deadly drought.

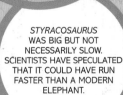

STYRACOSAURUS WAS BIG BUT NOT NECESSARILY SLOW. SCIENTISTS HAVE SPECULATED THAT IT COULD HAVE RUN FASTER THAN A MODERN ELEPHANT.

TRICERA-TOPS

tri-SERR-uh-tops

NAME *Triceratops*

MEANING "Three-horned face"

PERIOD 72 to 65 million years ago, Late Cretaceous

FOUND Western Canada and western U.S.

FOSSILS About 50 skulls and some partial skeletons

LENGTH 25 feet (8 meters) long

TWO *TRICERATOPS* in battle—a scary sight. But did it happen? Fossils of *Triceratops* skull frills show scrapes and holes. But it is unlikely that these thin horns and bones could have done deadly damage.

THE LAST HORNED DINOSAUR

Triceratops was the last and largest of the horned dinosaurs. It may have been one of the most common dinosaurs in the North American West at the time of *Tyrannosaurus rex* (p. 91). These dinosaurs are often pictured traveling in large groups, but the biggest gathering of *Triceratops* ever found consisted of three youngsters. Perhaps it lived only in family groups.

Triceratops nipped at low-growing plants with its beak and cut them with its 800 little teeth. When walking, *Triceratops*'s toes pointed outward, a primitive posture common to most dinosaurs. Given its multi-ton weight, it did not walk quickly.

THE DINOSAUR NAMED **"TOROSAURUS"** HAS RECENTLY BEEN SHOWN TO BE A **TRICERATOPS**, NOT A DIFFERENT KIND OF DINOSAUR.

PENTACERA TOPS

PEN-ta-SER-ah-tops

NAME *Pentaceratops*

MEANING "Five-horned face"

PERIOD 75 to 73 million years ago, Late Cretaceous

FOUND U.S. (New Mexico)

FOSSILS Nine skulls and some skeletons

LENGTH 28 feet (8 meters) long

FOOTPRINTS SHOW similar dinosaurs pushing off into water to swim, so it is possible that *Pentaceratops* swam, too.

A FANCY HEAD

Pentaceratops was among the most decorated of all horned dinosaurs. It is named for the five spikes that stuck out from its head. Two were horns that stood out over its eyes. Two more stuck out from its cheeks toward the back of its face. The fifth was on its nose. These horns look like powerful weapons, but they were too thin and breakable to be much use in fighting big predators. They may have been used just for showing off.

The long frill at the end of *Pentaceratops*'s skull had several knobs and two spikes at the top. It may have helped protect the *Pentaceratops*'s neck from attack.

PENTACERATOPS HAS THE LARGEST SKULL KNOWN OF ANY LAND ANIMAL. IN ALL, ITS HEAD WAS 9.8 FEET (3 M) LONG.

HETERODONTO-SAURUS

HET-er-oh-DON-toe-SORE-us

NAME *Heterodontosaurus*

MEANING "Different-tooth lizard"

PERIOD 200 to 195 million years ago, Early Jurassic

FOUND South Africa

FOSSILS Partial skeleton

LENGTH 4 feet (1.2 meters) long

HETERODONTOSAURUS HAD GOOD-SIZED cheeks, which would have been useful for storing food. The many styles of teeth in its mouth suggest to some scientists that it was an omnivore, eating small animals and insects as well as plants.

LITTLE CHOPPER

Heterodontosaurus was a little plant eater with close relatives all around the world. It is named for its three different kinds of teeth. In the front of its mouth were little choppers. Farther back were a set of tall, straight-bottomed teeth that were good for chewing. In front of its cheek teeth were peculiar little tusks, unlike the teeth of other small bird-hipped dinosaurs of the time. The tusks may have been used to fight other *Heterodontosaurus* for food or mates.

    Heterodontosaurus's hands were also very unusual. It could pinch objects between its first and fifth fingers, the way you can hold things between your thumb and pinkie.

HETERODONTOSAURUS'S PINKIE IS ON BACKWARDS. HOW THAT DESIGN MIGHT HAVE HELPED THIS FAST RUNNER IS NOT CLEAR.

LEAELLYN ASAURA

lee-EL-in-a-SAWR-a

NAME *Leaellynasaura*

MEANING "Leaellyn lizard" after daughter of the namers

PERIOD 106 million years ago, Early Cretaceous

FOUND Australia

FOSSILS Partial skull, isolated limb bones, ribs, vertebrae, jaws, and teeth

LENGTH 6.5 to 10 feet (2 to 3 meters) long

THE SCIENTISTS WHO DISCOVERED *Leaellynasaura* speculated that it had a large brain and large eyes to help it cope with months of winter darkness. But there is too little fossil evidence yet to be sure how big its brain and eyes truly were.

TWILIGHT WALKER

Leaellynasaura was a bird-hipped plant eater that was no larger than a small kangaroo. In *Leaellynasaura*'s time, Australia was located much farther south than it is now, in the Antarctic Circle. Occasionally it might have felt temperatures close to freezing, but it is unlikely that *Leaellynasaura*, or any other dinosaurs, ever saw snow.

Some researchers have suggested that *Leaellynasaura* may have dug burrows to protect itself from the cold. Some dinosaurs did dig holes, but there is no evidence that *Leaellynasaura* did.

LEAELLYN RICH WAS TWO YEARS OLD WHEN SHE ASKED TO HAVE HER "OWN DINOSAUR." SO HER PARENTS, PALEONTOLOGISTS TOM AND PATRICIA RICH, NAMED THE DINOSAUR THEY DISCOVERED FOR HER.

CAMPTO-SAURUS

CAMP-toe-SORE-us

NAME *Camptosaurus*

MEANING "Flexible lizard"

PERIOD 145 to 135 million years ago, Late Jurassic/Early Cretaceous

FOUND U.S. (Wyoming, Utah, North Dakota, Colorado); England

FOSSILS Mostly complete skeletons

LENGTH 23 feet (7 meters) long

***CAMPTOSAURUS* WAS PROBABLY NOT** a fast runner. So, without defenses, it may have been an easy target for this nasty and hungry pack of *Ceratosaurus*.

PRIMITIVE PLANT EATER

Camptosaurus was the most primitive of all the members of the iguanodontian group of plant eaters. Like other iguan-odontids, *Camptosaurus* had small hooves on its fingers and toes. But it had four toes while other iguanodontids had three, and *Camptosaurus* did not have the big thumb spike that is a special feature of the group. Also, its skull was narrower and longer, and its jaws were probably not as powerful for crushing plants as those of the other iguanodontids.

Camptosaurus is sometimes portrayed walking on its hind legs. But with hooves on each limb, it is more likely that it walked on all fours.

AT FIRST, *CAMPTOSAURUS* WAS NAMED *CAMPTONOTUS*, MEANING "FLEXIBLE BACK," UNTIL SCIENTISTS DISCOVERED THAT THE NAME WAS ALREADY IN USE FOR A KIND OF CRICKET.

MUTTABURRA-SAURUS

mutt-ah-BUHR-ah-SORE-us

NAME *Muttaburrasaurus*

MEANING "Muttaburra lizard"

PERIOD 100 to 97.5 million years ago, Early Cretaceous

FOUND Australia

FOSSILS Two fragmentary skeletons, broken skull

LENGTH 24 feet (7 meters) long

MUTTABURRASAURUS'S ODD NOSE may have helped increase its sense of smell. It could also have attracted mates, or it may have been a honker, increasing the volume of its calls.

STRONG JAW AND ODD NOSE

Muttaburrasaurus had very strong jaws. Its teeth were designed to slice through plants. Other iguanodontids had very different cheek teeth that were suited for grinding plants. So, *Muttaburrasaurus* may have had to digest plants more completely in its large stomach.

Its skull featured a big bump behind its nostrils. One other member of the iguanodontid family, an Asian *Iguanodon* (p. 165), had a similar bumpy head. The purpose of the bumps is uncertain.

ALTHOUGH THEY ARE TWO OF THE MOST COMPLETE DINOSAUR SKELETONS FOUND IN AUSTRALIA, THE SKELETONS OF MUTTABURRASAURUS LACK ARMS. SO WE DON'T KNOW IF THEY HAD THUMB SPIKES LIKE *IGUANODON* (P. 165) DID.

IGUANODON

ig-WAN-oh-don

NAME *Iguanodon*

MEANING "Iguana tooth"

PERIOD 130 to 110 million years ago, Early Cretaceous

FOUND England, Belgium, Germany, North Africa, Asia, parts of U.S.

FOSSILS Hundreds of fossils

LENGTH 33 feet (10 meters) long

IGUANODON **LIVED AT THE TIME** when flowering plants first developed. One scientist has suggested that its well-developed jaws and teeth were designed to grind up these plants. But its powerful jaws would have been even better suited to eat tougher and more ancient plants in its world.

SPIKED THUMBS

Iguanodon was the first dinosaur identified by a scientist more than 180 years ago. Workers in a British forest brought its fossil teeth to a local doctor, Gideon Mantell.

Iguanodon was a heavy plant eater, with leg bones built to support its bulk. Its hands had three strong middle fingers, and its wrist bones were joined together for extra strength. Its peculiar thumb spike was set off to the side, which would have been useful for stabbing predators or cutting plants. Its fifth finger was small. It might have been more easily moved to hold food that *Iguanodon*'s other fingers could not grasp alone.

WHEN **IGUANODON** WAS FIRST DISCOVERED IN 1825, ITS **THUMB SPIKE** WAS THOUGHT TO HAVE BEEN A **HORN ON ITS HEAD.**

This dinosaur ran on two legs. On its hind legs, *Iguanodon* had three short, thick toes that were probably padded. The foot pads would help spread the animal's weight so it could walk comfortably.

OURANO-SAURUS

oo-RAHN-oh-SAWR-us

NAME *Ouranosaurus*

MEANING "Brave lizard"

PERIOD 115 million years ago, Early Cretaceous

FOUND Niger

FOSSILS Two nearly complete skeletons

LENGTH 24 feet (7 meters) long

IN *OURANOSAURUS'S* TIME, NORTH AFRICA was a green plain of ferns and evergreen trees that flooded each year. *Spinosaurus* (p. 87), gigantic crocodiles, and other big predators might have attacked *Ouranosaurus*.

SAIL-BACKED PLANT GRINDER

Ouranosaurus was found in the Sahara desert. But until recent times, the Sahara wasn't a desert at all. It was a land of forests and rivers, where rain fell frequently.

Like other members of the iguanodontid family, *Ourano-saurus* chewed tough plants with many grinding cheek teeth. But the spines on its back were twice as tall as those on *Iguanodon* (p. 165). *Ouranosaurus* also had two wide and low bumps behind its nostrils. Many iguanodontids had odd snout shapes. It is possible that these nifty noses were display features for attracting mates. Perhaps its enormous crest was a display feature, too.

OURANOSAURUS'S "BRAVE" NAME COMES FROM THE BIG MONITOR LIZARD THAT THE NOMADIC PEOPLE OF THE SAHARA CALL "OURANE."

EOLAMBIA

EE-oh-LAM-bee-ah

NAME *Eolambia*

MEANING "Dawn lambeosaurine (crested hadrosaur)"

PERIOD 3 million years ago, Late Cretaceous

FOUND U.S. (Utah)

FOSSILS Many partial skeletons

LENGTH 23 to 33 feet (7 to 10 meters) long

EOLAMBIA WAS DRAWN TO THE LAKE shores in its warm, dry world. The dinosaur came to the water not just to drink but to reach the rich plant growth in the evergreen forests.

DUCKBILLS' DADDY

Eolambia was named as the earliest duck-billed dinosaur just a few years ago. It represents a link between the iguanodontids that came before it and the duck-billed plant eaters that came after it. But new studies identify *Eolambia* as an iguanodontid. Like *Iguanodon* (p. 165), it had large spikes on its thumbs, likely used for raking leaves off trees rather than for defense. Perhaps *Eolambia* had to make use of its thumb spikes to help it cut down plants to chewing size since it did not have a big beak designed for that task, as did other duck-billed dinosaurs.

Eolambia had hundreds of grinding teeth, which are typical of duck-billed dinosaurs. It also had features of both crested and noncrested duckbills. This type of evidence makes it clear that *Eolambia* lived at the "dawn" of duck-billed dinosaur time.

EOLAMBIA WAS NAMED IN 1998 BY PALEONTOLOGIST **JAMES KIRKLAND**, WHO ALSO NAMED THE DEADLY *UTAHRAPTOR* (P. 97) AND THE ARMORED *GASTONIA* (P. 133) FROM THE SAME REGION.

CORYTHO-SAURUS

co-RITH-oh-SORE-us

NAME *Corythosaurus*

MEANING "Helmet lizard"

PERIOD 76 to 72 million years ago, Late Cretaceous

FOUND U.S. (Montana); Canada (Alberta)

FOSSILS Many nearly complete skeletons

LENGTH 30 feet (9 meters) long

CORYTHOSAURUS "HELMETS" came in different sizes. Perhaps *Corythosaurus* with the largest crests were males that used the crest to attract females. Young *Corythosaurus* may not have had crests at all.

HORN BLOWER

Like all the crested duckbills, *Corythosaurus* breathed through its bony, curved crest just the way we humans breathe through our sinuses. It's also likely it could blast trumpet sounds through the crest to communicate with its herd.

This dinosaur spent much of its day chewing on tough plants. It crushed them with its hundreds of tiny linked teeth. Then it ground food in three directions—up and down, back and forth, and in and out to the sides. No other animals ever chewed in as many ways as duckbills.

THE FIRST *CORYTHOSAURUS* SKELETON EVER FOUND, WHICH HAD IMPRESSIONS OF FOSSILIZED SKIN, WAS PLACED ON A SHIP THAT WAS SUNK IN WORLD WAR I AND NEVER FOUND AGAIN.

PARASAURO LOPHUS

PAR-ah-saw-RAH-loh-fuss

NAME	*Parasaurolophus*
MEANING	"Like crested lizard"
PERIOD	76 to 65 million years ago, Late Cretaceous
FOUND	U.S. (New Mexico, Utah); Canada (Alberta)
FOSSILS	Many skeletons and skulls
LENGTH	33 feet (10 meters) long

PARASAUROLOPHUS LIVED ALONG the shores of the great inland seaway that once covered much of central and western North America. Its habitat was rich in evergreen trees and below them, ferns. Flowering plants were also present in smaller numbers.

TUBE-HEADED DUCKBILL

Parasaurolophus is one of the last and best known crested duckbills. Like other duckbills, it probably traveled in herds. The fancy crest of this big plant eater has long been of interest to scientists. One paleontologist speculated that it held scent glands, or salt, or helped the animal breathe underwater.

But it was, in fact, a trumpet. Experiments have shown that *Parasaurolophus*'s crest produced a low B-flat sound similar to the sounds elephants and whales make when communicating to their own kind over long distances.

PALEONTOLOGIST DAVID WEISHAMPEL DETERMINED THE **SOUND MADE** BY PARASAUROLOPHUS'S CREST BY RECREATING ONE OUT OF **BATHROOM TUBING** AND BLOWING THROUGH IT!

TSINTAO-SAURUS

sin-tau-SORE-us

NAME *Tsintaosaurus*

MEANING "Lizard from Tsintao"

PERIOD 70 million years ago, Late Cretaceous

FOUND China

FOSSILS Complete skeleton

LENGTH 33 feet (10 meters) long

WHAT WAS THE PURPOSE OF *Tsintaosaurus*'s unicorn-like horn? It appears to have been a decoration. To a female *Tsintaosaurus*, the male's horn might have been an attractive feature.

UNICORN-SPIKED MUNCHER

Of all the strange headgear on duckbills, *Tsintaosaurus*'s skull bones may have been the strangest of all. *Tsintaosaurus* had a spike, a bit like the mythical unicorn's, standing out from atop its skull.

When Chinese researcher C. C. Yang first described this long skull bone in 1958, scientists in other countries thought it was too strange to be true. They thought the spike was misplaced from somewhere else on the dinosaur's body. But when a second *Tsintaosaurus* skull was found with the same strange head spike, scientists were convinced that Dr. Yang was right after all.

TSINTAOSAURUS WAS NAMED BY YANGZHONGIAN, WHO WAS CALLED THE FATHER OF CHINESE PALEONTOLOGY. HE ALSO NAMED MAMENCHISAURUS AND WAS A CLASSMATE OF CHINA'S FIRST PREMIER, MAO ZEDONG.

EDMONTO-SAURUS

ed-MON-toh-SORE-us

NAME *Edmontosaurus*

MEANING "Edmonton lizard"

PERIOD 73 to 65 million years ago, Late Cretaceous

FOUND U.S. (Montana, Alaska); Canada (Alberta)

FOSSILS Several complete skeletons with skulls

LENGTH 42 feet (13 meters) long

HUGE HERDS OF ED-MONTOSAURUS roamed the North American West all the way to what is now northern Alaska. Scientists think that the animals may have migrated as many as 1,600 miles (2,575 km) a year.

DIAMOND-TOOTHED BROWSER

Edmontosaurus was one of the last of the noncrested duck-billed dinosaurs. It moved in enormous herds in the world of *Tyrannosaurus rex* (p. 91) and *Triceratops* (p. 153). It ground tough plants with hundreds of tiny diamond-shaped teeth. In winter, it lived along the shores of a great inland sea in Montana and south-western Canada. When the weather was warmer, it traveled north for the rich plant life of Arctic summers. One fossil bed of *Edmontosaurus* is thought to stretch for more than 2 miles (3 km) and contain as many as 25,000 fossils. What could have killed so many animals at once? Only a disaster such as a flood or a volcanic eruption.

ONE **EDMONTOSAURUS** WAS FOUND WITH HEALED TOOTHMARKS IN ITS JAWS. IT HAD SURVIVED AN **ATTACK** FROM SMALLER **MEAT-EATING DINOSAURS.**

RIOJA-SAURUS

REE-oh-hah-SORE-us

NAME *Riojasaurus*

MEANING "Reptile from La Rioja"

PERIOD 225 million years ago, Late Triassic

FOUND Argentina

FOSSILS One partial skeleton and one skull

LENGTH 36 feet (11 meters) long

RIOJASAURUS **FED IN THE** southern forests of Pangaea, the single landmass that then stretched across the middle of the Earth.

FIRST GIANT DINOSAUR

Riojasaurus was one of the earliest giant plant eaters and an ancestor of the largest of all plant eaters. Its neck and tail were long and thin, but its body and legs were heavy. Unlike other prosauropods, *Riojasaurus* had many holes in its enormous vertebrae. These holes lightened the weight of the bones to make it easier for *Riojasaurus* to move. It also had one more vertebra at its hips than did other prosauropods. Many of its smaller relatives could stand on hind legs to reach high into the trees, but *Riojasaurus* may have been too heavy to get up on two legs. Its legs were of equal length, so perhaps it was most comfortable on all fours.

RIOJASAURUS HAD ONLY **FIVE TEETH** IN THE FRONT OF ITS TOP JAW AND 24 **MORE BEHIND THEM.** SO CHANCES ARE IT GULPED DOWN ITS FOOD AND DIGESTED PLANTS IN **ITS STOMACH.**

PLATEO-SAURUS

PLAT-ee-oh-SORE-us

NAME *Plateosaurus*

MEANING "Flat lizard"

PERIOD 222 to 200 million years ago, Late Triassic

FOUND Northern and central Europe

FOSSILS More than 100 skeletons

LENGTH 23 feet (7 meters) long

PLATEOSAURUS WAS AMONG THE largest dinosaurs of its time. But despite its weight, it was still able to tilt up on its hind legs to feed high in trees.

EUROPEAN TREE FEEDER

More than 100 skeletons of *Plateosaurus* have been found across Europe. A huge burial ground of skeletons was discovered in a brick quarry in Switzerland. That plateosaur burial ground may reach for more than 3 miles (4.8 km)!

Scientists think that *Plateosaurus* may have grown to more than 4 tons (3.5 MT) and lived up to 25 years. It had hands that could grasp plants, and its large thumb claws may have been used for defense or to tear down tree branches. Its teeth were sharp and wide and could crush and slice plants. *Plateosaurus* also had cheeks, which might have held food before the dinosaur chewed and swallowed.

PLATEOSAURUS CAME IN MANY SIZES OF ADULTS, FROM 16 FEET (5 M) LONG TO 33 FEET (10 M) LONG.

LESSEM-SAURUS

LESS-em-SORE-us

NAME *Lessemsaurus*

MEANING "Don Lessem's reptile" after the author of this book

PERIOD 210 million years ago, Late Triassic

FOUND Argentina

FOSSILS One partial spinal column

LENGTH 33 feet (10 meters) long

***LESSEMSAURUS* FED ON TOUGH PLANTS**
such as these ancient cycads. These primitive plants offered little nutrition. So *Lessemsaurus* probably ate a lot, and often!

EARLY SUPERGIANT?

Lessemsaurus was one of the first giant sauropod plant eaters ever to walk on the Earth. Dinosaurs began to grow truly enormous when sauropods developed from the nearly 30-foot-long (9-m-long) prosauropods. The new group of supergiants was too heavy to stand on two legs as the prosauropods sometimes did. And the sauropods' bodies went through many other changes, including growing longer necks and tails. We may never know which was the earliest sauropod dinosaur, but the heavy bones of *Lessemsaurus* are among the earliest yet.

THE ONLY FOSSILS WE HAVE OF **LESSEMSAURUS** ARE A FEW VERTEBRA. THEY ARE **NO BIGGER** THAN THOSE OF A **PROSAUROPOD,** BUT ARE SHAPED MORE LIKE THOSE OF A SAUROPOD— THEY HAVE TALLER ARCHES THAT PINCH INWARD.

EUROPA-SAURUS

yoo-ROPE-ah-SORE-us

NAME *Europasaurus*

MEANING "European lizard"

PERIOD 155 to 150 million years ago, Late Jurassic

FOUND Germany

FOSSILS Many partial skeletons

LENGTH 20 feet (6.2 meters) long

EUROPASAURUS ROAMED ISLANDS in an ocean that is now Europe. The forests might have looked dense, but there were few of them. To survive where food was limited, *Europasaurus* somehow slowed down its growth rate and stayed smaller than other sauropods.

THE ISLAND DWELLER

Europasaurus was one of the smallest members of the group that includes the largest of all dinosaurs. It was solidly built and larger than nearly all other European dinosaurs of its time. But it was tiny by comparison to its giant North American cousins that include *Brachiosaurus* (p. 189) and *Apatosaurus* (p. 191). *Europasaurus* "only" weighed 3 tons (3 MT) and grew 20 feet (6 m) long.

A dozen or more *Europasaurus* are known from fossils. The smallest was less than 6 feet (1.7 m) long—a tiny giant, perhaps only a few years old.

EUROPASAURUS MAY HAVE HAD A RIDGE ACROSS ITS SNOUT.

SHUNO-SAURUS

SHOO-noh-SORE-us

NAME *Shunosaurus*

MEANING "Szechuan lizard"

PERIOD 175 to 163 million years ago, Middle Jurassic

FOUND China

FOSSILS 20 skeletons with 5 skulls

LENGTH 40 feet (11 meters) long

SHUNOSAURUS MAY HAVE SWUNG its hard and heavy tail club to protect itself against predators. Here *Dsungaripterus* pterosaurs duck under the enormous waving tail.

CLUB-TAILED GIANT

Shunosaurus was discovered in one of the greatest fossil treasure piles ever unearthed. Gas company workers in central China found perfectly preserved *Shunosaurus* skeletons, complete from their skulls to the ends of their tails. It was as if someone had just laid the skeletons on their sides. It appears the dinosaurs died and were covered over gently with mud soon after their death.

When scientists began to examine the fossils, the discovery of a tail club on *Shunosaurus* was a big surprise. No other giant plant eaters were known to have such a bony lump.

THE ZIGONG MUSEUM IN CHINA WAS BUILT AROUND THE QUARRY WHERE SKELETONS OF *SHUNOSAURUS* WERE FOUND.

BRACHIO-SAURUS

BRACK-ee-oh-SORE-us

NAME *Brachiosaurus*

MEANING "Arm lizard"

PERIOD 156 to 145 million years ago, Late Jurassic

FOUND U.S. (Colorado)

FOSSILS Several incomplete skeletons, most without skulls

LENGTH 80 to 85 feet (24 to 26 meters) long

WITH LONG FRONT LEGS AND shorter rear legs, *Brachiosaurus* was built to feed high in trees.

HIGH TREE FEEDER

Brachiosaurus was a gigantic dinosaur. Scientists have estimated its weight at more than 28 tons (25 MT). Its neck and head stood up more than 40 feet (12 m) in the air. The most complete skeletons found belong to animals not yet fully grown. So *Brachiosaurus* probably grew even longer and taller than we know. Scientists once thought an animal this heavy could only support itself by living in water. The nostrils on top of its head seemed to support this theory. But the pressure of the water would have made it impossible for these animals to take in air.

IF *BRACHIOSAURUS* LIVED IN OUR WORLD, IT COULD LOOK INTO A WINDOW ON THE FIFTH FLOOR OF A BUILDING.

APATO-SAURUS

uh-PAT-uh-SORE-us

NAME *Apatosaurus*

MEANING "Deceptive lizard"

PERIOD 157 to 146 million years ago, Late Jurassic

FOUND U.S. (Colorado, Oklahoma, Utah, Wyoming)

FOSSILS A few partial skeletons, most without skulls

LENGTH 70 to 90 feet (21 to 27 meters) long

APATOSAURUS MAY HAVE MIGRATED in herds like other large plant eaters of the past and present. If so, it could have protected its young from predators by hiding them in the center of the herd.

WESTERN ROAMER

Apatosaurus is the correct name for the dinosaur once known as *Brontosaurus*. *Brontosaurus* was named in the late 1800s from bones of a dinosaur already named *Apatosaurus*. Scientists realized the mistake in 1911, but the name *Brontosaurus* stuck for many years.

By any name, *Apatosaurus* was a huge dinosaur. It roamed the North American west along with many other giant plant eaters, including *Diplodocus* (p. 193), *Barosaurus* (p. 219), *Brachiosaurus* (p. 189), and *Camarasaurus* (p. 222). How did all of these dinosaurs share the same food sources? Perhaps by feeding at different heights from the forest trees.

APATOSAURUS WAS DISPLAYED WITH THE WRONG HEAD FOR MANY YEARS. THE SKULL OF A *CAMARASAURUS* (P. 222), SHOWN HERE, WAS FOUND IN THE SAME QUARRY AND MISTAKENLY PUT ATOP A SKELETON OF *APATOSAURUS*.

DIPLODOCUS

dih-PLOD-uh-kus

NAME *Diplodocus*

MEANING "Double-beamed"

PERIOD 155 to 145 million years ago, Late Jurassic

FOUND U.S. (Colorado, Montana, Utah, Wyoming)

FOSSILS Many complete skeletons

LENGTH 90 feet (27 meters) long

DIPLODOCUS MIGHT HAVE SNAPPED its long tail like a bullwhip to defend itself from big meat eaters, such as *Allosaurus* (p. 75).

THE TAIL SNAPPER

Diplodocus is the largest dinosaur known from a complete skeleton. But *Diplodocus* was a lightly built dinosaur for its size, perhaps "only" 16 tons (14.5 MT). It had a very long tail that stretched more than 20 feet (6 m) with about 80 tail vertebrae, far more than other giant dinosaurs. The booming sound made by snapping its tail might have scared off hungry predators.

Its teeth were also very unusual. They were long and thin with a triangular point. They seem to be designed for stripping leaves from trees. But scientists disagree on whether or not *Diplodocus* held its head up high. It would have been difficult for its heart to pump blood that far upward.

DIPLODOCUS IS SEEN IN MUSEUMS **ACROSS THE WORLD. ANDREW CARNEGIE,** A 19TH-CENTURY AMERICAN BUSINESSMAN, GAVE REPRODUCTIONS OF ITS SKELETON TO THE RULERS OF MANY COUNTRIES.

SEISMO-SAURUS

SIZE-moh-SORE-us

NAME *Seismosaurus*

MEANING "Earthquake lizard"

PERIOD 156 to 145 million years ago, Late Jurassic

FOUND U.S. (New Mexico)

FOSSILS Incomplete skeleton, including some ribs, vertebrae, and partial hip

LENGTH Up to 110 feet (34 meters) long

SEISMOSAURUS HAD A LARGE TOE CLAW on each thumb. Perhaps the claw could be wielded in defense. But it is hard to imagine so big an animal moving its foot quickly to strike. Also, the claw was not firmly attached to bone, so it may not have been a powerful weapon.

THE EARTH SHAKER

Seismosaurus has just disappeared. This dinosaur was real, but now scientists identify it as a new species of *Diplodocus* (p. 193).

This dinosaur was once thought to have grown to 170 feet (52 m) long, which would have made it the largest of all dinosaurs. Then scientists discovered that the fossil bones from near *Seismosaurus*'s hips were mistakenly placed much closer to the tail. Once the bones were put in the right place, *Seismosaurus* was simply a very large dinosaur. And even though *Seismosaurus* is not as long as first thought, it still may be one of the longest of all dinosaurs.

SEISMOSAURUS WAS FOUND WITH MANY SMOOTH STONES NEAR ITS MIDSECTION. SOME SCIENTISTS THINK THESE WERE ROCKS SWALLOWED TO HELP DIGEST FOOD. OTHER SCIENTISTS DISAGREE.

PARALITITAN

pah-ral-e-TIE-tan

NAME *Paralititan*

MEANING "Tidal titan"

PERIOD 100 million years ago, Early Cretaceous

FOUND Egypt

FOSSILS Upper arm bone, other skeletal parts from one individual

LENGTH 78 to 100 feet (24 to 30 meters) long

PARALITITAN ROAMED AN ANCIENT swamp that is now part of the North African desert. In its time, this warm, moist environment supported rich plant life. The plants provided abundant food for this browsing giant. Mangrove forests are among the richest of habitats.

GIANT SWAMP DWELLER

Paralititan was one of the largest dinosaurs; it may have weighed up to 60 tons (54 MT). Its upper arm bone was nearly six feet (1.8 m) long. It was also the first dinosaur to be discovered from an ancient mangrove swamp. It lived in the mangroves at the edge of the shallow ocean that once flowed over the middle of the Earth. Today that land is the Sahara desert.

One might think a dinosaur as large as *Paralititan* would not need any defenses. But it looks as if *Paralititan* may have had some armor on its sides. The remains of *Paralititan* were found with tooth marks on the bones, showing that large meat eaters chewed on them, probably after it died of other causes.

PARALITITAN WAS FOUND IN 1999 AT A SITE WHERE GERMAN SCIENTISTS IN THE 1930S HAD FOUND **SPINOSAURUS** FOSSILS THAT WERE DESTROYED IN WORLD WAR II.

ARGENTINO-SAURUS

ahr-gen-TEEN-oh-SORE-us

NAME *Argentinosaurus*

MEANING "Argentina lizard"

PERIOD 100 million years ago, Late Cretaceous

FOUND Argentina

FOSSILS Vertebrae, sacrum, tibia, and ribs

LENGTH 130 to 140 feet (40 to 42 meters) long

ARGENTINOSAURUS STOOD MORE than 20 feet (6 m) high, but the huge trees of its world were almost five times taller. *Argentinosaurus* is long gone. But the Araucarian trees it munched on still live in Argentina.

THE HEAVYWEIGHT

Argentinosaurus was the largest animal ever to walk the Earth. Of all creatures, only the blue whale is larger. Some dinosaurs were as long as *Argentinosaurus*. Others stood taller. But *Argentinosaurus* was far heavier than other dinosaurs. It may have weighed 100 tons (91 MT), as much as 20 elephants. But even an animal as large as *Argentinosaurus* may not have been safe from predators. *Mapusaurus* (p. 83), the largest known meat eater, roamed its world.

This dinosaur is known from the parts of just a single skeleton. Those include vertebrae 5 feet (1.5 m) high and wide. Each vertebra fossil weighs 2 tons (2 MT).

THE RANCHER WHO DISCOVERED THE GIANT SHINBONE OF *ARGENTINOSAURUS* THOUGHT IT WAS A PIECE OF DRIFTWOOD.

REBBACHI-SAURUS

re-BASH-eh-SAWR-us

NAME *Rebbachisaurus*

MEANING "Rebbach-territory, Morocco lizard"

PERIOD 113 to 97.5 million years ago, Late Cretaceous

FOUND Morocco, Niger, Tunisia, Spain

FOSSILS Vertebrae

LENGTH 68 feet (20 meters) long

THE AFRICAN GIANT

Rebbachisaurus was a close relative of the North American *Diplodocus* (p. 193). Like *Diplodocus*, it had a long, thin neck and tail. But it lived far away and much later in time. *Rebbachisaurus* lived in Africa. A very similar giant, *Rayosaurus* (p. 250), lived in South America at the same time. The similarity of these dinosaurs shows that those two continents were still closely linked 100 million years ago.

Unlike other giant plant eaters, *Rebbachisaurus* had a tall ridge on its back. Other plant eaters from North Africa, as well as the meat eater *Spinosaurus* (p. 87), also had similar structures.

THE FOSSIL THAT MAY BE THE OLDEST KNOWN *REBBACHISAURUS* WAS FOUND IN SPAIN.

THE RIDGE ON *REBBACHISAURUS'S* back was part of a sail-like structure. Because it exposed more skin to the air, it may have helped the dinosaur cool down or heat up more quickly. After crashing through the forest, this *Rebbachisaurus* needed to cool down.

AMARGA-SAURUS

uh-MARG-uh-SORE-us

NAME *Amargasaurus*

MEANING "Lizard from La Amarga, Argentina"

PERIOD 131 to 125 million years ago, Early Cretaceous

FOUND Argentina

FOSSILS Mostly complete skeleton

LENGTH 33 feet (10 meters) long

LIKE OTHER SPINE-BACKED DINOSAURS, *Amargasaurus* lived in a dry, hot environment. So for many years, scientists have suggested that *Amargasaurus's* sails could have helped cool them off.

THE PUZZLING PLANT EATER

Amargasaurus was a very strange and puzzling dinosaur. It is unusually small for a giant plant eater. It resembles *Dicraeosaurus* (p. 226), a North African plant eater of the same size and time.

Amargasaurus had enormous spines in pairs on its back. The sail might have been a way of attracting mates or frightening rivals. Or perhaps it was simply a device to give off or take in heat. The spines that supported the sail were huge, more than six feet (1.8 m) long. The closest in size are those of *Dicraeosaurus* from Africa. But *Dicraeosaurus's* spines were only half as long.

AMARGASAURUS WAS DISCOVERED BY A GEOLOGIST WORKING FOR AN OIL COMPANY.

MAMENCHI SAURUS

mah-MEHN-chee-SORE-us

NAME *Mamenchisaurus*

MEANING "Mamenchi lizard" for place where fossils were first found

PERIOD 156 to 145 million years ago, Late Jurassic

FOUND China

FOSSILS Partial skeletons, skulls, neck material

LENGTH 70 feet (21 meters) long

MAMENCHISAURUS LIKELY USED its long neck to sweep across the land like a giant vacuum cleaner to grab plants. If the comparison of brain size to body size truly indicates intelligence, the enormous pea-brained *Mamenchisaurus* was one of the dopiest animals.

LONG-NECKED VACUUM CLEANER

Mamenchisaurus had the longest neck of any animal that ever lived. It stretched for more than 30 feet (9 m). Its neck was as long as the rest of its body, including its tail. And its brain was tiny. Its head was smaller than a horse's on a body longer than two school buses! *Mamenchisaurus* was so large that it might not have needed many weapons to defend itself. But one nearly complete skeleton shows four strongly linked vertebrae near the tip of its tail, which suggests that *Mamenchisaurus* may have also had a tail club like the earlier Chinese giant plant eater, *Shunosaurus* (p. 187).

LIKE MANY OTHER DINOSAURS, MAMENCHISAURUS WAS NOT DISCOVERED BY SCIENTISTS. WORKERS BUILDING A BRIDGE IN CENTRAL CHINA FOUND ITS BONES.

NURO-SAURUS

NEW-row-SORE-us

NAME *Nurosaurus*

MEANING "Nur lizard"

PERIOD 80 million years ago, Late Cretaceous

FOUND China

FOSSILS Partial skeleton

LENGTH 80 feet (25 meters) long

THE ENORMOUS NUROSAURUS roamed sandy desert lands, but it may have weighed too much for its own good. Fossils of the one known *Nurosaurus* show that it walked on a broken front foot.

ASIAN GIANT

Nurosaurus is one of the longest and maybe the heaviest of all Asian plant eaters. It weighed 25 tons (23 MT) or more. No other dinosaur in its world was anywhere close to this dinosaur in size.

Nurosaurus was excavated in the Gobi Desert of Inner Mongolia in the early 1990s. Chinese scientists put this dinosaur back together and displayed it around the world. Leading the excavation that discovered it was Dong Zhiming, the Chinese scientist who has named dozens of new kinds of dinosaurs. But Dong has never described *Nurosaurus* in a scientific paper. So it is still not officially a new dinosaur.

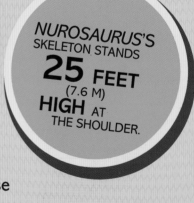

NUROSAURUS'S SKELETON STANDS **25** FEET (7.6 M) **HIGH** AT THE SHOULDER.

NOTH-RONYCHUS

NOTH-throw-NYE-cuss

NAME *Nothronychus*

MEANING "Slothful claw"

PERIOD 92 to 91 million years ago

FOUND U.S. (New Mexico)

FOSSILS Two nearly half-complete skeletons

LENGTH 20 feet (6.1 meters) long

HOW DID *NOTHRONY-CHUS* LIVE? Perhaps by snipping leaves and grabbing branches off of trees.

DINOSAUR SLOTH

Discovered in 2001, *Nothronychus* is the first known North American relative of the mysterious *Therizinosaurus* (p. 211) of Central Asia. Both animals had some odd features very different from most meat eaters.

Like its Asian cousin, *Nothronychus* had a bird-like hip structure and four toes turned forward on each foot. And both animals had huge arm claws, the biggest of any creatures ever. Scientists named it "slothful" because *Nothronychus* reminded them of the giant ground sloth, a huge, slow-moving, plant-eating mammal that lived during the Ice Age and ate a similar diet to *Nothronychus*.

NOTHRONYCHUS WAS DISCOVERED IN A PART OF **NEW MEXICO** THAT WAS ONCE THOUGHT TO BE UNDERWATER IN DINOSAUR TIME. IT WAS A **LAND DWELLER.** SO THE FIRST SCIENTIFIC STUDIES OF THE ANCIENT ENVIRONMENT WERE CLEARLY WRONG.

THERIZINO-SAURUS

THERE-ih-ZIN-oh-SORE-us

NAME *Therizinosaurus*

MEANING "Cut off reptile"

PERIOD 70 million years ago, Late Cretaceous

FOUND Mongolia, China

FOSSILS Several limb bones, including huge claws

LENGTH 36 feet (11 meters) long

ONE OF THE MANY MYSTERIES about *Therizinosaurus* is what it did with its huge but not sharp claws. Scientists have suggested that it might have used them to scrape away the ground to find ants, beetles, and other insects to eat.

SHARP-CLAWED FORAGER?

Therizinosaurus is one of the most mysterious of all dinosaurs. We know its 3-foot- (1-m) long claws, but we have few other bones of this giant. At first, scientists who found the bones thought they belonged to an ancient form of turtle. Instead, *Therizinosaurus* was among the last and largest of a strange group of giant plant eaters descended from meat eaters. From related animals, scientists picture *Therizinosaurus* as a small-headed, long-necked, and heavyset giant. Its enormous claws would have stretched from 8-foot- (2.5-m) long arms!

THE RUSSIAN SCIENTISTS WHO FIRST STUDIED *THERIZINOSAURUS* THOUGHT IT MIGHT BE A KIND OF GIANT TURTLE.

DINO DICTIONARY

Tens of thousands of dinosaurs lived during the 150 million years that they ruled the Earth. So far, we have found almost 1,000 of them, and each year we find more than twenty. In the last thirty years, scientists have named most of the dinosaurs we know. Still, most are identified from just a few bones or teeth. And with so little fossil information, scientists can make mistakes. Nearly half of all of the dinosaurs ever named turn out to be mistakes. Here, for now, are all the kinds of dinosaurs we know.

THIS CHART SHOWS THE DINOSAUR GROUPS FROM THE FAMILY TREE ON PAGES 22-23. THROUGH-OUT THE DICTIONARY, EACH DINOSAUR IS KEYED TO ITS FAMILY TREE GROUP.

MEAT EATER

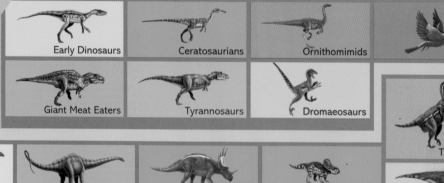

Early Dinosaurs · Ceratosaurians · Ornithomimids · Birds

Giant Meat Eaters · Tyrannosaurs · Dromaeosaurs

PLANT EATER

Prosauropods · Sauropods · Large Ceratopsians · Small Ceratopsians

Stegosaurs · Pachycephalosaurs · Anklyosaurs · Iguanodontians

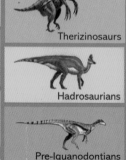

Therizinosaurs

Hadrosaurians

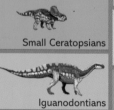

Pre-Iguanodontians

A

ABELISAURUS

MEANING: "Abel's lizard"

HOW TO SAY: ay-bel-uh-SORE-us

PERIOD: 75 to 70 million years ago, Late Cretaceous

WHERE FOUND: Argentina

FOSSILS: Incomplete skull

LENGTH: 21 to 26 feet (6.5 to 7.9 meters); Big

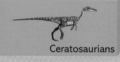
Ceratosaurians

ABYDOSAURUS

MEANING: After reptile from mythological Egyptian city containing head of god Osiris

HOW TO SAY: ah-BEE-do-SORE-us

PERIOD: 145 million years ago, Late Jurassic

WHERE FOUND: U.S. (Utah)

FOSSILS: Four skulls, one nearly complete

LENGTH: 50 feet (16 meters); Giant

Sauropods

ACROCANTHOSAURUS

MEANING: "High-spined lizard"

HOW TO SAY: AK-roh-CAN-thuh-SORE-us

PERIOD: 121 million years ago, Early Cretaceous

WHERE FOUND: U.S. (Oklahoma, Texas, Arizona)

FOSSILS: Two nearly complete skeletons

LENGTH: 40 feet (12.5 meters); Giant

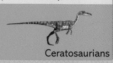
Ceratosaurians

ADEOPAPPOSAURUS

MEANING: "Far eating lizard"

HOW TO SAY: add-e-oh-PAP-oh-SORE-us

PERIOD: 200 to 190 million years ago, Early Jurassic

WHERE FOUND: Argentina

FOSSILS: Two partial skeletons with skulls, two without

LENGTH: Unknown

Prosauropods

AEOLOSAURUS

MEANING: "Aeolus's lizard"

HOW TO SAY: EE-oh-loh-SORE-us

PERIOD: 83 to 74 million years ago, Late Cretaceous

WHERE FOUND: Argentina

FOSSILS: Partial skeleton

LENGTH: 50 feet (15 meters); Giant

Sauropods

ABRICTOSAURUS

MEANING: "Awake lizard"

HOW TO SAY: uh-BRICK-tuh-SORE-us

PERIOD: 200 million years ago, Early Jurassic

WHERE FOUND: South Africa

FOSSILS: Skeleton and skull

LENGTH: 4.6 feet (1.2 meters); Small

Iguanodontians

ACHELOUSAURUS

MEANING: "Achelous lizard" after a river god who lost his horns

HOW TO SAY: ah-key-LOH-oh-SORE-us

PERIOD: 83 to 74 million years ago, Late Cretaceous

WHERE FOUND: U.S. (Montana)

FOSSILS: Partial skeleton

LENGTH: 20 feet (6 meters); Big

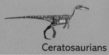
Ceratosaurians

ADAMANTISAURUS

MEANING: "Adamantina lizard"

HOW TO SAY: ah-da-MAN-ti-SORE-us

PERIOD: 93 to 70 million years ago, Late Cretaceous

WHERE FOUND: Brazil

FOSSILS: Six vertebrae

LENGTH: Unknown, but assumed to be large

Sauropods

AEGYPTOSAURUS

MEANING: "Egyptian lizard"

HOW TO SAY: ee-JIP-tuh-SORE-us

PERIOD: 99 to 93 million years ago, Late Cretaceous

WHERE FOUND: Egypt and Niger

FOSSILS: A few random bones

LENGTH: 50 feet (15 meters); Giant

Sauropods

AEROSTEON

MEANING: "Air bone"

HOW TO SAY: air-oh-STEE-on

PERIOD: 84 million years ago, Late Cretaceous

WHERE FOUND: Argentina

FOSSILS: Isolated bones including a tooth, part of a skull, and vertebrae

LENGTH: 30 feet (9 meters); Big

Ceratosaurians

ABROSAURUS

MEANING: "Delicate or gentle lizard"

HOW TO SAY: AB-roh-SORE-us

PERIOD: 168 to 161 million years ago, Middle Jurassic

WHERE FOUND: China

FOSSILS: Two skulls, fragmentary skeleton

LENGTH: 30 feet (9 meters); Big

Sauropods

ACHILLOBATOR

MEANING: "Achilles warrior/hero"

HOW TO SAY: ah-kill-oh-BATE-or

PERIOD: 90 million years ago, Late Cretaceous

WHERE FOUND: Mongolia

FOSSILS: Jaw, shoulder, ribs, vertebrae

LENGTH: 16 feet (5 meters); Big

Dromaeosaurs

ADASAURUS

MEANING: "Ada's lizard"

HOW TO SAY: AID-a-SORE-us

PERIOD: 74 to 65 million years ago, Late Cretaceous

WHERE FOUND: Mongolia

FOSSILS: Incomplete skeletons

LENGTH: 6 feet (2 meters); Small

Dromaeosaurs

ACROCANTHOSAURUS
PP. 76–77

AFROVENATOR

MEANING: "African hunter"

HOW TO SAY: af-roh-VEN-ah-tor

PERIOD: 130 million years ago, Early Cretaceous

WHERE FOUND: Niger

FOSSILS: Mostly complete skeleton

LENGTH: 27 to 30 feet (8 to 9 meters), Big

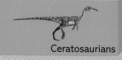
Ceratosaurians

AGROSAURUS

MEANING: "Wild country lizard"

HOW TO SAY: AG-roh-SORE-us

PERIOD: 225 to 213 million years ago, Late Triassic

WHERE FOUND: Wales

FOSSILS: A few isolated bones

LENGTH: 6.5 to 10 feet (2 to 3 meters); Small

Sauropods

ALAMOSAURUS

MEANING: "Alamo lizard"

HOW TO SAY: Al-uh-moe-SORE-us

PERIOD: 73 to 65 million years ago, Late Cretaceous

WHERE FOUND: U.S. (New Mexico, Texas, Utah)

FOSSILS: Partial skeletons without skulls

LENGTH: 69 feet (21 meters); Gigantic

Sauropods

ALBERTONYKUS

MEANING: "Alberta claw"

HOW TO SAY: al-BUR-toe-NY-cuss

PERIOD: 70 million years ago, Late Cretaceous

WHERE FOUND: Canada (Alberta)

FOSSILS: Several limbs

LENGTH: 2.5 feet (0.8 meters); Small

Dromaeosaurs

ALETOPELTA

MEANING: "Wandering shield"

HOW TO SAY: AL-et-oh-PELT-ah

PERIOD: 84 to 70 million years ago, Late Cretaceous

WHERE FOUND: U.S. (California)

FOSSILS: Partial skeleton

LENGTH: 20 feet (6 meters); Big

Anklyosaurs

AGILISAURUS

MEANING: "Agile lizard"

HOW TO SAY: AJ-il-eh-SORE-us

PERIOD: 170 million years ago, Middle Jurassic

WHERE FOUND: China

FOSSILS: Mostly complete skeleton

LENGTH: 3.5 to 4 feet (1.2 to 1.7 meters); Small

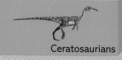
Pre-Iguanodontians

AGUJACERATOPS

MEANING: "Horned face from Aguja"

HOW TO SAY: ah-JAW-SER-ah-tops

PERIOD: 83 to 70 million years ago, Late Cretaceous

WHERE FOUND: U.S. (Texas)

FOSSILS: Partial skeleton without a skull

LENGTH: 16.5 feet (5 meters); Big

Large Ceratopsians

ALASKACEPHALE

MEANING: "Alaska head"

HOW TO SAY: ah-LAS-ka-seff-al-ee

PERIOD: 80 to 70 million years ago, Late Cretaceous

WHERE FOUND: U.S. (Alaska)

FOSSILS: Portion of a jaw

LENGTH: Probably about 8 feet (2.5 meters); Small

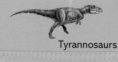
Pachycephalosaurs

ALBERTOSAURUS

MEANING: "Reptile from Alberta"

HOW TO SAY: al-BUR-toh-SORE-us

PERIOD: 70 million years ago, Late Cretaceous

WHERE FOUND: Canada (Alberta)

FOSSILS: Many skeletons

LENGTH: 25 feet (7.6 meters); Big

Tyrannosaurs

ALIORAMUS

MEANING: "Different branch"

HOW TO SAY: AL-ee-oh-RAY-mus

PERIOD: 73 to 65 million years ago, Late Cretaceous

WHERE FOUND: Mongolia

FOSSILS: Partial skeleton

LENGTH: 16 to 20 feet (5 to 6 meters); Big

Tyrannosaurs

AGNOSPHITYS

MEANING: "Unknown begetter"

HOW TO SAY: AG-no-SFEE-tis

PERIOD: 218 million years ago. Late Triassic

WHERE FOUND: England

FOSSILS: Partial skeleton

LENGTH: 2 feet (70 centimeters); Small

Early Dinosaurs

AGUSTINIA

MEANING: After Agustin Martinelli, the discoverer

HOW TO SAY: aw-GUST-tin-e-ah

PERIOD: 116 to 100 million years ago, Early Cretaceous

WHERE FOUND: Argentina

FOSSILS: Various bones, including vertebrae and nine plates or spikes, fibula, and tibia

LENGTH: 50 feet (15 meters); Giant

Sauropods

ALBERTACERATOPS

MEANING: "Alberta horn face"

HOW TO SAY: al-bert-ah-SERR-ah-tops

PERIOD: 100 to 70 million years ago, Late Cretaceous

WHERE FOUND: U.S. (Montana); Canada (Alberta)

FOSSILS: Complete skull

LENGTH: About 20 feet (6 meters); Big

Large Ceratopsians

ALECTROSAURUS

MEANING: "Unmarried lizard"

HOW TO SAY: ah-LECK-troh-SORE-us

PERIOD: 98 to 88 million years ago, Late Cretaceous

WHERE FOUND: Mongolia

FOSSILS: Partial skeletons, skull

LENGTH: 30 feet (9 meters); Big

Tyrannosaurs

ALIWALIA

MEANING: After Aliwal North, South Africa

HOW TO SAY: AL-ih-WAHL-ee-ah

PERIOD: 145 to 135 million years ago, Early Cretaceous

WHERE FOUND: South Africa

FOSSILS: A few bones

LENGTH: 25 feet (8 meters); Big

Prosauropods

ALLOSAURUS

MEANING: "Strange reptile"

HOW TO SAY: AL-oh-SORE-us

PERIOD: 145 million years ago, Late Jurassic

WHERE FOUND: U.S. (Colorado, Montana, Utah, Wyoming)

FOSSILS: Many skeletons

LENGTH: 28 feet (8.5 meters); Giant

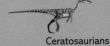

Ceratosaurians

ALOCODON

MEANING: "Furrowed tooth"

HOW TO SAY: a-LOK-oh-don

PERIOD: 164 million years ago, Late Jurassic

WHERE FOUND: Portugal

FOSSILS: One tooth

LENGTH: Unknown, probably 3 feet (1 meter); Small

Pre-Iguanodontians

ALTIRHINUS

MEANING: "High snout"

HOW TO SAY: al-ti-RINE-us

PERIOD: 120 to 100 million years ago, Early Cretaceous

WHERE FOUND: Mongolia

FOSSILS: Five partial skeletons, two skulls

LENGTH: 23 to 26 feet (7 to 8 meters); Big

Hadrosaurians

ALTISPINAX

MEANING: "High spine"

HOW TO SAY: AL-tee-SPY-nax

PERIOD: 123 to 119 million years ago, Early Cretaceous

WHERE FOUND: England

FOSSILS: One tooth

LENGTH: 30 feet (9 meters); Big

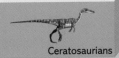

Ceratosaurians

ALVAREZSAURUS

MEANING: After Argentine historian Don Gregorio Alvarez

HOW TO SAY: Al-vuh-rez-SORE-us

PERIOD: 89 to 85 million years ago, Late Cretaceous

WHERE FOUND: Argentina

FOSSILS: A few bones, including vertebrae and pelvis

LENGTH: 6 feet (2 meters); Small

Dromaeosaurs

ALWALKERIA

MEANING: After British paleontologist Alick Walker

HOW TO SAY: al-wah-KERR-ee-a

PERIOD: 220 million years ago, Late Triassic

WHERE FOUND: India

FOSSILS: Partial skeleton

LENGTH: 3 feet (1 meter); Small

Early Dinosaurs

ALXASAURUS

MEANING: "Alxa (Desert) Lizard"

HOW TO SAY: AWL-shah-SORE-us

PERIOD: 99 million years ago, Middle Cretaceous

WHERE FOUND: Mongolia

FOSSILS: Several partial skeletons

LENGTH: 11.5 to 13 feet (3.5 to 4 meters); Small

Therizinosaurs

AMARGASAURUS

MEANING: "Lizard from La Amarga, Argentina"

HOW TO SAY: uh-MARG-uh-SORE-us

PERIOD: 131 to 125 million years ago, Early Cretaceous

WHERE FOUND: Argentina

FOSSILS: Mostly complete skeleton

LENGTH: 33 feet (10 meters); Giant

Sauropods

AMARGATITANIS

MEANING: "Amarga giant"

HOW TO SAY: am-ARE-gah-tye-TAN-us

PERIOD: 130 to 125 million years ago, Early Cretaceous

WHERE FOUND: Argentina

FOSSILS: Various bones, including shoulder, vertebrae, thighbone

LENGTH: Up to 40 feet (12 meters); Giant

Sauropods

AMAZONSAURUS

MEANING: "Amazon lizard"

HOW TO SAY: am-ah-zon-SORE-us

PERIOD: 125 to 100 million years ago, Early Cretaceous

WHERE FOUND: Brazil

FOSSILS: Various bones, including vertebrae, ribs, and pelvis

LENGTH: 40 feet (12 meters); Giant

Sauropods

AMMOSAURUS

MEANING: "Sandy-ground lizard"

HOW TO SAY: AM-oh-SORE-us

PERIOD: 198 to 187 million years ago, Early Jurassic

WHERE FOUND: U.S. (Connecticut, Arizona); Canada (Nova Scotia)

FOSSILS: Four partial skeletons

LENGTH: 14 feet (4 meters); Small

Prosauropods

AMPELOSAURUS

MEANING: "Vineyard lizard"

HOW TO SAY: AM-pel-o-SORE-us

PERIOD: 198 to 187 million years ago, Early Jurassic

WHERE FOUND: France

FOSSILS: Partial skeleton

LENGTH: 50 feet (15 meters); Giant

Sauropods

AMUROSAURUS

MEANING: "Amur lizard"

HOW TO SAY: am-er-oh-SORE-us

PERIOD: 74 to 65 million years ago, Late Cretaceous

WHERE FOUND: Russia, China

FOSSILS: Upper jaw

LENGTH: 20 feet (6 meters); Big

Hadrosaurians

AMYGDALODON

MEANING: "Almond tooth"

HOW TO SAY: am-ig-DAL-oh-don

PERIOD: 171 to 167 million years ago, Middle Jurassic

WHERE FOUND: Argentina

FOSSILS: One tooth

LENGTH: 11.5 feet (3.5 meters); Small

Sauropods

ANABISETIA

MEANING: After Argentine archaeologist Ana Biset

HOW TO SAY: an-ah-BISS-et-tee-ah

PERIOD: 95 to 92 million years ago, Late Cretaceous

WHERE FOUND: Argentina

FOSSILS: Skulls, various bones

LENGTH: 7 feet (2 meters); Small

Pre-Iguanodontians

ANATOTITAN

MEANING: "Giant duck"

HOW TO SAY: un-NAT-uh-TYE-tan

PERIOD: 70 to 65 million years ago, Late Cretaceous

WHERE FOUND: U.S. (Montana, South Dakota)

FOSSILS: Six individuals, several complete skeletons

LENGTH: 40 feet (12 meters); Giant

Hadrosaurians

ANCHIORNIS

MEANING: "Near bird"

HOW TO SAY: ANN-kee-OR-niss

PERIOD: 130 million years ago, Early Cretaceous

WHERE FOUND: China

FOSSILS: Partial skeleton

LENGTH: 1 foot (0.3 meters); Small

Dromaeosaurs

ANDESAURUS

MEANING: "Andes Mountain lizard"

HOW TO SAY: ANN-dee-SORE-us

PERIOD: 113 to 91 million years ago, Middle Cretaceous

WHERE FOUND: Argentina

FOSSILS: Vertebrae, arm and hip bones

LENGTH: 60 to 130 feet (18 to 40 meters); Gigantic

Sauropods

ANIKSOSAURUS

MEANING: "Spring lizard"

HOW TO SAY: an-ICK-so-SORE-us

PERIOD: 95 million years ago, Middle Cretaceous

WHERE FOUND: Argentina

FOSSILS: Incomplete skeleton without skull

LENGTH: 8 feet (2 meters); Small

Dromaeosaurs

ANASAZISAURUS

MEANING: "Anasazi lizard"

HOW TO SAY: AN-ah-saz-ee-SORE-us

PERIOD: 74 million years ago, Late Cretaceous

WHERE FOUND: U.S. (New Mexico)

FOSSILS: Skull

LENGTH: 33 feet (10 meters); Giant

Hadrosaurians

ANCHICERATOPS

MEANING: "Horn-near-face"

HOW TO SAY: AN-key-SERR-ah-tops

PERIOD: 73 to 70 million years ago, Late Cretaceous

WHERE FOUND: Canada (Alberta)

FOSSILS: Six skulls

LENGTH: 15 to 20 feet (4.5 to 6 meters); Big

Large Ceratopsians

ANCHISAURUS

MEANING: "Near bird"

HOW TO SAY: AN-key-SORE-us

PERIOD: 200 to 188 million years ago, Early Jurassic

WHERE FOUND: U.S. (Connecticut, Massachusetts)

FOSSILS: Mostly complete skeletons

LENGTH: 6.5 to 8 feet (2 to 2.5 meters); Small

Sauropods

ANGATURAMA

MEANING: "Noble one"

HOW TO SAY: ANN-gah-two-RAH-ma

PERIOD: 112 to 100 million years ago, Early Cretaceous

WHERE FOUND: Brazil

FOSSILS: Partial skull

LENGTH: 20 to 27 feet (6 to 8 meters); Big

Giant Meat Eaters

ANIMANTARX

MEANING: "Living citadel"

HOW TO SAY: ANN-ee-MAN-tarks

PERIOD: 106 to 97 million years ago, Late Cretaceous

WHERE FOUND: U.S. (Montana)

FOSSILS: Partial skeleton, lower jaw, part of skull, various limbs

LENGTH: 10 feet (3 meters); Small

Anklyosaurs

ANGULOMASTICATOR

MEANING: "Bend chewer"

HOW TO SAY: ANN-goo-lo-MAS-tick-a-tor

PERIOD: 70 million years ago, Late Cretaceous

WHERE FOUND: U.S. (Texas)

FOSSILS: Partial jaw

LENGTH: 10 feet (3 meters)

Hadrosaurians

ANKYLOSAURUS

MEANING: "Fused lizard"

HOW TO SAY: AN-kye-loh-SORE-us

PERIOD: 70 to 65 million years ago, Late Cretaceous

WHERE FOUND: U.S. (Montana); Canada (Alberta)

FOSSILS: Two skulls and three partial skeletons

LENGTH: 25 to 35 feet (7.5 to 10.7 meters); Giant

Anklyosaurs

ARCHAEOPTERYX
P. 116–117

ANODONTOSAURUS

MEANING: "Toothless lizard"

HOW TO SAY: an-oh-DONT-oh-SORE-us

PERIOD: 76 to 70 million years ago, Late Cretaceous

WHERE FOUND: U.S. (Montana); Canada (Alberta)

FOSSILS: Forty individuals, including 15 skulls and several nearly complete skeletons

LENGTH: 20 feet (6 meters); Big

Anklyosaurs

ANTARCTOPELTA

MEANING: "Antarctic shield"

HOW TO SAY: ant-ARK-toe-PELT-ah

PERIOD: 74 to 70 million years ago, Late Cretaceous

WHERE FOUND: Antarctica

FOSSILS: Three teeth, part of jaw and skull, various partial limbs

LENGTH: 13 feet (4 meters); Small

Anklyosaurs

APATOSAURUS

MEANING: "Deceptive lizard"

HOW TO SAY: uh-PAT-uh-SORE-us

PERIOD: 157 to 146 million years ago, Late Jurassic

WHERE FOUND: U.S. (Colorado, Oklahoma, Utah, Wyoming)

FOSSILS: A few partial skeletons, most without skulls

LENGTH: 70 to 90 feet (21 to 27 meters); Gigantic

Sauropods

ARALOSAURUS

MEANING: "Aral Sea lizard"

HOW TO SAY: AR-a-lo-SORE-us

PERIOD: 95 to 80 million years ago, Late Cretaceous

WHERE FOUND: Kazakhstan

FOSSILS: Partial skeleton

LENGTH: 30 feet (9 meters); Big

Hadrosaurians

ARCHAEOPTERYX

MEANING: "Ancient feather" or "Ancient wing"

HOW TO SAY: ARK-ee-OP-turr-icks

PERIOD: 145 million years ago, Late Jurassic

WHERE FOUND: Germany

FOSSILS: 11 skeletons

LENGTH: 1.6 feet (0.5 meters); Small

Birds

ANOPLOSAURUS

MEANING: "No-weapon lizard"

HOW TO SAY: an-OP-loh-SORE-us

PERIOD: 98 million years ago, Early Cretaceous

WHERE FOUND: England

FOSSILS: Very incomplete skeleton

LENGTH: Unknown, but small

Anklyosaurs

ANTARCTOSAURUS

MEANING: "Opposite-of-northern lizard"

HOW TO SAY: ant-ARK-toe-SORE-us

PERIOD: 83 to 65 million years ago, Late Cretaceous

WHERE FOUND: Argentina, Uruguay, Chile

FOSSILS: Partial skeleton, skull, various bones

LENGTH: 60 to 100 feet (19 to 30 meters); Gigantic

Sauropods

APPALACHIOSAURUS

MEANING: "Appalachian lizard"

HOW TO SAY: app-ah-LAY-sha-SORE-us

PERIOD: 77 million years ago, Late Cretaceous

WHERE FOUND: U.S. (Alabama)

FOSSILS: Partial skull, pelvis and lower jaw, vertebrae

LENGTH: 23 feet (7 meters); Big

Tyrannosaurs

ARCHAEOCERATOPS

MEANING: "Ancient horned face"

HOW TO SAY: AHR-kee-oh-SERR-a-tops

PERIOD: 140 to 130 million years ago, Early Cretaceous

WHERE FOUND: China

FOSSILS: Partial skeleton

LENGTH: 3 feet (1 meter); Small

Small Ceratopsians

ARCHAEORNITHOIDES

MEANING: "Archaeornis-like"

HOW TO SAY: AHR-kee-OR-nith-OI-deez

PERIOD: 75 million years ago, Late Cretaceous

WHERE FOUND: Mongolia

FOSSILS: Partial skull

LENGTH: 3 feet (1 meter); Small

Dromaeosaurs

ANSERIMIMUS

MEANING: "Goose mimic"

HOW TO SAY: AN-ser-i-MIME-us

PERIOD: 75 to 70 million years ago, Late Cretaceous

WHERE FOUND: Mongolia

FOSSILS: One skeleton without skull

LENGTH: 3 feet (1 meter); Small

Ornithomimids

ANTETONITRUS

MEANING: "Before the thunder"

HOW TO SAY: AN-tee-TON-ee-truss

PERIOD: 221 to 210 million years ago, Late Triassic

WHERE FOUND: South Africa

FOSSILS: Various bones from two individuals

LENGTH: 33 feet (10 meters); Giant

Sauropods

ARAGOSAURUS

MEANING: "Aragon lizard"

HOW TO SAY: AHR-ah-go-SORE-us

PERIOD: 130 to 120 million years ago, Early Cretaceous

WHERE FOUND: Spain

FOSSILS: Partial skeleton

LENGTH: 60 feet (18 meters); Giant

Sauropods

ARCHAEODONTO–SAURUS

MEANING: "Ancient-toothed lizard"

HOW TO SAY: AHR-kee-oh-don-toe-SORE-us

PERIOD: 167 to 164 million years ago, Middle Jurassic

WHERE FOUND: Madagascar

FOSSILS: Jaw with several teeth

LENGTH: 37 to 43 feet (11 to 13 meters); Giant

Sauropods

ARCHAEORNITHO–MIMUS

MEANING: "Ancient bird mimic"

HOW TO SAY: AHR-kee-or-NI-thoh-MIME-us

PERIOD: 80 million years ago, Late Cretaceous

WHERE FOUND: China, Uzbekhistan

FOSSILS: More than 20 skeletons up to 90% complete

LENGTH: 11 feet (3 meters); Small

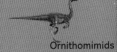
Ornithomimids

ARGENTINOSAURUS

MEANING: "Argentina lizard"

HOW TO SAY: ahr-gen-TEEN-oh-SORE-us

PERIOD: 100 million years ago, Late Cretaceous

WHERE FOUND: Argentina

FOSSILS: Vertebrae, sacrum, tibia, and ribs

LENGTH: 130 to 140 feet (40 to 42 meters); Gigantic

Sauropods

ARRHINOCERATOPS

MEANING: "Without nose horn face"

HOW TO SAY: aye-RYE-no-SER-ah-tops

PERIOD: 72 to 68 million years ago, Late Cretaceous

WHERE FOUND: Canada (Alberta)

FOSSILS: Skull

LENGTH: 20 feet (6 meters); Big

Large Ceratopsians

ATLASAURUS

MEANING: "Atlas lizard" after Greek God who held up the Earth

HOW TO SAY: AT-luh-SORE-us

PERIOD: 165 million years ago, Middle Jurassic

WHERE FOUND: Morocco

FOSSILS: Mostly complete skeleton

LENGTH: 50 feet (15 meters); Giant

Sauropods

AUCASAURUS

MEANING: "Reptile from Auca (in Patagonia)"

HOW TO SAY: AW-kuh-SORE-us

PERIOD: 84 million years ago, Late Cretaceous

WHERE FOUND: Argentina

FOSSILS: One nearly complete skeleton

LENGTH: 14 feet (4.3 meters); Small

Ceratosaurians

AUSTRALOVENATOR

MEANING: "Southern hunter"

HOW TO SAY: awst-ra-LO-ven-ate-or

PERIOD: 100 million years ago, Early Cretaceous

WHERE FOUND: Australia

FOSSILS: Partial skeleton with partial skull

LENGTH: 20 feet (6 meters); Big

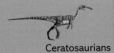
Ceratosaurians

ARGYROSAURUS

MEANING: "Silver lizard"

HOW TO SAY: AH-gear-o-SORE-us

PERIOD: 73 to 65 million years ago, Late Cretaceous

WHERE FOUND: Argentina, Uruguay

FOSSILS: Various limbs

LENGTH: 70 feet (21 meters); Gigantic

Sauropods

ASIACERATOPS

MEANING: "Asian horned face"

HOW TO SAY: AY-zha-SER-ah-tops

PERIOD: 97.5 to 90 million years ago, Late Cretaceous

WHERE FOUND: Kazakhstan

FOSSILS: Various bones

LENGTH: 6 to 7 feet (2 meters); Small

Small Ceratopsians

ATLASCOPCOSAURUS

MEANING: "Atlas Copco lizard" for drilling company that donated equipment

HOW TO SAY: AT-las-KOP-co-SORE-us

PERIOD: 125 to 100 million years ago, Early Cretaceous

WHERE FOUND: Australia

FOSSILS: Jaw and teeth

LENGTH: 6.5 to 10 feet (2 to 3 meters); Small

Pre-Iguanodontians

AURORACERATOPS

MEANING: "Dawn horn face"

HOW TO SAY: AW-roar-ah-SERR-a-tops

PERIOD: 125 to 112 million years ago, Early Cretaceous

WHERE FOUND: China

FOSSILS: Mostly complete skull

LENGTH: 4 feet (1.2 meters)

Small Ceratopsians

AUSTRORAPTOR

MEANING: "Southern thief"

HOW TO SAY: AW-stroh-rap-TORE

PERIOD: 70 million years ago, Late Cretaceous

WHERE FOUND: Argentina

FOSSILS: Partial skeleton w/fragmentary skull

LENGTH: 16 feet (5 meters); Big

Dromaeosaurs

ATROCIRAPTOR

MEANING: "Cruel thief"

HOW TO SAY: at-ROW-sih-RAP-tore

PERIOD: 70 to 65 million years ago, Late Cretaceous

WHERE FOUND: Canada (Alberta)

FOSSILS: Jaw, teeth

LENGTH: 2.3 feet (0.7 meters); Small

Dromaeosaurs

AUSTRALODOCUS

MEANING: "Southern beam"

HOW TO SAY: AW-stra-LOW-doe-cuss

PERIOD: 150 million years ago, Late Jurassic

WHERE FOUND: Tanzania

FOSSILS: Various bones, including vertebrae

LENGTH: 66 feet (20 meters)

Sauropods

AUSTROSAURUS

MEANING: "Southern lizard"

HOW TO SAY: AW-stroh-SORE-us

PERIOD: 113 to 98 million years ago, Early Cretaceous

WHERE FOUND: Australia

FOSSILS: Partial skulls, teeth

LENGTH: 50 feet (15 meters); Giant

Sauropods

ARCHAEORNITHOMIMUS
P. 92–93

B

AVACERATOPS

MEANING: "Horned face"

HOW TO SAY: AY-vuh-SER-uh-tops

PERIOD: 77 to 73 million years ago, Late Cretaceous

WHERE FOUND: U.S. (Montana)

FOSSILS: Partial skulls

LENGTH: 7 to 14 feet (2 to 4 meters); Small

Large Ceratopsians

AVIATYRANNIS

MEANING: "Jurassic grandmother tyrant"

HOW TO SAY: AVE-e-ah-TIE-ran-is

PERIOD: 145 million years ago, Late Jurassic

WHERE FOUND: Portugal

FOSSILS: Pelvis

LENGTH: About 3 feet (0.8 meters); Small

Tyrannosaurs

AVIMIMUS

MEANING: "Bird mimic"

HOW TO SAY: AH-vee-MIME-us

PERIOD: 85 to 75 million years ago, Late Cretaceous

WHERE FOUND: Mongolia

FOSSILS: Four partial skeletons

LENGTH: 5 feet (1.5 meters); Small

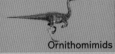

Ornithomimids

BACTROSAURUS

MEANING: "Club-spined lizard"

HOW TO SAY: BACK-tra-SORE-us

PERIOD: 97 to 85 million years ago, Late Cretaceous

WHERE FOUND: Mongolia, China

FOSSILS: Six partial skeletons

LENGTH: 20 feet (6 meters); Big

Hadrosaurians

BAGACERATOPS

MEANING: "Small-horned face"

HOW TO SAY: BAG-uh-SER-ah-TOPS

PERIOD: 80 million years ago, Late Cretaceous

WHERE FOUND: Mongolia

FOSSILS: Five complete skulls, many partial skulls

LENGTH: 3 feet (1 meter); Small

Small Ceratopsians

BAGARAATAN

MEANING: "Small hunter"

HOW TO SAY: BAG-ah-RAH-tahn

PERIOD: 70 to 65 million years ago, Late Cretaceous

WHERE FOUND: Mongolia

FOSSILS: incomplete skeleton

LENGTH: 11.5 feet (3.5 meters); Small

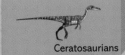

Ceratosaurians

BAHARIASAURUS

MEANING: "Oasis lizard"

HOW TO SAY: bah-hah-REE-ya-SORE-us

PERIOD: 95 million years ago, Late Cretaceous

WHERE FOUND: Egypt

FOSSILS: None (original specimen was destroyed in WWII bombing of Germany)

LENGTH: 20 to 40 feet (6 to 12 meters); Big

Ceratosaurians

BAINOCERATOPS

MEANING: "Mountain horned face"

HOW TO SAY: BANE-oh-SER-ah-tops

PERIOD: 84 to 70 million years ago, Late Cretaceous

WHERE FOUND: Mongolia

FOSSILS: Backbones

LENGTH: About 10 feet (3 meters); Small

Small Ceratopsians

BALOCHISAURUS

MEANING: "Balochi lizard"

HOW TO SAY: BAH-lo-chi-SORE-us

PERIOD: 70 to 65 million years ago, Late Cretaceous

WHERE FOUND: Pakistan

FOSSILS: Seven vertebrae

LENGTH: 66 feet (20 meters)

Sauropods

BAMBIRAPTOR

MEANING: After Bambi, the young deer of the Disney animated movie

HOW TO SAY: BAM-be-RAP-tore

PERIOD: 75 million years ago, Late Cretaceous

WHERE FOUND: U.S. (Montana)

FOSSILS: Nearly complete skull

LENGTH: 3 feet (1 meter); Small

Dromaeosaurs

BARAPASAURUS

MEANING: "Big-legged lizard"

HOW TO SAY: buh-RAH-pah-SORE-us

PERIOD: 200 million years ago, Early Jurassic

WHERE FOUND: India

FOSSILS: Six partial skeletons without skulls or feet

LENGTH: 60 feet (20 meters); Giant

Sauropods

BAROSAURUS

MEANING: "Heavy lizard"

HOW TO SAY: BAR-oh-SORE-us

PERIOD: 156 to 145 million years ago, Late Jurassic

WHERE FOUND: Western U.S.; East Africa

FOSSILS: Mostly complete skeleton, various bones, and partial skeletons

LENGTH: 60 to 88 feet (20 to 27 meters); Giant

Sauropods

BARROSASAURUS

MEANING: Lizard from Barrosa Hill

HOW TO SAY: BARR-oh-sa-SORE-us

PERIOD: 80 million years ago, Late Cretaceous

WHERE FOUND: Argentina

FOSSILS: Three incomplete vertebrae

LENGTH: 95 feet (30 meters); Gigantic

Sauropods

BARSBOLDIA

MEANING: After Mongolian paleontologist Rinchen Barsbold

HOW TO SAY: BARS-bold-ee-yah

PERIOD: 70 million years ago, Late Cretaceous

WHERE FOUND: Mongolia

FOSSILS: Partial back bones, partial pelvis, some ribs

LENGTH: 30 feet (10 meters); Big

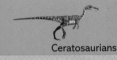

Hadrosaurians

BARYONYX

MEANING: "Heavy claw"

HOW TO SAY: BARE-ee-ON-icks

PERIOD: 125 million years ago, Early Cretaceous

WHERE FOUND: England, Niger, Spain

FOSSILS: One nearly complete skeleton, claws, and part of a skull

LENGTH: 28 feet (8.5 meters); Big

Giant Meat Eaters

BAURUTITAN

MEANING: "Bauru giant"

HOW TO SAY: BAR-oo-TEH-tan

PERIOD: 100 to 65 million years ago, Late Cretaceous

WHERE FOUND: Brazil

FOSSILS: Vertebrae

LENGTH: 79 feet (24 meters); Gigantic

Sauropods

BECKLESPINAX

MEANING: "Beckles' spine"

HOW TO SAY: BECK-el-SPIN-icks

PERIOD: 125 million years ago, Early Cretaceous

WHERE FOUND: England

FOSSILS: Three vertebrae, teeth

LENGTH: 15 feet (5 meters); Small

Giant Meat Eaters

BEIPIAOSAURUS

MEANING: "Beipiao lizard"

HOW TO SAY: bay-pyow-SORE-us

PERIOD: 124 million years ago, Early Cretaceous

WHERE FOUND: China

FOSSILS: Partial skeleton

LENGTH: 7.3 feet (2.2 meters); Small

Therizinosaurs

BEISHANLONG

MEANING: "Beishan dragon"

HOW TO SAY: BAY-shan-long

PERIOD: 125 to 100 million years ago, Early Cretaceous

WHERE FOUND: China

FOSSILS: Partial skeleton

LENGTH: 17 feet (5 meters); Big

Ornithomimids

BELLUSAURUS

MEANING: "Beautiful lizard"

HOW TO SAY: BEL-uh-SORE-us

PERIOD: 188 to 163 million years ago, Middle Jurassic

WHERE FOUND: China

FOSSILS: 17 individuals

LENGTH: 16 feet (5 meters); Big

Sauropods

BERBEROSAURUS

MEANING: "Berber lizard" after Berber people of Morocco

HOW TO SAY: BUR-bear-oh-SORE-us

PERIOD: 189 to 176 million years ago, Early Jurassic

WHERE FOUND: Morocco

FOSSILS: Partial skeleton, femur, tibia, and fibulae

LENGTH: About 20 feet (6 meters); Big

Ceratosaurians

BIENOSAURUS

MEANING: "Bien's lizard" after Chinese geologist Mei Nien Bien

HOW TO SAY: BEE-en-oh-SORE-us

PERIOD: 200 to 196 million years ago, Early Jurassic

WHERE FOUND: China

FOSSILS: Jaw and teeth, parts of a skull

LENGTH: 3.3 to 10 feet (1 to 3 meters); Small

Anklyosaurs

BIHARIOSAURUS

MEANING: "Bihor lizard"

HOW TO SAY: bi-HAHR-ee-oh-SORE-us

PERIOD: 153 to 145 million years ago, Late Jurassic

WHERE FOUND: Romania

FOSSILS: Partial bones

LENGTH: 10 feet (3 meters); Small

Iguanodontians

BISSEKTIPELTA

MEANING: "Bissekt shield"

HOW TO SAY: BIH-seck-tih-PELT-ah

PERIOD: 94 to 86 million years ago, Late Cretaceous

WHERE FOUND: Uzbekistan

FOSSILS: Incomplete skull, teeth

LENGTH: 20 to 23 feet (6 to 7 meters); Big

Anklyosaurs

BISTAHIEVERSOR

MEANING: "Destroyer from Bisti (WIlderness Area)"

HOW TO SAY: BISS-tah-HE-ee-VER-sore

PERIOD: 75 million years ago, Late Cretaceous

WHERE FOUND: U.S. (New Mexico)

FOSSILS: Two fairly complete skulls and skeletons

LENGTH: 20 feet (6.5 meters); Big

Tyrannosaurs

BLIKANASAURUS

MEANING: "Blikana lizard"

HOW TO SAY: bli-KAHN-ah-SORE-us

PERIOD: 225 to 215 million years ago, Late Triassic

WHERE FOUND: South Africa

FOSSILS: Partial back limb

LENGTH: 10 to 16 feet (3 to 5 meters); Small

Sauropods

BOATIANMAN–SAURUS

MEANING: "Boatianman lizard"

HOW TO SAY: BOW-tee-en-man-SORE-us

PERIOD: 80 to 60 million years ago, Late Cretaceous

WHERE FOUND: China

FOSSILS: Vertebrae

LENGTH: 82 feet (25 meters); Giant

Sauropods

BONATITAN

MEANING: After Argentine paleontologist Jose Fernando Bonaparte

HOW TO SAY: BON-a-TIE-tan

PERIOD: 83 to 65 million years ago, Late Cretaceous

WHERE FOUND: Argentina

FOSSILS: Partial skeleton with skull

LENGTH: Up to 40 feet (12 meters); Giant

Sauropods

BONITASAURA

MEANING: After the site, "La Bonita"

HOW TO SAY: BAH-neat-tah-SORE-ah

PERIOD: 80 million years ago, Late Cretaceous

WHERE FOUND: Argentina

FOSSILS: Partial skeleton

LENGTH: 30 feet (9 meters); Big

Sauropods

BOREALOSAURUS

MEANING: "North lizard"

HOW TO SAY: BORE-ee-al-luh-SORE-us

PERIOD: 86 to 83 million years ago, Early Cretaceous

WHERE FOUND: China

FOSSILS: Vertebrae

LENGTH: 40 feet (12 meters); Giant

Sauropods

BOROGOVIA

MEANING: After *Alice in Wonderland* author Lewis Carroll's characters called borogoves

HOW TO SAY: bor-oh-GOH-vee-a

PERIOD: 80 to 70 million years ago, Late Cretaceous

WHERE FOUND: Mongolia

FOSSILS: Partial leg bones

LENGTH: 6.5 feet (2 meters); Small

Dromaeosaurs

BOTHRIOSPONDYLUS

MEANING: "Trench vertebra"

HOW TO SAY: BOTH-ree-o-SPON-dye-luss

PERIOD: 170 to 156 million years ago, Middle Jurassic

WHERE FOUND: England, Madagascar

FOSSILS: Vertebrae, some hip and limb fragments

LENGTH: 65 feet (20 meters); Gigantic

Sauropods

BRACHIOSAURUS

MEANING: "Arm lizard"

HOW TO SAY: BRACK-ee-oh-SORE-us

PERIOD: 156 to 145 million years ago, Late Jurassic

WHERE FOUND: U.S. (Colorado)

FOSSILS: Several incomplete skeletons, most without skulls

LENGTH: 80 to 85 feet (24 to 26 meters); Gigantic

Sauropods

BRACHYCERATOPS

MEANING: "Short-horned face"

HOW TO SAY: BRACK-ee-SER-a-tops

PERIOD: 80 to 70 million years ago, Late Cretaceous

WHERE FOUND: U.S. (Montana)

FOSSILS: Five partial skeletons of young Brachyceratops

LENGTH: 6 feet (1.8 meters); Small

Small Ceratopsians

BRACHYLOPHO–SAURUS

MEANING: "Short crested lizard"

HOW TO SAY: BRACK-ee-LOW-fo-SORE-us

PERIOD: 75 million years ago, Late Cretaceous

WHERE FOUND: U.S. (Montana); Canada (Alberta)

FOSSILS: Complete skeleton, partial skeletons

LENGTH: 22 feet (7 meters); Big

Hadrosaurians

BRACHYTRACHELO–PAN

MEANING: "Short-necked Pan" for the Greek god of shepherds (skeleton was found by a shepherd)

HOW TO SAY: BRACK-ee-tra-CHELL-o-pan

PERIOD: 150 to 145 million years ago, Late Jurassic

WHERE FOUND: Argentina

FOSSILS: Incomplete skeleton

LENGTH: Up to 33 feet (10 meters); Big

Sauropods

BREVICERATOPS

MEANING: "Short-horned face"

HOW TO SAY: BREV-eh-SER-ah-tops

PERIOD: 100 to 65 million years ago, Late Cretaceous

WHERE FOUND: Mongolia

FOSSILS: Five skulls, some of a skeleton

LENGTH: 7 feet (2 meters); Small

Small Ceratopsians

BROHISAURUS

MEANING: "Reptile from Brohi"

HOW TO SAY: BRO-he-SORE-us

PERIOD: 145 million years ago, Late Jurassic

WHERE FOUND: Pakistan

FOSSILS: Limbs

LENGTH: 98 feet (30 meters)

Sauropods

BUITRERAPTOR

MEANING: Thief from La Buitrera

HOW TO SAY: BWEE-tre-RAP-tore

PERIOD: 90 million years ago, Late Cretaceous

WHERE FOUND: Argentina

FOSSILS: Complete skeleton

LENGTH: 3 feet (1 meter); Small

Dromaeosaurs

BYRONOSAURUS

MEANING: "Byron lizard" after Byron Jaffe

HOW TO SAY: by-RON-oh-SORE-us

PERIOD: 76 to 70 million years ago, Late Cretaceous

WHERE FOUND: Mongolia

FOSSILS: Two skulls, two young skulls

LENGTH: 5 feet (1.5 meters); Small

Dromaeosaurs

C

CAENAGNATHASIA

MEANING: "Asian recent jaw"

HOW TO SAY: see-NAG-na-THAY-zhee-a

PERIOD: 90 million years ago, Late Cretaceous

WHERE FOUND: Asia

FOSSILS: Jawbones

LENGTH: 3 feet (1 meter); Small

Dromaeosaurs

CAENAGNATHUS

MEANING: "Recent jaw"

HOW TO SAY: SEE-nag-NAY-thus

PERIOD: 75 million years ago, Late Cretaceous

WHERE FOUND: Western U.S.

FOSSILS: Lower jaw

LENGTH: 6.5 feet (2 meters); Small

Likely invalid, *see Chirostenotes, page 223*

Dromaeosaurs

CALLOVOSAURUS

MEANING: "Callovian lizard"

HOW TO SAY: call-oh-vo-SORE-us

PERIOD: 166 million years ago, Middle Jurassic

WHERE FOUND: England

FOSSILS: Fragmentary bones

LENGTH: 11.5 feet (3.5 meters); Small

Iguanodontians

BUITRERAPTOR P. 106–107

CAMARASAURUS

MEANING: "Chambered lizard"

HOW TO SAY: KAM-ah-rah-SORE-us

PERIOD: 156 to 145 million years ago, Late Jurassic

WHERE FOUND: U.S. (Colorado, New Mexico, Utah, Wyoming)

FOSSILS: Many complete skeletons

LENGTH: 60 feet (18 meters); Giant

Sauropods

CAMELOTIA

MEANING: After Camelot

HOW TO SAY: kam-eh-LOH-tee-ah

PERIOD: 219 to 213 million years ago, Late Triassic

WHERE FOUND: England

FOSSILS: Partial skeleton

LENGTH: 30 feet (9 meters); Big

Prosauropods

CAMPOSAURUS

MEANING: "Camp's lizard"

HOW TO SAY: CAMP-oh-SORE-us

PERIOD: 227 to 220 million years ago, Late Triassic

WHERE FOUND: U.S. (Arizona)

FOSSILS: Parts of leg bones

LENGTH: About 10 feet (3 meters); Small

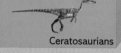
Ceratosaurians

CAMPTOSAURUS

MEANING: "Flexible lizard"

HOW TO SAY: CAMP-toe-SORE-us

PERIOD: 145 to 135 million years ago, Late Jurassic/Early Cretaceous

WHERE FOUND: U.S. (Wyoming, Utah, North Dakota, Colorado); England

FOSSILS: Mostly complete skeletons

LENGTH: 23 feet (7 meters); Big

Iguanodontians

CARCHARODONTO–SAURUS

MEANING: "Shark-toothed reptile"

HOW TO SAY: CAR-care-oh-DON-toe-SORE-us

PERIOD: 110 million years ago, Late Cretaceous

WHERE FOUND: Algeria, Egypt, Morocco, Niger

FOSSILS: Two skeletons and several other fossils

LENGTH: 40 feet (12.2 meters); Giant

Giant Meat Eaters

CARNOTAURUS

MEANING: "Meat-eating bull lizard"

HOW TO SAY: KAR-no-TORE-us

PERIOD: 80 million years ago, Late Cretaceous

WHERE FOUND: Argentina

FOSSILS: Nearly complete skeleton with skin impressions

LENGTH: 25 feet (7.6 meters); Big

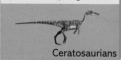
Ceratosaurians

CASEOSAURUS

MEANING: "Case's lizard" after Ermine Cowles Case

HOW TO SAY: KAY-so-SORE-us

PERIOD: 223 million years ago, Late Triassic

WHERE FOUND: U.S. (Texas)

FOSSILS: Hip and other partial fossils

LENGTH: 10 feet (3 meters)

Early Dinosaurs

CATHARTESAURUS

MEANING: "Vulture lizard"

HOW TO SAY: CATH-art-eh-SAWR-us

PERIOD: 100 to 86 million years ago, Late Cretaceous

WHERE FOUND: Argentina

FOSSILS: Partial skeleton

LENGTH: 49 to 55 feet (15 to 17 meters); Giant

Sauropods

CATHETOSAURUS

MEANING: "Upright lizard"

HOW TO SAY: ca-THEE-toh-SORE-us

PERIOD: 156 to 145 million years ago, Late Jurassic

WHERE FOUND: U.S. (Colorado)

FOSSILS: Very incomplete skeleton

LENGTH: 59 feet (18 meters); Giant

Sauropods

CAUDIPTERYX

MEANING: "Tail feather"

HOW TO SAY: caw-DIP-ter-iks

PERIOD: 136 to 120 million years ago, Early Cretaceous

WHERE FOUND: China

FOSSILS: Two, possibly more, complete skeletons

LENGTH: 3 feet (1 meter); Small

Dromaeosaurs

CEDAROSAURUS

MEANING: "Cedar (Mountain) lizard"

HOW TO SAY: SEED-er-oh-SAWR-us

PERIOD: 130 to 125 million years ago, Early Cretaceous

WHERE FOUND: U.S. (Utah)

FOSSILS: Partial skeleton

LENGTH: 49 feet (15 meters); Giant

Sauropods

CEDARPELTA

MEANING: "Cedar (Mountain) shield"

HOW TO SAY: SEE-dar-PELL-tuh

PERIOD: 112 to 100 million years ago, Early Cretaceous

WHERE FOUND: U.S. (Utah)

FOSSILS: Incomplete skull, various bones

LENGTH: 25 to 28 feet (7.5 to 8.5 meters); Big

Anklyosaurs

CEDRORESTES

MEANING: "Cedar (Mountain) dweller"

HOW TO SAY: SEE-dro-RESS-tees

PERIOD: 130 to 125 million years ago, Early Cretaceous

WHERE FOUND: U.S. (Utah)

FOSSILS: Incomplete skeleton

LENGTH: Up to 20 feet (6 meters); Big

Hadrosaurians

CERASINOPS

MEANING: "Lesser horned face"

HOW TO SAY: SERR-ah-SIN-ops

PERIOD: 84 to 70 million years ago, Late Cretaceous

WHERE FOUND: U.S. (Montana)

FOSSILS: Mostly complete skeleton

LENGTH: 6.5 feet (2 meters); Small

Small Ceratopsians

CERATONYKUS

MEANING: "Horned claw"

HOW TO SAY: SERR-ah-toh-nye-kuss

PERIOD: 80 million years ago, Late Cretaceous

WHERE FOUND: Mongolia

FOSSILS: Partial skeleton

LENGTH: 6 to 9 feet (1 to 2 meters); Small

Dromaeosaurs

CERATOSAURUS

MEANING: "Horned lizard"

HOW TO SAY: ser-RAT-uh-SORE-us

PERIOD: 156 to 145 million years ago, Late Jurassic

WHERE FOUND: U.S. (Colorado, Utah); Tanzania

FOSSILS: Many skeletons

LENGTH: 20 feet (6 meters); Big

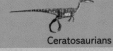

Ceratosaurians

CHANGCHUNSAURUS

MEANING: "Changchun lizard"

HOW TO SAY: CHANG-chim-SORE-us

PERIOD: 120 million years ago, Early Cretaceous

WHERE FOUND: China

FOSSILS: Skull and skeleton

LENGTH: 3.3 feet (1 meter); Small

Pre-Iguanodontians

CHASMOSAURUS

MEANING: "Opening lizard"

HOW TO SAY: KAS-mo-SORE-us

PERIOD: 76 to 70 million years ago, Late Cretaceous

WHERE FOUND: U.S. (Texas); Canada (Alberta)

FOSSILS: Many skeletons

LENGTH: 16 to 26 feet (5 to 8 meters); Big

Large Ceratopsians

CHILANTAISAURUS

MEANING: After lake Chilantai, "Chilantai's lizard"

HOW TO SAY: chee-LONN-ti-SORE-us

PERIOD: 113 to 97 million years ago, Early Cretaceous

WHERE FOUND: Mongolia, China, Russia

FOSSILS: Incomplete skeletons

LENGTH: 10 feet (3 meters); Small

Giant Meat Eaters

CHINSHAKIANGO–SAURUS

MEANING: "Chinshakian lizard"

HOW TO SAY: CHIN-sha-key-ANG-o-SORE-us

PERIOD: 200 to 175 million years ago, Early Jurassic

WHERE FOUND: China

FOSSILS: Partial jawbone, vertebrae, scapulae, limbs, and pelvis

LENGTH: 37 to 43 feet (11 to 13 meters); Giant

Sauropods

CETIOSAURISCUS

MEANING: "Whale-lizardlike"

HOW TO SAY: SEE-tee-oh-sore-IS-kuss

PERIOD: 181 to 169 million years ago, Middle Jurassic

WHERE FOUND: England, Switzerland

FOSSILS: Vertebrae

LENGTH: 50 feet (15 meters); Giant

Sauropods

CHAOYANGSAURUS

MEANING: "Chaoyang lizard"

HOW TO SAY: chow-yahng-SORE-us

PERIOD: 156 million years ago, Late Jurassic

WHERE FOUND: China

FOSSILS: Incomplete skeleton

LENGTH: 5 to 7 feet (1.5 to 2 meters); Small

Small Ceratopsians

CHEBSAURUS

MEANING: "Teenager lizard"

HOW TO SAY: cheb-SORE-us

PERIOD: 175 to 161 million years ago, Middle Jurassic

WHERE FOUND: Algeria

FOSSILS: complete skeleton

LENGTH: 27 to 30 feet (8 to 9 meters); Big

Sauropods

CHINDESAURUS

MEANING: "Chinde (Point) lizard"

HOW TO SAY: CHIN-dee-SORE-us

PERIOD: 220 million years ago, Late Triassic

WHERE FOUND: U.S. (Arizona, New Mexico)

FOSSILS: Partial skeleton, teeth

LENGTH: 6.5 feet (2 meters); Small

Early Dinosaurs

CHIROSTENOTES

MEANING: "Narrow handed"

HOW TO SAY: KIE-roh-STEN-oh-teez

PERIOD: 80 million years ago, Late Cretaceous

WHERE FOUND: Canada (Alberta)

FOSSILS: Partial skeletons

LENGTH: 9.5 feet (2.9 meters); Small

Dromaeosaurs

CETIOSAURUS

MEANING: "Whale-like lizard"

HOW TO SAY: see-TIE-o-SORE-us

PERIOD: 181 to 169 million years ago, Middle Jurassic

WHERE FOUND: England, Morocco

FOSSILS: Partial skeletons

LENGTH: 49 to 53 feet (15 to 16 meters); Giant

Sauropods

CHARONOSAURUS

MEANING: "Charon's lizard"

HOW TO SAY: Char-ON-oh-SORE-us

PERIOD: 70 to 65 million years ago, Late Cretaceous

WHERE FOUND: China

FOSSILS: Partial skull

LENGTH: 42.5 feet (13 meters); Giant

Hadrosaurians

CHIALINGOSAURUS

MEANING: "Chialing lizard"

HOW TO SAY: CHEE-ah-LING-oh-SORE-us

PERIOD: 163 to 150 million years ago, Middle Jurassic

WHERE FOUND: China

FOSSILS: Very incomplete skeletons

LENGTH: 13 feet (4 meters); Small

Stegosaurs

CHINGKANKOUSAURUS

MEANING: "Ch'ing-kang-kou lizard"

HOW TO SAY: CHING-can-co-SORE-rus

PERIOD: 88.5 to 65 million years ago, Late Cretaceous

WHERE FOUND: China

FOSSILS: Right shoulder bone

LENGTH: Unknown

Giant Meat Eaters

CHUANDONGO–COELURUS

MEANING: "Chuandong hollow tail"

HOW TO SAY: CHWAHN-DUNG-o-see-LOOR-us

PERIOD: 165 million years ago, Middle Jurassic

WHERE FOUND: China

FOSSILS: Partial skeleton

LENGTH: 7.8 feet (2.4 meters); Small

Ceratosaurians

CHUANJIESAURUS

MEANING: "Chuanjie lizard"

HOW TO SAY: CHEW-on-gee-SORE-us

PERIOD: 164 to 161 million years ago, Middle Jurassic

WHERE FOUND: China

FOSSILS: Few bones

LENGTH: 45 to 56 feet (14 to 17 meters); Giant

Sauropods

CITIPATI

MEANING: "Lord of the funeral pyre"

HOW TO SAY: CHITT-i-putt-ee

PERIOD: 84 to 75 million years ago, Late Cretaceous

WHERE FOUND: Mongolia

FOSSILS: Nearly complete skeleton

LENGTH: 9 feet (3 meters); Small

Birds

COELOPHYSIS

MEANING: "Hollow form"

HOW TO SAY: SEE-low-FIE-sis

PERIOD: 200 million years ago, Late Triassic

WHERE FOUND: U.S. (Arizona, New Mexico)

FOSSILS: Many complete skeletons

LENGTH: Less than 9 feet (3 meters); Small

Ceratosaurians

COLORADISAURUS

MEANING: "Lizard from the Los Colorados Formation"

HOW TO SAY: kol-oh-RAHD-uh-SORE-us

PERIOD: 225 to 219 million years ago, Late Triassic

WHERE FOUND: Argentina

FOSSILS: Skull and neck

LENGTH: 10 to 13 feet (3 to 4 meters); Small

Prosauropods

CONCHORAPTOR

MEANING: "Conch shell robber"

HOW TO SAY: KONK-oh-RAP-tore

PERIOD: 83 to 70 million years ago, Late Cretaceous

WHERE FOUND: Mongolia, China

FOSSILS: Partial skeletons

LENGTH: 5 feet (1.5 meters); Small

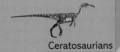
Ceratosaurians

CHUBUTISAURUS

MEANING: "Chubut lizard"

HOW TO SAY: shoe-BOO-tee-SORE-us

PERIOD: 113 to 97 million years ago, Early Cretaceous

WHERE FOUND: Argentina

FOSSILS: Two partial skeletons

LENGTH: 75 feet (23 meters); Gigantic

Sauropods

CLAOSAURUS

MEANING: "Broken lizard"

HOW TO SAY: CLAY-oh-SORE-us

PERIOD: 80 to 75 million years ago, Late Cretaceous

WHERE FOUND: U.S. (Kansas)

FOSSILS: Skeleton without a skull

LENGTH: 12 feet (3.5 meters); Small

Hadrosaurians

COELURUS

MEANING: "Hollow tail"

HOW TO SAY: see-LURE-us

PERIOD: 156 to 145 million years ago, Late Jurassic

WHERE FOUND: U.S. (Wyoming)

FOSSILS: Partial skeleton

LENGTH: 6 feet (1.8 meters); Small

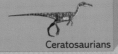
Ceratosaurians

COMPSOGNATHUS

MEANING: "Delicate jaw"

HOW TO SAY: KOMP-sog-NAH-thus or komp-SOG-no-thus

PERIOD: 155 to 145 million years ago, Late Jurassic

WHERE FOUND: Germany, France

FOSSILS: Two complete skeletons

LENGTH: 2 to 4.6 feet (0.7 to 1.4 meters); Small

Dromaeosaurs

CONDORRAPTOR

MEANING: "Condor robber"

HOW TO SAY: KON-door-RAP-tore

PERIOD: 162 million years ago, Middle Jurassic

WHERE FOUND: Argentina

FOSSILS: Incomplete skeleton

LENGTH: About 16.5 feet (5 meters); Big

Ceratosaurians

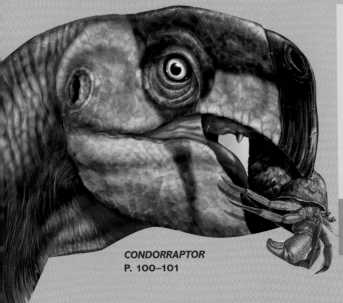

CONDORRAPTOR
P. 100–101

COLEPIOCEPHALE

MEANING: "Knuckle head"

HOW TO SAY: COLE-ep-ee-oh-SEFF-al-ee

PERIOD: 84 to 70 million years ago, Late Cretaceous

WHERE FOUND: Canada (Alberta)

FOSSILS: Skull

LENGTH: 3 feet (1 meter)

Pachycephalosaurs

COMPSOSUCHUS

MEANING: "Elegant crocodile"

HOW TO SAY: COMP-so-SOOK-us

PERIOD: 70 to 65 million years ago, Late Cretaceous

WHERE FOUND: India

FOSSILS: A few vertebrae

LENGTH: About 3 feet (1 meter); Small

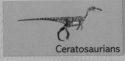
Ceratosaurians

CORYTHOSAURUS

MEANING: "Helmet lizard"

HOW TO SAY: co-RITH-oh-SORE-us

PERIOD: 76 to 72 million years ago, Late Cretaceous

WHERE FOUND: U.S. (Montana); Canada (Alberta)

FOSSILS: Many nearly complete skeletons

LENGTH: 30 feet (9 meters); Big

Hadrosaurians

CRASPEDODON

MEANING: "Edge tooth"

HOW TO SAY: kras-PEE-doh-don

PERIOD: 87.5 to 83 million years ago, Late Cretaceous

WHERE FOUND: Belgium

FOSSILS: Two teeth

LENGTH: About 20 feet (6 meters); Big

Large Ceratopsians

CRICHTONSAURUS

MEANING: After Jurassic Park author Michael Crichton

HOW TO SAY: CRY-ton-SORE-us

PERIOD: 100 to 90 million years ago, Late Cretaceous

WHERE FOUND: China

FOSSILS: Skull and partial skeleton

LENGTH: 8.2 to 11 feet (2.5 to 3.5 meters); Small

Anklyosaurs

CRYOLOPHOSAURUS

MEANING: "Frozen-crested reptile"

HOW TO SAY: CRY-oh-LOW-fo-SORE-us

PERIOD: 195 million years ago, Early Jurassic

WHERE FOUND: Antarctica

FOSSILS: Partial skeleton with skull

LENGTH: 20 feet (6.1 meters); Big

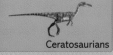

Ceratosaurians

D

DAANOSAURUS

MEANING: "Daan (District of Szechuan Province, China) lizard"

HOW TO SAY: DAN-oh-SORE-us

PERIOD: 161 to 145 million years ago, Late Jurassic

WHERE FOUND: China

FOSSILS: Skull and other bones

LENGTH: 18 feet (5 meters); Big

Sauropods

CRYPTOSAURUS

MEANING: "Hidden lizard"

HOW TO SAY: KRIP-toe-SORE-us

PERIOD: 156 million years ago, Late Jurassic

WHERE FOUND: England

FOSSILS: Partial femur

LENGTH: unknown

Anklyosaurs

CRYPTOVOLANS

MEANING: "Hidden flyer"

HOW TO SAY: KRIP-toe-VUL-ans

PERIOD: 120 million years ago, Early Cretaceous

WHERE FOUND: China

FOSSILS: Three individuals

LENGTH: 3 feet (0.9 meters); Small

Dromaeosaurs

DACENTRURUS

MEANING: "Very sharp point tail"

HOW TO SAY: dah-sen-TROO-russ

PERIOD: 163 to 150 million years ago, Late Jurassic

WHERE FOUND: Portugal, England, France

FOSSILS: Incomplete skeletons

LENGTH: 15 feet (4.4 meters); Small

Stegosaurs

DAKOTADO

MEANING: After South Dakota

HOW TO SAY: DACK-oh-tah-DO

PERIOD: 130 to 125 million years ago, Early Cretaceous

WHERE FOUND: U.S. (South Dakota)

FOSSILS: Partial skull

LENGTH: Unknown

Iguanodontians

DALIANRAPTOR

MEANING: "Dalian thief"

HOW TO SAY: DAH-lee-an-RAP-tore

PERIOD: 120 million years ago, Early Cretaceous

WHERE FOUND: China

FOSSILS: Skeleton

LENGTH: 31 inches (90 centimeters)

Dromaeosaurs

DASHANPUSAURUS

MEANING: "Dashanpu lizard"

HOW TO SAY: DA-shan-poo-SORE-us

PERIOD: 175 to 163 million years ago, Middle Jurassic

WHERE FOUND: China

FOSSILS: Many partial bones and vertebrae, partial pelvis from one individual, other bones

LENGTH: 56 feet (17 meters); Giant

Sauropods

DASPLETOSAURUS

MEANING: "Frightful reptile"

HOW TO SAY: dass-PLEE-toe-SORE-us

PERIOD: 77 million to 74 million years ago, Late Cretaceous

WHERE FOUND: U.S. (Montana); Canada

FOSSILS: Complete skeleton and partial skeleton

LENGTH: 30 feet (9 meters); Large

Tyrannosaurs

DATOUSAURUS

MEANING: "Chieftain lizard"

HOW TO SAY: DAH-toe-SORE-us

PERIOD: 170 million years ago, Middle Jurassic

WHERE FOUND: China

FOSSILS: Two partial skeletons without skulls, one skull from a different individual

LENGTH: 50 feet (15 meters); Giant

Sauropods

DAXIATITAN

MEANING: "Daxia giant"

HOW TO SAY: DOCKS-ee-ah-TIE-tan

PERIOD: 120 million years ago, Early Cretaceous

WHERE FOUND: China

FOSSILS: Neck vertebrae, thigh bone

LENGTH: 98 feet (30 meters); Gigantic

Sauropods

DEINOCHEIRUS

MEANING: "Terrible hand"

HOW TO SAY: DINE-oh-KYE-russ

PERIOD: 70 million years ago, Late Cretaceous

WHERE FOUND: Mongolia

FOSSILS: Two arm bones

LENGTH: 23 to 38 feet (7 to 12 meters); Big

Therizinosaurs

DEINONYCHUS

MEANING: "Terrible claw"

HOW TO SAY: die-NON-ny-kuss

PERIOD: 119 to 93 million years ago, Cretaceous

WHERE FOUND: U.S. (Montana, Utah, Wyoming)

FOSSILS: Eight skeletons

LENGTH: 10 feet (3 meters); Small

Dromaeosaurs

DELTADROMEUS

MEANING: "Delta runner"

HOW TO SAY: DEL-ta-DROME-ee-us

PERIOD: 95 million years ago, Late Cretaceous

WHERE FOUND: Morocco

FOSSILS: Partial skeleton

LENGTH: 26 feet (8 meters); Big

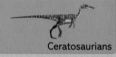

Ceratosaurians

DIAMANTINASAURUS

MEANING: Diamantina River lizard

HOW TO SAY: dye-ah-man-tin-ah-SORE-us

PERIOD: 100 million years ago, Early Cretaceous

WHERE FOUND: Australia

FOSSILS: Front and hind legs, hips and some ribs

LENGTH: 50 feet (15 meters); Giant

Sauropods

DICERATUS

MEANING: "Two-horned"

HOW TO SAY: DIE-serr-A-tuss

PERIOD: 65 million years ago, Late Cretaceous

WHERE FOUND: U.S. (Wyoming)

FOSSILS: partial skeleton

LENGTH: 30 feet (9.1 meters); Big

Large Ceratopsians

DICRAEOSAURUS

MEANING: "Two-forked lizard"

HOW TO SAY: die-CREE-oh-SORE-us

PERIOD: 156 to 150 million years ago, Late Jurassic

WHERE FOUND: East Africa

FOSSILS: Partial skeletons

LENGTH: 45 feet (13 meters); Giant

Sauropods

DILONG

MEANING: "Emperor dragon"

HOW TO SAY: DYE-long

PERIOD: 130 million years ago, Early Cretaceous

WHERE FOUND: China

FOSSILS: Nearly complete skeleton

LENGTH: 6.5 feet (2 meters); Small

Tyrannosaurs

DILOPHOSAURUS

MEANING: "Double-crested reptile"

HOW TO SAY: DIE-low-fo-SORE-us

PERIOD: 195 million years ago, Early Jurassic

WHERE FOUND: U.S. (Arizona); China

FOSSILS: Several nearly complete skeletons

LENGTH: 20 feet (6 meters); Big

Sauropods

DINHEIROSAURUS

MEANING: "Porto Dinheiro lizard"

HOW TO SAY: deen-YAYR-o-SORE-us

PERIOD: 155 to 150 million years ago, Late Jurassic

WHERE FOUND: Portugal

FOSSILS: Partial skeleton

LENGTH: 56 to 72 feet (17 to 22 meters); Giant

Sauropods

DIPLODOCUS

MEANING: "Double-beamed"

HOW TO SAY: dih-PLOD-uh-kus

PERIOD: 155 to 145 million years ago, Late Jurassic

WHERE FOUND: U.S. (Colorado, Montana, Utah, Wyoming)

FOSSILS: Many complete skeletons

LENGTH: 90 feet (27 meters); Gigantic

Sauropods

DOLLODON

MEANING: After Louis Dollo

HOW TO SAY: DOLL-oh-don

PERIOD: 130 to 125 million years ago, Early Cretaceous

WHERE FOUND: Belgium, possibly Germany

FOSSILS: Complete skeleton

LENGTH: 20 feet (6 meters); Big

Iguanodontians

DONGBEITITAN

MEANING: "Dongbe giant"

HOW TO SAY: DONG-beh-tie-tan

PERIOD: 133 to 120 million years ago, Early Cretaceous

WHERE FOUND: China

FOSSILS: Partial skeleton

LENGTH: 66 feet (20 meters); Giant

Sauropods

DONGYANGOSAURUS

MEANING: "Reptile from Dongyang city, China"

HOW TO SAY: DONG-yang-oh-SORE-us

PERIOD: 90 million years ago, Late Cretaceous

WHERE FOUND: China

FOSSILS: Partial skeleton

LENGTH: 82 feet (25 meters); Gigantic

Sauropods

DRACONYX

MEANING: "Dragon claw"

HOW TO SAY: drack-ON-iks

PERIOD: 155 million years ago, Late Jurassic

WHERE FOUND: Portugal

FOSSILS: Many partial bones from one individual, femur from another

LENGTH: 20 to 27 feet (6 to 8 meters); Big

Iguanodontians

DRACOPELTA

MEANING: "Shield bearer"

HOW TO SAY: drack-oh-PELL-ta

PERIOD: 156 to 150 million years ago, Late Jurassic

WHERE FOUND: Portugal

FOSSILS: Partial skeleton

LENGTH: 6.5 feet (2 meters); Small

Anklyosaurs

DRACOREX

MEANING: "Dragon king"

HOW TO SAY: DRAY-CO-Rex

PERIOD: 70 to 65 million years ago, Late Cretaceous

WHERE FOUND: U.S. (South Dakota)

FOSSILS: Nearly complete skull, four backbones

LENGTH: 10 feet (3 meters); Small

Pachycephalosaurs

DRACOVENATOR

MEANING: "Dragon hunter"

HOW TO SAY: DUH-rake-oh-VEN-ate-or

PERIOD: 196 to 189 million years ago, Early Jurassic

WHERE FOUND: South Africa

FOSSILS: Partial skull

LENGTH: 18 to 21 feet (5.5 to 6.5 meters); Big

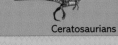

Ceratosaurians

DRINKER

MEANING: After paleontologist Edward Drinker Cope

HOW TO SAY: DRINK-er

PERIOD: 156 to 145 million years ago, Late Jurassic

WHERE FOUND: U.S. (Wyoming)

FOSSILS: Two partial skeletons

LENGTH: 6.5 feet (2 meters); Small

Pre-Iguanodontians

DROMAEOSAURUS

MEANING: "Fast-running lizard"

HOW TO SAY: DROH-mee-oh-SORE-us

PERIOD: 76 to 72 million years ago, Late Cretaceous

WHERE FOUND: U.S. (Montana); Canada (Alberta)

FOSSILS: Incomplete skeletons

LENGTH: 6 feet (1.8 meters); Small

Dromaeosaurs

DROMAEOSAURO–IDES

MEANING: "Dromaeosaurus like"

HOW TO SAY: DRO-may-oh-SORE-oy-deeze

PERIOD: 140 to 136 million years ago, Early Cretaceous

WHERE FOUND: Denmark

FOSSILS: Two teeth

LENGTH: 10 to 13 feet (3 to 4 meters); Small

Ceratosaurians

DROMICEIOMIMUS

MEANING: "Emu mimic"

HOW TO SAY: droh-MEE-see-oh-MY-us

PERIOD: 75 to 70 million years ago, Late Cretaceous

WHERE FOUND: Canada (Alberta)

FOSSILS: Partial skeletons

LENGTH: 12 feet (3.6 meters); Small

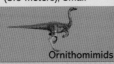

Ornithomimids

DRYOSAURUS

MEANING: "Tree lizard"

HOW TO SAY: DRY-oh-SORE-us

PERIOD: 156 to 145 million years ago, Late Jurassic

WHERE FOUND: U.S. (Colorado, Wyoming, Utah); East Africa

FOSSILS: Complete skeletons

LENGTH: 10 to 12 feet (3 to 3.5 meters); Small

Pre-Iguanodontians

DRYPTOSAURUS

MEANING: "Wounding lizard"

HOW TO SAY: DRIP-toh-SORE-us

PERIOD: 70 to 65 million years ago, Late Cretaceous

WHERE FOUND: U.S. (New Jersey)

FOSSILS: Partial skeleton

LENGTH: 20 feet (6 meters); Big

Tyrannosaurs

DUBREUILLOSAURUS

MEANING: "Dubreuillo lizard"

HOW TO SAY: doo-brew-ee-low-SORE-us

PERIOD: 167 to 164 million years ago, Middle Jurassic

WHERE FOUND: France

FOSSILS: Partial skull

LENGTH: 30 feet (9 meters); Big

Giant Meat Eaters

DURIAVENATOR

MEANING: "Duria hunter"

HOW TO SAY: DUR-ee-ah-VEN-ay-tor

PERIOD: 170 million years ago, Middle Jurassic

WHERE FOUND: England

FOSSILS: Incomplete skeleton

LENGTH: 30 feet (9 meters); Big

Giant Meat Eaters

DYOPLOSAURUS

MEANING: "Double-armored lizard"

HOW TO SAY: DIE-oh-plo-SORE-us

PERIOD: 76 to 70 million years ago, Late Cretaceous

WHERE FOUND: Canada (Alberta)

FOSSILS: An almost complete armor

LENGTH: 20 to 23 feet (6 to 7 meters); Big

Anklyosaurs

DYSLOCOSAURUS

MEANING: "Hard-to-place lizard"

HOW TO SAY: dis-low-co-SORE-us

PERIOD: 150 to 145 million years ago, Late Cretaceous

WHERE FOUND: U.S. (Wyoming)

FOSSILS: Leg bones

LENGTH: 55 to 60 feet (17 to 18 meters); Giant

Sauropods

DYSTROPHAEUS

MEANING: "Coarse joint"

HOW TO SAY: DIS-tro-FEE-us

PERIOD: 154 to 150 million years ago, Late Jurassic

WHERE FOUND: U.S. (Utah)

FOSSILS: Partial skeleton

LENGTH: 33 to 47 feet (10 to 14 m); Giant

Sauropods

E

ECHINODON

MEANING: "Spiny tooth"

HOW TO SAY: ee-KINE-oh-don

PERIOD: 145 million years ago, Late Jurassic

WHERE FOUND: England

FOSSILS: Very incomplete skeleton

LENGTH: 2 feet (0.7 meters); Small

Pre-Iguanodontians

EDMARKA

MEANING: After Colorado scientist William Edmark

HOW TO SAY: ed-MARK-ah

PERIOD: 150 to 145 million years ago, Late Jurassic

WHERE FOUND: U.S. (Wyoming)

FOSSILS: Several bones

LENGTH: 36 feet (11 meters); Giant

Giant Meat Eaters

EDMONTONIA

MEANING: "From Edmonton"

HOW TO SAY: ed-mon-TONE-ee-ah

PERIOD: 76 to 68 million years ago, Late Cretaceous

WHERE FOUND: U.S. (Montana, South Dakota, Texas); Canada (Alberta)

FOSSILS: Partial skulls

LENGTH: 20 to 23 feet (6 to 7 meters); Big

Anklyosaurs

EDMONTOSAURUS

MEANING: "Edmonton lizard"

HOW TO SAY: ed-MON-toh-SORE-us

PERIOD: 73 to 65 million years ago, Late Cretaceous

WHERE FOUND: U.S. (Montana); Canada (Alberta)

FOSSILS: Several complete skeletons with skulls

LENGTH: 42 feet (13 meters); Giant

Hadrosaurians

EINIOSAURUS

MEANING: "Bison lizard"

HOW TO SAY: eye-nee-oh-SORE-us

PERIOD: 71 million years ago, Late Cretaceous

WHERE FOUND: U.S. (Montana)

FOSSILS: Three skulls, some bones

LENGTH: 20 feet (6 meters); Big

Large Ceratopsians

EKRIXINATOSAURUS

MEANING: "Explosion-born lizard"

HOW TO SAY: ek-RICKS-ee-NA-tow-SORE-us

PERIOD: 112 to 93 million years ago, Middle Cretaceous

WHERE FOUND: Argentina

FOSSILS: Nearly complete disconnected skeleton

LENGTH: About 20 feet (6 meters); Big

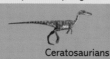
Ceratosaurians

ELAPHROSAURUS

MEANING: "Light lizard"

HOW TO SAY: EL-ah-fro-SORE-us)

PERIOD: 155 million years ago, Late Jurassic

WHERE FOUND: Tanzania

FOSSILS: Nearly complete skeleton, no skull

LENGTH: 17 feet (5 meters); Big

Large Ceratopsians

ELMISAURUS

MEANING: "Foot lizard"

HOW TO SAY: ELM-ee-SORE-us

PERIOD: 80 to 70 million years ago, Late Cretaceous

WHERE FOUND: Mongolia

FOSSILS: Hands and feet bones

LENGTH: 6.5 feet (2 meters); Small

Dromaeosaurs

EMAUSAURUS

MEANING: "Ernst-Moritz-Arndt University (Germany) lizard"

HOW TO SAY: EE-mau-SORE-us

PERIOD: 194 to 188 million years ago, Early Jurassic

WHERE FOUND: Germany

FOSSILS: Skull and some bones

LENGTH: 6.5 feet (2 meters); Small

Stegosaurs

EOBRONTOSAURUS

MEANING: "Dawn thunder lizard"

HOW TO SAY: EE-oh-BRON-toh-SORE-us

PERIOD: 154 to 150 million years ago, Late Jurassic

WHERE FOUND: U.S. (Wyoming)

FOSSILS: Partial skeleton

LENGTH: 68 to 78 feet (21 to 26 meters); Gigantic

Sauropods

EOCARCHARIA

MEANING: "Dawn shark"

HOW TO SAY: EO-car-KEY-ya

PERIOD: 112 million years ago, Early Cretaceous

WHERE FOUND: Niger

FOSSILS: Jaw, ribs, hips, and vertebrae

LENGTH: 33 feet (10 meters); Giant

Giant Meat Eaters

EOCURSOR

MEANING: "Dawn runner"

HOW TO SAY: EE-oh-KUR-sore

PERIOD: 210 million years ago, Late Triassic

WHERE FOUND: South Africa

FOSSILS: Partial skeleton

LENGTH: 3 feet (1 meter); Small

Pre-Iguanodontians

EOLAMBIA

MEANING: "Dawn lambeosaurine (crested hadrosaur)"

HOW TO SAY: EE-oh-LAM-bee-ah

PERIOD: 3 million years ago, Late Cretaceous

WHERE FOUND: U.S. (Utah)

FOSSILS: Many partial skeletons

LENGTH: 23 to 33 feet (7 to 10 meters); Giant

Hadrosaurians

EOMAMENCHISAURUS

MEANING: "Dawn Mamenchisaurus"

HOW TO SAY: EE-oh-MAH-men-chi-SORE-us

PERIOD: 170 million years ago, Middle Jurassic

WHERE FOUND: China

FOSSILS: Incomplete skeleton

LENGTH: 30 to 50 feet (9 to 15 meters); Giant

Sauropods

EORAPTOR

MEANING: "Dawn raptor"

HOW TO SAY: EE-oh-RAP-tore

PERIOD: 225 million years ago, Late Triassic

WHERE FOUND: Argentina

FOSSILS: Skull, leg bones

LENGTH: 5 feet (1.5 meter); Small

Early Dinosaurs

EOTRICERATOPS

MEANING: "Dawn three-horn face"

HOW TO SAY: EE-oh-trie-SERR-a-tops

PERIOD: 70 to 65 million years ago, Late Cretaceous

WHERE FOUND: Canada (Alberta)

FOSSILS: Skull

LENGTH: 30 feet (9 meters); Big

Large Ceratopsians

EOTYRANNUS

MEANING: "Dawn tyrant"

HOW TO SAY: EE-oh-tih-RAN-us

PERIOD: 125 to 120 million years ago, Early Cretaceous

WHERE FOUND: England

FOSSILS: Partial skeletons

LENGTH: 12 to 16 feet (4 to 5 meters); Small

Tyrannosaurs

EPACHTHOSAURUS

MEANING: "Ponderous lizard"

HOW TO SAY: ee-PAK-tho-SORE-us

PERIOD: 87.5 million years ago, Late Cretaceous

WHERE FOUND: Argentina

FOSSILS: Partial skeleton

LENGTH: 50 to 65 feet (15 to 20 meters); Giant

Sauropods

EQUIJUBUS

MEANING: "Horse mane"

HOW TO SAY: ee-kwi-JUH-bus

PERIOD: 130 to 125 million years ago, Early Cretaceous

WHERE FOUND: China

FOSSILS: Complete skull

LENGTH: 33 to 34 feet (10 to 10.5 meters); Giant

Hadrosaurians

EORAPTOR
P. 54–55

EPIDENDROSAURUS

MEANING: "Upon-tree lizard"

HOW TO SAY: ep-EH-den-dro-SORE-us

PERIOD: 154 million years ago, Late Jurassic

WHERE FOUND: China

FOSSILS: Very incomplete skeleton

LENGTH: Unknown

Dromaeosaurs

ERECTOPUS

MEANING: "Upright foot"

HOW TO SAY: ee-RECK-toh-pus

PERIOD: 113 to 97.5 million years ago, Middle Cretaceous

WHERE FOUND: France, Portugal, Egypt

FOSSILS: partial skeleton

LENGTH: 10-20 feet (3-6 meters); Big

Giant Meat Eaters

ERLIANSAURUS

MEANING: "Erlian, China, lizard"

HOW TO SAY: er-LEE-on-SORE-us

PERIOD: 83 to 70 million years ago, Late Cretaceous

WHERE FOUND: China

FOSSILS: Partial skeleton

LENGTH: 10 feet (3 meters); Small

Therizinosaurs

ESHANOSAURUS

MEANING: "Eshan country lizard"

HOW TO SAY: eh-SHAH-no-SORE-us

PERIOD: 200 to 196 million years ago, Early Jurassic

WHERE FOUND: China

FOSSILS: Lower jaw

LENGTH: 6.5 feet (2 meters); Small

Therizinosaurs

EUOPLOCEPHALUS

MEANING: "Well-armored head"

HOW TO SAY: YOU-oh-plo-SEF-ah-lus

PERIOD: 76 to 70 million years ago, Late Cretaceous

WHERE FOUND: Canada (Alberta)

FOSSILS: 40 individuals—several mostly complete skeletons, 15 skulls, teeth

LENGTH: 20 to 23 feet (6 to 7 meters); Big

Anklyosaurs

EPIDEXIPTERYX

MEANING: "Display feather"

HOW TO SAY: EP-ee-DEX-ip-terr-icks

PERIOD: 168 to 152 million years ago, Late Jurassic

WHERE FOUND: Mongolia

FOSSILS: Partial skeleton

LENGTH: 10 inches (0.3 meters); Small

Ceratosaurians

ERKETU

MEANING: After Erketu Tengri, the Buddhist god of creation

HOW TO SAY: err-KEH-too

PERIOD: 112 to 100 million years ago, Early Cretaceous

WHERE FOUND: Mongolia

FOSSILS: Partial skeleton without skull

LENGTH: Up to 50 feet (15 meters); Giant

Sauropods

ERLIKOSAURUS

MEANING: "Erlik's (Buddhist king of the dead) lizard"

HOW TO SAY: ER-lik-oh-SORE-us

PERIOD: 80 million years ago, Late Cretaceous

WHERE FOUND: Mongolia

FOSSILS: Partial skeleton with skull

LENGTH: 16 to 20 feet (5 to 6 meters); Big

Therizinosaurs

EUHELOPUS

MEANING: "Good marsh foot"

HOW TO SAY: you-HELL-oh-pus

PERIOD: 156 to 150 million years ago, Late Jurassic

WHERE FOUND: China

FOSSILS: Nearly complete skeleton

LENGTH: 34 feet (10 meters); Giant

Sauropods

EURONYCHODON

MEANING: "European claw-tooth"

HOW TO SAY: your-on-EE-koh-don

PERIOD: Late Cretaceous

WHERE FOUND: Portugal

FOSSILS: Teeth

LENGTH: 6.5 feet (2 meters); Small

Dromaeosaurs

EUSTREPTO–SPONDYLUS

MEANING: "Well-curved vertebrae"

HOW TO SAY: you-STREP-toh-SPON-dye-luss

PERIOD: 165 million years ago, Middle Jurassic

WHERE FOUND: England

FOSSILS: Mostly complete skeleton

LENGTH: 23 to 30 feet (7 to 9 meters); Big

Giant Meat Eaters

FERGANOCEPHALE

MEANING: "Fergana (Valley) head"

HOW TO SAY: fer-GAH-no-SEFF-all-ee

PERIOD: 164 to 161 million years ago, Late Jurassic

WHERE FOUND: Kyrgyzstan

FOSSILS: Teeth

LENGTH: Unknown

Pachycephalosaurs

FUKUISAURUS

MEANING: "Lizard from Fukui"

HOW TO SAY: foo-KOO-ee-SORE-us

PERIOD: 112 to 100 million years ago, Middle Cretaceous

WHERE FOUND: Japan

FOSSILS: Skull

LENGTH: 16 feet (5 meters); Big

Hadrosaurians

FUTALOGNKO–SAURUS

MEANING: "Giant chief lizard"

HOW TO SAY: FOO-ta-long-koh-SORE-us

PERIOD: 94 to 85 million years ago, Middle Cretaceous

WHERE FOUND: Argentina

FOSSILS: Three partial skeletons

LENGTH: 105 to 112 feet (32 to 34 meters); Gigantic

Sauropods

EUROPASAURUS

MEANING: "European lizard"

HOW TO SAY: yoo-ROPE-ah-SORE-us

PERIOD: 155 to 150 million years ago, Late Jurassic

WHERE FOUND: Germany

FOSSILS: Many partial skeletons

LENGTH: 20 feet (6.2 meters); Big

Sauropods

F

FALCARIUS

MEANING: "Sickle-maker"

HOW TO SAY: fal-KEH-ree-us

PERIOD: 130 to 125 million years ago, Early Cretaceous

WHERE FOUND: U.S. (Utah)

FOSSILS: Several skeletons

LENGTH: Up to 15 feet (4 meters); Small

Therizinosaurs

FRUITADENS

MEANING: "Fruita tooth"

HOW TO SAY: FROO-ta-dens

PERIOD: 150 million years ago, Late Jurassic

WHERE FOUND: U.S. (Colorado)

FOSSILS: Partial skulls and skeletons

LENGTH: 26 to 30 inches (65 to 75 cm); Small

Pre-Iguanodontians

FULGUROTHERIUM

MEANING: "Lightning beast"

HOW TO SAY: FULL-gur-oh-THEER-ee-um

PERIOD: 140 to 136 million years ago, Early Cretaceous

WHERE FOUND: Australia

FOSSILS: Very incomplete fossils

LENGTH: 6.5 feet (2 meters); Small

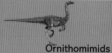

Pre-Iguanodontians

G

GALLIMIMUS

MEANING: "Rooster mimic"

HOW TO SAY: gal-ih-MIME-mus

PERIOD: 75 to 70 million years ago, Late Cretaceous

WHERE FOUND: Mongolia

FOSSILS: Many complete skeletons

LENGTH: 17 feet (5.5 meters); Big

Ornithomimids

EUSKELOSAURUS

MEANING: "Good-limbed lizard"

HOW TO SAY: YOO-skel-oh-SORE-us

PERIOD: 216 to 203 million years ago, Late Triassic

WHERE FOUND: South Africa, Zimbabwe

FOSSILS: Hundreds of bones

LENGTH: 30 to 40 feet (9 to 12 meters); Giant

Prosauropods

FERGANASAURUS

MEANING: "Fergana (Valley) lizard"

HOW TO SAY: fer-GAH-na-SORE-us

PERIOD: 164 to 161 million years ago, Late Jurassic

WHERE FOUND: Kyrgyzstan

FOSSILS: Very little material

LENGTH: 49 to 52 feet (15 to 16 meters); Giant

Sauropods

FUKUIRAPTOR

MEANING: "Fukui robber"

HOW TO SAY: foo-KOO-ee-RAP-tor

PERIOD: 112 to 100 million years ago, Middle Cretaceous

WHERE FOUND: Japan

FOSSILS: Complete skeleton

LENGTH: 14 to 20 feet (4.2 to 6 meters); Big

Dromaeosaurs

FUSUISAURUS

MEANING: "Fusui lizard"

HOW TO SAY: FOO-su-ee-SORE-us

PERIOD: 120 million years ago, Early Cretaceous

WHERE FOUND: China

FOSSILS: Partial skull, ribs, some various bones

LENGTH: 82 feet; (25 meters); Gigantic

Sauropods

GALVEOSAURUS

MEANING: "Galve lizard"

HOW TO SAY: GAL-vee-o-SORE-us

PERIOD: 150 to 145 million years ago, Late Jurassic

WHERE FOUND: Spain

FOSSILS: Vertebrae, humeri, some ribs, and other various bones

LENGTH: 62 to 72 feet (19 to 22 meters); Gigantic

Sauropods

GARGOYLEOSAURUS

MEANING: "Gargoyle lizard"

HOW TO SAY: GAR-goil-oh-SORE-us

PERIOD: 154 to 144 million years ago, Late Jurassic

WHERE FOUND: U.S. (Wyoming)

FOSSILS: Mostly complete skeleton with skull

LENGTH: 10 feet (3 meters); Small

Anklyosaurs

GASPARINISAURA

MEANING: "(Argentine paleontologist Zulma) Gasparini's lizard"

HOW TO SAY: gas-pa-REEN-ah-SAWR-ah

PERIOD: 90 to 83 million years ago, Late Cretaceous

WHERE FOUND: Argentina

FOSSILS: Partial skeleton

LENGTH: 2.5 feet (0.7 meters); Small

Pre-Iguanodontians

GENYODECTES

MEANING: "Biting jaw"

HOW TO SAY: JEN-eeh-o-DECK-teez

PERIOD: 112 to 100 million years ago, Early Cretaceous

WHERE FOUND: Argentina

FOSSILS: Teeth, part of snout, and jaw

LENGTH: 24 feet (7 meters); Big

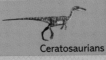

Ceratosaurians

GIGANTORAPTOR

MEANING: "Gigantic robber"

HOW TO SAY: jie-GAN-toe-RAP-tore

PERIOD: 100 to 93 million years ago, Early Cretaceous

WHERE FOUND: China

FOSSILS: Incomplete skeleton

LENGTH: Up to 27 feet (8 meters); Big

Dromaeosaurs

GLACIALISAURUS

MEANING: "Frozen lizard"

HOW TO SAY: GLAY-see-al-ih-SORE-us

PERIOD: 200 to 175 million years ago, Early Jurassic

WHERE FOUND: Antarctica

FOSSILS: Hind limb and foot

LENGTH: 20 to 25 feet (6 to 7.5 meters); Big

Prosauropods

GARUDIMIMUS

MEANING: "Garuda (bird from Asian myths) mimic"

HOW TO SAY: ga-ROOD-uh-MIME-us

PERIOD: 89 to 83 million years ago, Late Cretaceous

WHERE FOUND: Mongolia

FOSSILS: Skull and various bones

LENGTH: 12 to 13 feet (3.5 to 4 meters); Small

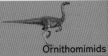

Ornithomimids

GASTONIA

MEANING: After discoverer, artist Robert Gaston

HOW TO SAY: gas-TONE-ee-ah

PERIOD: 125 million years ago, Early Cretaceous

WHERE FOUND: U.S. (Utah)

FOSSILS: Four or five individuals

LENGTH: 13 to 16 feet (4 to 5 meters); Big

Anklyosaurs

GERANOSAURUS

MEANING: "Crane lizard"

HOW TO SAY: JER-an-oh-SORE-us

PERIOD: 208 to 194 million years ago, Early Jurassic

WHERE FOUND: U.S.; South Africa

FOSSILS: Incomplete jaw

LENGTH: 5 feet (1.5 meters); Small

Pre-Iguanodontians

GIGANTOSPINO–SAURUS

MEANING: "Giant-spined lizard"

HOW TO SAY: jigh-GANT-toe-spin-oh-SORE-us

PERIOD: Late Jurassic

WHERE FOUND: China

FOSSILS: Partial skeleton without skull

LENGTH: 15 feet (4 meters); Small

Giant Meat Eaters

GLYPTODONTOPELTA

MEANING: "Glyptodont (Ice Age armor-shelled animal) shield"

HOW TO SAY: GLIP-toe-DONT-oh-pelt-ah

PERIOD: 70 million years ago, Late Cretaceous

WHERE FOUND: U.S. (New Mexico)

FOSSILS: Bony armor

LENGTH: 16 feet (5 meters)

Anklyosaurs

GASOSAURUS

MEANING: "Gas lizard" after gas company that discovered it

HOW TO SAY: GAS-oh-SORE-us

PERIOD: 175 to 163 million years ago, Middle Jurassic

WHERE FOUND: China

FOSSILS: Incomplete skeletons

LENGTH: 12 feet (3.5 meters); Small

Ceratosaurians

GENUSAURUS

MEANING: "Knee reptile"

HOW TO SAY: JEN-oo-SORE-us

PERIOD: 112 to 100 million years ago, Middle Cretaceous

WHERE FOUND: France

FOSSILS: Partial skeleton

LENGTH: 10 feet (3 meters); Small

Small Ceratopsians

GIGANOTOSAURUS

MEANING: "Giant reptile of the south"

HOW TO SAY: JYE-ga-NO-toe-SORE-us

PERIOD: 100 million years ago, Early Cretaceous

WHERE FOUND: Argentina

FOSSILS: One nearly complete skeleton and jawbone

LENGTH: 45 feet (13 meters); Giant

Giant Meat Eaters

GILMOREOSAURUS

MEANING: After American paleontologist Charles Gilmore

HOW TO SAY: GIL-more-o-SORE-us

PERIOD: 99 to 65 million years ago, Late Cretaceous

WHERE FOUND: China

FOSSILS: Incomplete skeletons

LENGTH: 26 feet (8 meters); Big

Prosauropods

GOBICERATOPS

MEANING: "Gobi horn face"

HOW TO SAY: GO-bee-SERR-ah-tops

PERIOD: 83 million years ago, Late Cretaceous

WHERE FOUND: Mongolia

FOSSILS: Skull

LENGTH: 3 feet (1 meter); Small

Small Ceratopsians

GOBISAURUS

MEANING: "Gobi (Desert) lizard"

HOW TO SAY: GO-bee-SORE-us

PERIOD: 112 to 100 million years ago, Early Cretaceous

WHERE FOUND: China

FOSSILS: Skull

LENGTH: 22 feet (6 meters); Big

Small Ceratopsians

GOBITITAN

MEANING: "Gobi (Desert) giant"

HOW TO SAY: GO-bee-TIE-tan

PERIOD: 130 to 125 million years ago, Early Cretaceous

WHERE FOUND: China

FOSSILS: Hind limb and a few vertebrae

LENGTH: 33 to 37 feet (10 to 11 meters); Giant

Sauropods

GOJIRASAURUS

MEANING: After Japanese name for movie monster Godzilla

HOW TO SAY: go-JEER-a-SORE-us

PERIOD: 216 to 203 million years ago, Early Triassic

WHERE FOUND: U.S. (New Mexico)

FOSSILS: Partial skeleton

LENGTH: 18 feet (5.5 meters); Big

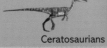

Ceratosaurians

GONDWANATITAN

MEANING: "Gondwana titan"

HOW TO SAY: gon-DWAN-uh-TIE-tan

PERIOD: 100 to 94 million years ago, Middle Cretaceous

WHERE FOUND: Brazil

FOSSILS: Partial skeleton without skull

LENGTH: 23 to 30 feet (7 to 9 meters); Big

Sauropods

GONGBUSAURUS

MEANING: "Kung Pu lizard"

HOW TO SAY: GUNG-boo-SORE-us

PERIOD: 167 to 164 million years ago, Late Jurassic

WHERE FOUND: China

FOSSILS: Very incomplete skeleton

LENGTH: 3 to 5 feet (1 to 1.5 meters); Small

Pre-Iguanodontians

GONGXIANOSAURUS

MEANING: "Gongxian, China lizard"

HOW TO SAY: GONG-she-yen-o-SORE-us

PERIOD: 200 to 175 million years ago, Early Jurassic

WHERE FOUND: China

FOSSILS: Nearly complete skeleton/ no skull

LENGTH: 46 feet (14 meters); Giant

Prosauropods

GOYOCEPHALE

MEANING: "Decorated head"

HOW TO SAY: GOH-yo-SEFF-ah-lee

PERIOD: 85 to 80 million years ago, Late Cretaceous

WHERE FOUND: Mongolia

FOSSILS: Skull and very partial skeleton

LENGTH: 5 to 6.5 feet (1.5 to 2 meters); Small

Pachycephalosaurs

GRACILICERATOPS

MEANING: "Thin horn-face"

HOW TO SAY: GRAS-ill-i-SER-a-tops

PERIOD: 100 to 94 million years ago, Middle Cretaceous

WHERE FOUND: Mongolia

FOSSILS: Partial skeleton

LENGTH: 3 to 5 feet (0.8 to 1.5 meters); Small

Small Ceratopsians

GRACILIRAPTOR

MEANING: "Thin hunter"

HOW TO SAY: GRAS-ill-i-RAP-tore

PERIOD: 130 to 125 million years ago, Early Cretaceous

WHERE FOUND: China

FOSSILS: Teeth, part of a jaw, fore and hind legs, partial vertebrae

LENGTH: 4 to 5 feet (1.2 to 1.5 meters); Small

Dromaeosaurs

GRYPOSAURUS

MEANING: "Hook-nose lizard"

HOW TO SAY: GRIP-oh-SORE-us

PERIOD: 76 to 72 million years ago, Late Cretaceous

WHERE FOUND: Canada (Alberta)

FOSSILS: Ten skulls and a few bones

LENGTH: 30 feet (9 meters); Giant

Hadrosaurians

GUAIBASAURUS

MEANING: "Rio Guaiba Basin lizard"

HOW TO SAY: GWY-bah-SORE-us

PERIOD: 228 to 215 million years ago, Late Triassic

WHERE FOUND: Brazil

FOSSILS: Two partial skeletons

LENGTH: 5 to 10 feet (1.5 to 2.9 meters); Small

Early Dinosaurs

HETERODONTOSAURUS
P. 156–157

GUANLONG

MEANING: "Crown dragon"

HOW TO SAY: GWAN-long

PERIOD: 161 to 155 million years ago, Late Jurassic

WHERE FOUND: China

FOSSILS: Two mostly complete skeletons

LENGTH: Up to 10 feet (3 meters); Small

Tyrannosaurs

H

HAGRYPHUS

MEANING: "Ha (Egyptian god of the western desert) four-footed bird"

HOW TO SAY: HAH-griff-fuss

PERIOD: 83.5 to 70 million years ago, Late Cretaceous

WHERE FOUND: U.S. (Utah)

FOSSILS: Complete limb bone

LENGTH: 8.5 to 11.5 feet (2.6 to 3.5 meters); Small

Dromaeosaurs

HANSSUESIA

MEANING: After paleontologist Hans Dieter Sues

HOW TO SAY: hons-SUE-see-ia

PERIOD: 75 to 70 million years ago, Late Cretaceous

WHERE FOUND: U.S. (Montana); Canada (Alberta)

FOSSILS: Skull and incomplete skeleton

LENGTH: 10 feet (3 meters); Small

Pachycephalosaurs

HAPLOCANTHO–SAURUS

MEANING: "Single spine lizard"

HOW TO SAY: hap-lo-KAN-tho-SORE-us

PERIOD: 156 to 145 million years ago, Late Jurassic

WHERE FOUND: U.S. (Wyoming, Colorado)

FOSSILS: Partial skeletons

LENGTH: 70 feet (21 meters); Gigantic

Sauropods

HARPYMIMUS

MEANING: "Harpy (monster of Greek mythology) mimic"

HOW TO SAY: HAR-pee-MIME-us

PERIOD: 119 to 97.5 million years ago, Middle Cretaceous

WHERE FOUND: Mongolia

FOSSILS: Skull and some bones

LENGTH: 6.5 feet (2 meters); Small

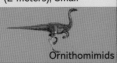
Ornithomimids

HELIOCERATOPS

MEANING: "Sun horned dinosaur"

HOW TO SAY: HEEL-ee-oh-SER-ah-tops

PERIOD: 110 million years ago, Early Cretaceous

WHERE FOUND: China

FOSSILS: Parts of jaws

LENGTH: 29 inches (72 cm); Small

Small Ceratopsians

HERRERASAURUS

MEANING: "Herrera's lizard," for discoverer Don Victorino Herrera

HOW TO SAY: huh-RARE-ah-SORE-us

PERIOD: 225 million years ago, Late Triassic

WHERE FOUND: Argentina

FOSSILS: Skull

LENGTH: 16.5 feet (5 meters); Big

Early Dinosaurs

HESPERISAURUS

MEANING: "Western lizard"

HOW TO SAY: hes-PARE-uh-SORE-us

PERIOD: 150 million years ago, Late Jurassic

WHERE FOUND: U.S. (Wyoming)

FOSSILS: Nearly complete skull, partial skeleton

LENGTH: 23 feet (7 meters); Big

Stegosaurs

HESPERONYCHUS

MEANING: "West claw"

HOW TO SAY: hess-PER-o-ny-kuss

PERIOD: 75 million years ago, Late Cretaceous

WHERE FOUND: Canada (Alberta)

FOSSILS: Partial skeleton

LENGTH: Under 3.3 feet (1 meter); Small

Dromaeosaurs

HETERODONTO–SAURUS

MEANING: "Different-tooth lizard"

HOW TO SAY: HET-er-oh-DON-toe-SORE-us

PERIOD: 200 to 195 million years ago, Early Jurassic

WHERE FOUND: South Africa

FOSSILS: Partial skeleton

LENGTH: 4 feet (1.2 meters); Small

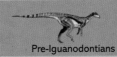
Pre-Iguanodontians

HEXINLUSAURUS

MEANING: After Chinese paleontologist He Xin-Lu

HOW TO SAY: hay-SHIN-loo-SORE-us

PERIOD: 171 to 168 million years ago, Middle Jurassic

WHERE FOUND: China

FOSSILS: Mostly complete skull, incomplete skeleton

LENGTH: 4 feet (1.2 meters); Small

Pre-Iguanodontians

HEYUANNIA

MEANING: "(Huang's) Heyuan City one"

HOW TO SAY: HEY-yoo-on-neé-ya

PERIOD: 89 to 80 million years ago, Late Cretaceous

WHERE FOUND: China

FOSSILS: Many fossils

LENGTH: 6.5 feet (2 meters); Small

Dromaeosaurs

HISTRIASAURUS

MEANING: "Istrian lizard"

HOW TO SAY: HIS-tree-ah-SORE-us

PERIOD: 126 to 125 million years ago, Early Cretaceous

WHERE FOUND: Croatia

FOSSILS: Incomplete vertebrae and limb bones

LENGTH: 20 feet

Sauropods

HOMALOCEPHALE

MEANING: "Level head"

HOW TO SAY: HOMM-ah-low-seh-FAH-lee

PERIOD: 80 to 70 million years ago, Late Cretaceous

WHERE FOUND: Mongolia

FOSSILS: Nearly complete skeleton

LENGTH: 5 feet (1.5 meters); Small

Pachycephalosaurs

HONGSHANOSAURUS

MEANING: "Red Hill lizard"

HOW TO SAY: hong-SHAN-oh-SORE-us

PERIOD: 130 to 125 million years ago, Early Cretaceous

WHERE FOUND: China

FOSSILS: Two skulls

LENGTH: 6.5 feet (2 meters); Small

Small Ceratopsians

HOPLITOSAURUS

MEANING: "Hoplite lizard"

HOW TO SAY: huh-PLEE-toh-SORE-us

PERIOD: 135 to 119 million years ago, Early Cretaceous

WHERE FOUND: U.S. (South Dakota)

FOSSILS: Incomplete skeleton

LENGTH: 13 to 16 feet (4 to 5 meters); Small

Anklyosaurs

HUAYANGOSAURUS

MEANING: "Lizard from Huayang"

HOW TO SAY: hwah-YANG-oh-SORE-us

PERIOD: 170 million years ago, Middle Jurassic

WHERE FOUND: China

FOSSILS: 12 mostly complete skeletons

LENGTH: 13 feet (4 meters); Small

Stegosaurs

HUNGAROSAURUS

MEANING: "Lizard from Hungary"

HOW TO SAY: HUN-gare-o-SORE-us

PERIOD: 85 to 83 million years ago, Late Cretaceous

WHERE FOUND: Hungary

FOSSILS: Several nearly complete skeletons

LENGTH: Up to 13 feet (4 meters); Small

Anklyosaurs

HYPSELOSAURUS

MEANING: "High ridge lizard"

HOW TO SAY: HIP-seh-low-SORE-us

PERIOD: 73 to 65 million years ago, Late Cretaceous

WHERE FOUND: France, Spain

FOSSILS: Bones from 10 individuals, many eggs

LENGTH: 27 feet (8 meters); Big

Sauropods

ILIOSUCHUS

MEANING: "Crocodile hipped"

HOW TO SAY: ILL-ee-o-SOO-cuss

PERIOD: 167 to 164 million years ago, Middle Jurassic

WHERE FOUND: England

FOSSILS: Two individuals

LENGTH: 5 feet (1.5 meters); Small

Tyrannosaurs

HUABEISAURUS

MEANING: "Huabei, China reptile"

HOW TO SAY: hwah-bay-SORE-us

PERIOD: 84 to 70 million years ago, Late Cretaceous

WHERE FOUND: China

FOSSILS: Teeth, partial limbs, partial vertebrae

LENGTH: 67 feet (20 meters); Gigantic

Sauropods

HUDIESAURUS

MEANING: "Butterfly reptile"

HOW TO SAY: HOO-dee-eh-SORE-us

PERIOD: 150 to 145 million years ago, Late Jurassic

WHERE FOUND: China

FOSSILS: Partial skeleton, vertebrae

LENGTH: 98 feet (20 meters); Gigantic

Sauropods

HYLAEOSAURUS

MEANING: "Woodland lizard"

HOW TO SAY: hie-LEE-oh-SORE-us

PERIOD: 135 to 119 million years ago, Early Cretaceous

WHERE FOUND: England

FOSSILS: Mostly complete skeleton

LENGTH: 20 feet (6 meters); Big

Anklyosaurs

HYPSILOPHODON

MEANING: "High-crested lizard"

HOW TO SAY: hip-seh-LOAF-oh-don

PERIOD: 125 to 115 million years ago, Early Cretaceous

WHERE FOUND: England

FOSSILS: Many complete skeletons

LENGTH: 7.5 feet (2.3 meters); Small

Pre-Iguanodontians

ILOKELESIA

MEANING: "Flesh-eating reptile"

HOW TO SAY: EE-loh-kay-LAY-see-yuh

PERIOD: 100 to 93 million years ago, Middle Cretaceous

WHERE FOUND: Argentina

FOSSILS: Very incomplete skull and skeleton

LENGTH: 20 to 26 feet (6 to 8 meters); Big

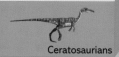

Ceratosaurians

HUANGHETITAN

MEANING: "Yellow River titan"

HOW TO SAY: hwah-ENG-he-TIE-tan

PERIOD: 120 to 115 million years ago, Early Cretaceous

WHERE FOUND: China

FOSSILS: Two vertebrae, base of the spine, partial rib pieces, left shoulder girdle

LENGTH: 80 to 90 feet (25 to 30 meters); Gigantic

Sauropods

HULSANPES

MEANING: "Khulsan foot"

HOW TO SAY: HOOL-sahn-pees

PERIOD: 83 to 70 million years ago, Late Cretaceous

WHERE FOUND: Mongolia

FOSSILS: Partial foot

LENGTH: 1.3 feet (0.4 meters); Small

Dromaeosaurs

HYPACROSAURUS

MEANING: "Under the top lizard"

HOW TO SAY: hi-PACK-row-SORE-us

PERIOD: 72 to 70 million years ago, Late Cretaceous

WHERE FOUND: U.S. (Montana); Canada (Alberta)

FOSSILS: Mostly skulls

LENGTH: 30 feet (9 meters); Big

Hadrosaurians

I

IGUANODON

MEANING: "Iguana tooth"

HOW TO SAY: ig-WAN-oh-don

PERIOD: 130 to 110 million years ago, Early Cretaceous

WHERE FOUND: England, Belgium, Germany, North Africa, parts of U.S.

FOSSILS: Hundreds of fossils

LENGTH: 33 feet (10 meters); Giant

Iguanodontians

INDOSAURUS

MEANING: "Lizard from India"

HOW TO SAY: IN-doh-SORE-us

PERIOD: 70 to 65 million years ago, Late Cretaceous

WHERE FOUND: India

FOSSILS: Partial skull

LENGTH: 12 to 15 feet (4 to 5 meters); Small

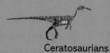

Ceratosaurians

INDOSUCHUS

MEANING: "Indian crocodile"

HOW TO SAY: IN-doh-SOO-cuss

PERIOD: 70 to 65 million years ago, Late Cretaceous

WHERE FOUND: India

FOSSILS: Partial skull

LENGTH: 20 feet (6 meters); Big

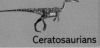
Ceratosaurians

ITEMIRUS

MEANING: After Itemir, Mongolia

HOW TO SAY: EYE-te-MEER-us

PERIOD: 90 million years ago, Middle Cretaceous

WHERE FOUND: Mongolia

FOSSILS: Braincase

LENGTH: 5 feet (1.5 meters); Small

Dromaeosaurs

JIANGJUNOSAURUS

MEANING: "General lizard"

HOW TO SAY: JEE-ang-june-oh-SORE-us

PERIOD: 161 to 155 million years ago, Late Jurassic

WHERE FOUND: China

FOSSILS: Partial skull, complete jaw, 11 vertebrae, some ribs

LENGTH: 30 feet (9 meters); Big

Stegosaurs

JINZHOUSAURUS

MEANING: "Jinzhou lizard"

HOW TO SAY: jins-how-oo-SORE-us

PERIOD: 130 to 125 million years ago, Early Cretaceous

WHERE FOUND: China

FOSSILS: Nearly complete skeleton

LENGTH: 23 feet (7 meters); Big

Iguanodontians

JURAVENATOR

MEANING: "Jurassic hunter"

HOW TO SAY: JOO-rah-ven-AY-tore

PERIOD: 150 to 145 million years ago, Late Jurassic

WHERE FOUND: Germany

FOSSILS: Complete skeleton

LENGTH: Up to 1.3 feet (0.4 meters); Small

Dromaeosaurs

IRRITATOR

MEANING: "The irritating one"

HOW TO SAY: IRR-uh-TAY-tore

PERIOD: 112 to 100 million years ago, Middle Cretaceous

WHERE FOUND: Brazil

FOSSILS: Skull

LENGTH: 25.5 feet (8 meters); Big

Giant Meat Eaters

J

JANENSCHIA

MEANING: After Werner Janensch

HOW TO SAY: yah-NEN-chee-ah

PERIOD: 156 to 150 million years ago, Late Jurassic

WHERE FOUND: Africa

FOSSILS: Two forelimbs, three hindlimbs, and some vertebrae

LENGTH: 80 feet (24 meters); Gigantic

Sauropods

JIANGSHANOSAURUS

MEANING: "Jiangshan lizard"

HOW TO SAY: JEE-ang-shan-oh-SORE-us

PERIOD: 112 to 100 million years ago, Middle Cretaceous

WHERE FOUND: China

FOSSILS: Incomplete shoulder, back, pelvis, femur, and tail

LENGTH: 66 to 72 feet (20 to 22 meters); Gigantic

Sauropods

JIUTAISAURUS

MEANING: "Jiutai lizard" after the city

HOW TO SAY: ju-TA-ee-SORE-us

PERIOD: 145 to 100 million years ago, Middle Cretaceous

WHERE FOUND: China

FOSSILS: 18 vertebrae

LENGTH: 26 to 32 feet (8 to 10 meters); Big

Sauropods

K

KAIJIANGOSAURUS

MEANING: "Kai River lizard"

HOW TO SAY: kie-JANG-oh-SORE-us

PERIOD: 175 to 163 million years ago, Middle Jurassic

WHERE FOUND: China

FOSSILS: A few vertebrae

LENGTH: About 30 feet (9 meters); Big

Giant Meat Eaters

ISANOSAURUS

MEANING: "Isan lizard"

HOW TO SAY: ee-sahn-o-SORE-us

PERIOD: 203 to 200 million years ago, Late Triassic

WHERE FOUND: Thailand

FOSSILS: Very incomplete fossils

LENGTH: 21 feet (6.5 meters); Big

Sauropods

JEHOLOSAURUS

MEANING: "Jehol group lizard"

HOW TO SAY: jeh-HOH-lo-SORE-us

PERIOD: 130 to 125 million years ago, Early Cretaceous

WHERE FOUND: China

FOSSILS: Incomplete skulls, partial skeletons

LENGTH: 2.6 feet (0.8 meters); Small

Pre-Iguanodontians

JINGSHANOSAURUS

MEANING: "Jingshan lizard"

HOW TO SAY: jing-shan-oh-SORE-us

PERIOD: 200 to 196 million years ago, Early Jurassic

WHERE FOUND: China

FOSSILS: Nearly complete skeleton

LENGTH: 25 feet (7.5 meters); Big

Prosauropods

JOBARIA

MEANING: "Jobar's (mythical creature of the Tuareg desert people)"

HOW TO SAY: joh-BAHR-ee-uh

PERIOD: 135 million years ago, Early Cretaceous

WHERE FOUND: Niger

FOSSILS: Nearly complete skeleton

LENGTH: 70 feet (21 meters); Gigantic

Sauropods

KAKURU

MEANING: "Rainbow serpent"

HOW TO SAY: ka-KOO-roo

PERIOD: 119 to 113 million years ago, Early Cretaceous

WHERE FOUND: Australia

FOSSILS: Leg bones

LENGTH: 7.8 feet (2.4 meters); Small

Dromaeosaurs

KANGNASAURUS

MEANING: "Kangna lizard"

HOW TO SAY: KANG-na-SORE-us

PERIOD: 130 to 120 million years ago, Early Cretaceous

WHERE FOUND: South Africa

FOSSILS: Tooth and possible partial skull

LENGTH: 13 feet (4 meters); Small

Iguanodontians

KEMKEMIA

MEANING: After Kem Kem formation of Morocco

HOW TO SAY: KEM-kem-ee-ya

PERIOD: 75 million years, Late Cretaceous

WHERE FOUND: Morocco

FOSSILS: Vertebra

LENGTH: 17 feet (5 meters); Big

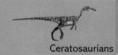
Ceratosaurians

KHAAN

MEANING: "Lord"

HOW TO SAY: KAAN

PERIOD: 83 to 70 million years ago, Late Cretaceous

WHERE FOUND: Mongolia

FOSSILS: Nearly complete skeleton

LENGTH: 4 feet (1.2 meters); Small

Dromaeosaurs

KLAMELISAURUS

MEANING: "Klameli lizard"

HOW TO SAY: klah-MEH-lee-SORE-us

PERIOD: 161 to 155 million years ago, Late Jurassic

WHERE FOUND: China

FOSSILS: Complete fossil

LENGTH: 55 feet (17 meters); Giant

Sauropods

KOTASAURUS

MEANING: "Kota (formation) lizard"

HOW TO SAY: KOH-tah-SORE-us

PERIOD: 200 to 188 million years ago, Early Jurassic

WHERE FOUND: India

FOSSILS: Partial skeleton without a skull

LENGTH: 30 feet (9 meters); Big

Sauropods

KARONGASAURUS

MEANING: "Karong lizard"

HOW TO SAY: CAR-ong-ah-SORE-us

PERIOD: 116 million years ago, Early Cretaceous

WHERE FOUND: Malawi, Africa

FOSSILS: Some teeth and lower jaw

LENGTH: 30 feet (9 meters); Big

Sauropods

KENTROSAURUS

MEANING: "The spiked lizard"

HOW TO SAY: KEN-troh-SORE-us

PERIOD: 156 to 150 million years ago, Late Jurassic

WHERE FOUND: Tanzania

FOSSILS: Fragmentary skeleton

LENGTH: 17 feet (5 meters); Big

Stegosaurs

KHETRANISAURUS

MEANING: "Khetran lizard"

HOW TO SAY: KET-ran-ee-SORE-us

PERIOD: 70 to 65 million years ago, Late Cretaceous

WHERE FOUND: Pakistan

FOSSILS: Tail vertebrae

LENGTH: Unknown

Sauropods

KOL

MEANING: "Foot" in Mongolian

HOW TO SAY: COAL

PERIOD: 80 million years ago, Late Cretaceous

WHERE FOUND: Mongolia

FOSSILS: Right foot

LENGTH: 6 feet (1.8 meters); Small

Dromaeosaurs

KOUTALISAURUS

MEANING: "Spoon lizard"

HOW TO SAY: ko-TAH-lee-SORE-us

PERIOD: 70 to 65 million years ago, Late Cretaceous

WHERE FOUND: Spain

FOSSILS: One dentary

LENGTH: 20 to 23 feet (6 to 7 meters); Big

Hadrosaurians

KELMAYISAURUS

MEANING: "Kelmayi (city in China) lizard"

HOW TO SAY: KELL-may-ee-SORE-us

PERIOD: 119 to 97.5 million years ago, Early Cretaceous

WHERE FOUND: China

FOSSILS: Very incomplete skeleton

LENGTH: 36 feet (11 meters); Giant

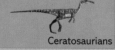
Ceratosaurians

KERBEROSAURUS

MEANING: "Kerberos lizard"

HOW TO SAY: CUR-berr-oh-SORE-us

PERIOD: 70 to 65 million years ago, Late Cretaceous

WHERE FOUND: Russia

FOSSILS: Partial skull

LENGTH: 29.5 feet (9 meters); Big

Hadrosaurians

KINNAREEMIMUS

MEANING: After Kinnaree bird-woman of Thai mythology

HOW TO SAY: KIN-a-ree-MIME-us

PERIOD: 130 million years ago, Early Cretaceous

WHERE FOUND: Thailand

FOSSILS: Vertebrae, parts of legs and hips

LENGTH: 2.5 feet (0.7 meters); Small

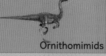
Ornithomimids

KOPARION

MEANING: "Scalpel tooth"

HOW TO SAY: co-PARR-ee-on

PERIOD: 155 to 150 million years ago, Late Jurassic

WHERE FOUND: U.S. (Utah)

FOSSILS: One tooth

LENGTH: 1.5 feet (0.5 meters); Small

Dromaeosaurs

KRYPTOPS

MEANING: "Covered face"

HOW TO SAY: KRIP-tops

PERIOD: 125 to 100 million years ago, Early Cretaceous

WHERE FOUND: Niger

FOSSILS: Partial skeleton

LENGTH: 23 to 26 feet (7 to 8 meters); Big

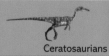
Ceratosaurians

KULCERATOPS

MEANING: "Lake-horned face"

HOW TO SAY: kool-SERR-ah-tops

PERIOD: 112 to 100 million years ago, Early Cretaceous

WHERE FOUND: Uzbekhistan

FOSSILS: Jaw bone

LENGTH: Unknown

Small Ceratopsians

LAMACERATOPS

MEANING: "Lama horn face"

HOW TO SAY: LAM-ah-SERR-ah-tops

PERIOD: 85 to 83 million years ago, Late Cretaceous

WHERE FOUND: Mongolia

FOSSILS: Skull

LENGTH: 6.5 feet (2 meters); Small

Small Ceratopsians

LAMPLUGHSAURA

MEANING: After Pamela Lamplugh

HOW TO SAY: lamb-plug-SORE-ah

PERIOD: 196 to 190 million years ago, Early Jurassic

WHERE FOUND: India

FOSSILS: Several partial skeletons

LENGTH: 33 feet (10 meters); Giant

Sauropods

LAPLATASAURUS

MEANING: "La Plata lizard"

HOW TO SAY: lah-PLAT-ah-SORE-us

PERIOD: 83 to 65 million years ago, Late Cretaceous

WHERE FOUND: Argentina, Madagascar

FOSSILS: Bones and body armor

LENGTH: 60 feet (18 meters); Giant

Sauropods

LEPTOCERATOPS

MEANING: "Slim horned face"

HOW TO SAY: LEP-toe-SERR-ah-tops

PERIOD: 68 to 65 million years ago, Late Cretaceous

WHERE FOUND: U.S. (Wyoming); Canada (Alberta)

FOSSILS: Five skulls and incomplete skeleton

LENGTH: 6 feet (1.8 meters); Small

Small Ceratopsians

L

LABOCANIA

MEANING: "La Bocana Roja (Formation) one"

HOW TO SAY: lah-boh-KAH-nee-ah

PERIOD: 83 to 73 million years ago, Late Cretaceous

WHERE FOUND: Mexico

FOSSILS: Incomplete skeleton

LENGTH: 20 feet (6 meters); Big

Tyrannosaurs

LAMBEOSAURUS

MEANING: After paleontologist Lawrence Lambe

HOW TO SAY: LAM-bee-oh-SORE-us

PERIOD: 83 to 65 million years ago, Late Cretaceous

WHERE FOUND: U.S. (Montana); Canada (Alberta)

FOSSILS: Many complete skeletons

LENGTH: 30 to 50 feet (9 to 15 meters); Giant

Hadrosaurians

LANASAURUS

MEANING: "Woolly lizard"

HOW TO SAY: LAY-na-SORE-us

PERIOD: 200 to 190 million years ago, Early Jurassic

WHERE FOUND: Africa

FOSSILS: Partial jaw bone

LENGTH: 4 feet (1.2 meters); Small

Pre-Iguanodontians

LANZHOUSAURUS

MEANING: "Lanzhou lizard"

HOW TO SAY: LAN-jo-SORE-us

PERIOD: 120 to 110 million years ago, Early Cretaceous

WHERE FOUND: China

FOSSILS: Partial skeleton

LENGTH: 29.5 to 33 feet (9 to 10 meters); Giant

Iguanodontians

LAPPARENTOSAURUS

MEANING: "Lapparent lizard," after paleontologist Albert De Lapparent

HOW TO SAY: LAP-uh-REN-tuh-SORE-us

PERIOD: 167 to 165 million years ago, Middle Jurassic

WHERE FOUND: Madagascar

FOSSILS: Incomplete juvenile skeleton

LENGTH: 6 feet (1.8 meters); Small

Sauropods

LEAELLYNASAURA

MEANING: "Leaellyn lizard," after daughter of the discoverers

HOW TO SAY: lee-EL-in-a-SORE-a

PERIOD: 106 million years ago, Early Cretaceous

WHERE FOUND: Australia

FOSSILS: Partial skull, isolated limb bones, ribs, vertebrae, jaws, and teeth

LENGTH: 6.5 to 10 feet (2 to 3 meters); Small

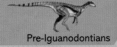

Pre-Iguanodontians

LESOTHOSAURUS

MEANING: "Lizard from Lesotho"

HOW TO SAY: le-SOH-tho-SORE-us

PERIOD: 208 to 200 million years ago, Lower Jurassic

WHERE FOUND: Lesotho

FOSSILS: Four skulls and incomplete skeleton

LENGTH: 3 feet (1 meter); Small

Pre-Iguanodontians

LESSEMSAURUS

MEANING: "Don Lessem's reptile," after the author of this book

HOW TO SAY: LESS-em-SORE-us

PERIOD: 210 million years ago, Late Triassic

WHERE FOUND: Argentina

FOSSILS: One partial spinal column

LENGTH: 33 feet (10 meters); Giant

Sauropods

LEAELLYNASAURA
PP. 158–159

LEVNESOVIA

MEANING: After Russian paleontologist Lev Nesov

HOW TO SAY: LEV-nuh-SO-vee-a

PERIOD: 90 million years ago, Late Cretaceous

WHERE FOUND: Uzbekistan

FOSSILS: Skull, vertebrae

LENGTH: 26 feet (8 meters); Big

Iguanodontians

LEXOVISAURUS

MEANING: "Lexovian lizard"

HOW TO SAY: LEX-oh-vee-SORE-us

PERIOD: 169 to 156 million years ago, Middle Jurassic

WHERE FOUND: England, France

FOSSILS: Pieces of armor and limbs

LENGTH: 17 feet (5 meters); Big

Stegosaurs

LIAOCERATOPS

MEANING: "Liao horned face"

HOW TO SAY: LEE-ow-SER-a-tops

PERIOD: 130 to 125 million years ago, Early Cretaceous

WHERE FOUND: China

FOSSILS: Two nearly complete skeletons

LENGTH: 3.3 feet (1 meter); Small

Small Ceratopsians

LIAONINGOSAURUS

MEANING: "Liaoning lizard"

HOW TO SAY: LEE-ow-ning-oh-SORE-us

PERIOD: 130 to 125 million years ago, Early Cretaceous

WHERE FOUND: China

FOSSILS: Very young complete skeleton

LENGTH: Unknown, skeleton was only 1.1 feet (34 cm); Small

Anklyosaurs

LIGABUEINO

MEANING: "Ligabue's small one" after dinosaur research supporter Giancarlo Ligabue

HOW TO SAY: lig-ah-BWAY-ee-no

PERIOD: 130 to 125 million years ago, Early Cretaceous

WHERE FOUND: Argentina

FOSSILS: Femur, ilium, pubis, phalanx, and some vertebrae

LENGTH: 2 feet (0.7 meters); Small

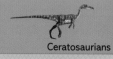
Ceratosaurians

LIGABUESAURUS

MEANING: "Ligabue's lizard" after dinosaur research supporter Giancarlo Ligabue

HOW TO SAY: LIG-ay-BWAY-SORE-us

PERIOD: 121 to 99 million years ago, Early Cretaceous

WHERE FOUND: Argentina

FOSSILS: Jawbone with teeth, six vertebrae, girdle, and limb bones

LENGTH: 79 feet (24 meters); Gigantic

Sauropods

LILIENSTERNUS

MEANING: After paleontologist Hugo Ruhle von Lilienstern

HOW TO SAY: LIL-ee-en-STERN-us

PERIOD: 222 to 219 million years ago, Late Triassic

WHERE FOUND: Germany, France

FOSSILS: Broken skeletons of two or more individuals

LENGTH: 16 feet (5 meters); Big

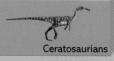
Ceratosaurians

LIMAYSAURUS

MEANING: "Limay lizard"

HOW TO SAY: LIM-ay-SORE-us

PERIOD: 100 to 94 million years ago, Middle Cretaceous

WHERE FOUND: Argentina

FOSSILS: Mostly complete skeleton

LENGTH: 56 feet (17 meters); Giant

Sauropods

LIMUSAURUS

MEANING: "Mud lizard"

HOW TO SAY: LEE-moo-SORE-us

PERIOD: 155 million years ago, Middle Jurassic

WHERE FOUND: China

FOSSILS: 3 nearly complete skeletons

LENGTH: 5.5 feet (1.7 meters); Small

Ceratosaurians

LINHERAPTOR

MEANING: "Linhe (area in Inner Mongolia) thief"

HOW TO SAY: LIN-he-RAP-tore

PERIOD: 80 million years ago, Late Cretaceous

WHERE FOUND: China

FOSSILS: Complete skeleton

LENGTH: 7 feet (2 meters) Small

Dromaeosaurs

LIRAINOSAURUS

MEANING: "Slim lizard"

HOW TO SAY: LEER-ane-oh-SORE-us

PERIOD: 84 to 65 million years ago, Late Cretaceous

WHERE FOUND: Spain

FOSSILS: Very incomplete individual

LENGTH: 59 feet (18 meters); Giant

Sauropods

LOPHORHOTHON

MEANING: "Crested snout"

HOW TO SAY: LOF-or-HOH-thon

PERIOD: 83 to 73 million years ago, Late Cretaceous

WHERE FOUND: U.S. (Alabama, North Carolina, Mississippi)

FOSSILS: Partial skeletons and skulls

LENGTH: 15 feet (4.5 meters); Big

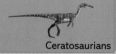
Ceratosaurians

LOPHOSTROPHEUS

MEANING: "Crested vertebrae"

HOW TO SAY: LO-fo-STROW-fee-us

PERIOD: 200 to 196 million years ago, Early Jurassic

WHERE FOUND: France

FOSSILS: Partial skeleton

LENGTH: 16 to 19 feet (5 to 6 meters); Big

Stegosaurs

LORICATOSAURUS

MEANING: "Armored lizard"

HOW TO SAY: LOHR-ik-at-oh-SORE-us

PERIOD: 164 to 161 million years ago, Middle Jurassic

WHERE FOUND: England, France

FOSSILS: Two partial skeletons

LENGTH: 13 feet (4 meters); Small

Stegosaurs

LOSILLASAURUS

MEANING: "Losilla lizard"

HOW TO SAY: loh-SIL-yah-SORE-us

PERIOD: 145 million years ago, Late Jurassic

WHERE FOUND: Spain

FOSSILS: Incomplete individuals

LENGTH: 85 to 88 feet (26 to 27 meters); Gigantic

Sauropods

LOURINHANOSAURUS

MEANING: "Reptile from Lourinha"

HOW TO SAY: lew-reen-ha-no-SORE-us

PERIOD: 145 million years ago, Late Jurassic

WHERE FOUND: Portugal

FOSSILS: Partial skeleton, no skull

LENGTH: 26 feet (8 meters); Big

Giant Meat Eaters

LOURINHASAURUS

MEANING: "Reptile from Lourinha"

HOW TO SAY: loh-reen-yah-SORE-us

PERIOD: 145 million years ago, Late Jurassic

WHERE FOUND: Portugal

FOSSILS: Three partial skeletons and about 100 gastroliths (stones that were swallowed to help digestion)

LENGTH: 57 feet (17 meters); Giant

Sauropods

LUANCHUANRAPTOR

MEANING: "Luanchuan robber"

HOW TO SAY: LOO-an-CHEW-an-RAP-tore

PERIOD: 80 million years ago, Late Cretaceous

WHERE FOUND: China

FOSSILS: Partial skeleton

LENGTH: 5 feet (1.5 meters); Small

Dromaeosaurs

LUFENGOSAURUS

MEANING: "Lufeng lizard"

HOW TO SAY: LOO-FUHNG-oh-SORE-us

PERIOD: 208 to 200 million years ago, Early Jurassic

WHERE FOUND: China

FOSSILS: Complete skeleton

LENGTH: 20 feet (6 meters); Big

Prosauropods

LUKOUSAURUS

MEANING: "Lukou lizard"

HOW TO SAY: LOO-KOH-SORE-us

PERIOD: 200 to 196 million years ago, Early Jurassic

WHERE FOUND: China

FOSSILS: Three skulls

LENGTH: 6.5 feet (2 meters); Small

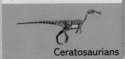

Ceratosaurians

LURDUSAURUS

MEANING: "Heavy reptile"

HOW TO SAY: LOOR-duh-SORE-us

PERIOD: 125 to 112 million years ago, Early Cretaceous

WHERE FOUND: Niger

FOSSILS: Nearly complete skeleton

LENGTH: 27.5 to 30 feet (8.4 to 9 meters); Big

Iguanodontians

LUSITANOSAURUS

MEANING: "Portuguese lizard"

HOW TO SAY: loos-i-TAYN-o-SORE-us

PERIOD: Early Jurassic

WHERE FOUND: Portugal

FOSSILS: Partial snout with teeth

LENGTH: 13 feet (4 meters); Small

Anklyosaurs

LUSOTITAN

MEANING: "Portuguese giant"

HOW TO SAY: loos-oh-TIE-tan

PERIOD: 150 to 145 million years ago, Late Jurassic

WHERE FOUND: Portugal

FOSSILS: Partial skeleton without skull

LENGTH: 72 feet (22 meters); Gigantic

Sauropods

LYCORHINUS

MEANING: "Wolf snout"

HOW TO SAY: LIE-koe-RINE-us

PERIOD: 208 to 200 million years ago, Early Jurassic

WHERE FOUND: South Africa

FOSSILS: Lower jaw bone and some teeth

LENGTH: 6.5 feet (2 meters); Small

Pre-Iguanodontians

M
....

MACROGRYPHO–SAURUS

MEANING: "Big puzzling lizard"

HOW TO SAY: MACK-ro-GRIFF-o-SORE-us

PERIOD: 93 to 86 million years ago, Late Cretaceous

WHERE FOUND: Argentina

FOSSILS: Partial skeleton without skull

LENGTH: 20 feet (6 meters); Big

Iguanodontians

MACRUROSAURUS

MEANING: "Long-tail lizard"

HOW TO SAY: ma-KROOR-o-SORE-us

PERIOD: 130 million years ago, Early Cretaceous

WHERE FOUND: England

FOSSILS: Incomplete skeleton

LENGTH: 40 feet (12 meters); Giant

Sauropods

MAGNIROSTRIS

MEANING: "Large beak"

HOW TO SAY: MAG-nee-ROSS-tris

PERIOD: 100 to 65 million years ago, Late Cretaceous

WHERE FOUND: China

FOSSILS: Complete skull

LENGTH: 3.3 feet (1 meter); Small

Small Ceratopsians

MAGNOSAURUS

MEANING: "Large lizard"

HOW TO SAY: MAG-no-SORE-us

PERIOD: 175 to 167 million years ago, Middle Jurassic

WHERE FOUND: England

FOSSILS: Partial skeletal remains

LENGTH: 13 feet (4 meters); Small

Giant Meat Eaters

MAGYAROSAURUS

MEANING: "Magyar lizard" for Hungarian people

HOW TO SAY: MAG-yar-o-SORE-us

PERIOD: 70 to 65 million years ago, Late Cretaceous

WHERE FOUND: Hungary and Romania

FOSSILS: Scattered fossils, possible eggs

LENGTH: 16 to 20 feet (5 to 6 meters); Big

Sauropods

MAHAKALA

MEANING: After a Tibetan Buddhist god

HOW TO SAY: Mah-hah-kah-lah

PERIOD: 84 to 70 million years ago, Late Cretaceous

WHERE FOUND: China

FOSSILS: Partial skull and skeleton

LENGTH: 2 feet (0.7 meters); Small

Dromaeosaurs

MAIASAURA

MEANING: "Good mother lizard"

HOW TO SAY: MA-ya-SORE-a

PERIOD: 83 to 70 million years ago, Late Cretaceous

WHERE FOUND: U.S. (Montana)

FOSSILS: Thousands of fossils from dinosaurs of all ages and some eggs

LENGTH: 30 feet (9 meters); Giant

Hadrosaurians

MAJUNGASAURUS

MEANING: "Madagascar lizard"

HOW TO SAY: mah-JOONG-ah-SORE-us

PERIOD: 83 to 73 million years ago, Late Cretaceous

WHERE FOUND: Madagascar

FOSSILS: Teeth and tail vertebrae

LENGTH: 27 feet (8 meters); Big

Ceratosaurians

MALEEVUS

MEANING: "Maleev's one"

HOW TO SAY: mahl-YAY-ev-us

PERIOD: 99 to 90 million years ago, Middle Cretaceous

WHERE FOUND: Mongolia

FOSSILS: Partial skull

LENGTH: 19.5 feet (6 meters); Big

Anklyosaurs

MALARGUESAURUS

MEANING: "Malargu lizard"

HOW TO SAY: MA-lar-gway-SORE-us

PERIOD: 89 million years ago, Late Cretaceous

WHERE FOUND: Argentina

FOSSILS: Tail vertebrae, ribs, limb bones

LENGTH: 82 feet (25 meters); Gigantic

Sauropods

MAMENCHISAURUS

MEANING: "Mamenchi lizard" for place where fossils were first found

HOW TO SAY: mah-MEHN-chee-SORE-us

PERIOD: 156 to 145 million years ago, Late Jurassic

WHERE FOUND: China

FOSSILS: Partial skeletons, skulls, neck material

LENGTH: 70 feet (21 meters); Gigantic

Sauropods

MALAWISAURUS

MEANING: "Malawi lizard"

HOW TO SAY: mah-LAA-we-SORE-us

PERIOD: 125 to 112 million years ago, Early Cretaceous

WHERE FOUND: Malawi

FOSSILS: Incomplete individual with some skull material

LENGTH: 35 feet (10.5 meters); Giant

Sauropods

MANTELLISAURUS

MEANING: After 19th-century British physician Gideon Mantell, who named the first dinosaur

HOW TO SAY: man-TEL-ee-SORE-us

PERIOD: 125 to 112 million years ago, Early Cretaceous

WHERE FOUND: England

FOSSILS: Skeletons, one with complete skull

LENGTH: 21 to 23 feet (6.5 to 7 meters); Big

Iguanodontians

MAPUSAURUS
P. 82–83

MAPUSAURUS

MEANING: "Lizard of the Mapuche Indians," after Indians of South America

HOW TO SAY: MAP-oo-SORE-us

PERIOD: 100 million years ago, Late Cretaceous

WHERE FOUND: Argentina

FOSSILS: Seven partial skeletons

LENGTH: 46 feet (14 meters); Giant

Giant Meat Eaters

MASIAKASAURUS

MEANING: "Vicious lizard"

HOW TO SAY: mah-SHEE-ah-kah-SORE-us)

PERIOD: 70 to 65 million years ago, Late Cretaceous

WHERE FOUND: Madagascar

FOSSILS: Very incomplete skeleton, parts of a jaw

LENGTH: 6 feet (2 meters); Small

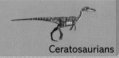
Ceratosaurians

MEGALOSAURUS

MEANING: "Great reptile"

HOW TO SAY: MEG-ah-low-SORE-us

PERIOD: 166 million years ago, Middle Jurassic

WHERE FOUND: England, France, Portugal

FOSSILS: Many bones, but no complete skeletons

LENGTH: 27 feet (8.5 meters); Big

Giant Meat Eaters

MELANOROSAURUS

MEANING: "Black mountain lizard"

HOW TO SAY: muh-LAN-or-oh-SORE-us

PERIOD: 228 to 219 million years ago, Late Triassic

WHERE FOUND: South Africa

FOSSILS: Complete skull, some bones

LENGTH: 40 feet (12 meters); Giant

Prosauropods

MICROCERATUS

MEANING: "Small horned"

HOW TO SAY: MY-crow-SER-at-us

PERIOD: 65 million years ago, Late Cretaceous

WHERE FOUND: Mongolia

FOSSILS: Incomplete skeleton

LENGTH: 2 feet (0.6 meters); Small

Small Ceratopsians

MARISAURUS

MEANING: "Mari lizard"

HOW TO SAY: mare-ee-SORE-us

PERIOD: 70 to 65 million years ago, Late Cretaceous

WHERE FOUND: Pakistan

FOSSILS: Many vertebrae, partial skull, some limb bones

LENGTH: 82 feet (25 meters); Gigantic

Sauropods

MASSOSPONDYLUS

MEANING: "Elongated vertebrae"

HOW TO SAY: mass-oh-SPON-duh-lus

PERIOD: 205 to 194 million years ago, Early Jurassic

WHERE FOUND: Namibia, Zimbabwe, South Africa

FOSSILS: Complete skeleton

LENGTH: 13 feet (4 meters); Small

Prosauropods

MEGARAPTOR

MEANING: "Huge robber"

HOW TO SAY: meg-ah-RAP-tore

PERIOD: 90 million years ago, Middle Cretaceous

WHERE FOUND: Argentina

FOSSILS: Very incomplete skeleton

LENGTH: 26 feet (8 meters); Big

Giant Meat Eaters

MENDOZASAURUS

MEANING: "Reptile from Mendoza Province"

HOW TO SAY: men-DOZE-ah-SORE-us

PERIOD: 93 to 90 million years ago, Middle Cretaceous

WHERE FOUND: Argentina

FOSSILS: Partial skeleton

LENGTH: 82 feet (25 meters); Gigantic

Sauropods

MICRORAPTOR

MEANING: "Small thief"

HOW TO SAY: MY-crow-RAP-tore

PERIOD: 124 million years ago, Early Cretaceous

WHERE FOUND: China

FOSSILS: More than 20 nearly complete skeletons

LENGTH: 22 inches (55.9 cm); Small

Dromaeosaurs

MARSHOSAURUS

MEANING: "Othniel Marsh's lizard"

HOW TO SAY: MARSH-oh-SORE-us

PERIOD: 151 to 142 million years ago, Late Jurassic

WHERE FOUND: U.S. (Utah, Colorado)

FOSSILS: Three, possibly four, partial skeletons

LENGTH: 16 feet (5 meters); Big

Giant Meat Eaters

MAXAKALISAURUS

MEANING: "Maxakali lizard"

HOW TO SAY: MAX-ah-KAL-ee-SORE-us

PERIOD: 83 to 70 million years ago, Late Cretaceous

WHERE FOUND: Brazil

FOSSILS: Mostly complete skeleton

LENGTH: Up to 43 feet (13 meters); Giant

Sauropods

MEI

MEANING: "Soundly sleeping dragon"

HOW TO SAY: MAY

PERIOD: 130 to 125 million years ago, Early Cretaceous

WHERE FOUND: China

FOSSILS: Mostly complete skeleton

LENGTH: 1.7 to 3.3 feet (0.5 to 1 meter); Small

Dromaeosaurs

METRIACANTHO–SAURUS

MEANING: "Moderate-spined lizard"

HOW TO SAY: MET-ri-ah-CAN-thuh-SORE-us

PERIOD: 160 million years ago, Late Jurassic

WHERE FOUND: England

FOSSILS: Partial skeleton without skull

LENGTH: 26 feet (8 meters); Big

Giant Meat Eaters

MICROVENATOR

MEANING: "Small hunter"

HOW TO SAY: MY-cro-ve-NAY-tore

PERIOD: 113 million years ago, Early Cretaceous

WHERE FOUND: U.S. (Montana)

FOSSILS: Partial skeleton

LENGTH: 4 feet (1.2 meters); Small

Giant Meat Eaters

N

MINMI

MEANING: After Minmi Crossing, Australia, where it was found

HOW TO SAY: MIN-mee

PERIOD: 119 to 113 million years ago, Early Cretaceous

WHERE FOUND: Australia

FOSSILS: Mostly complete skeleton and some fragments

LENGTH: 6.6 feet (2 meters); Small

Anklyosaurs

MIRISCHIA

MEANING: "Wonderful pelvis"

HOW TO SAY: Meer-ISCH-ee-ya

PERIOD: 108 million years ago, Early Cretaceous

WHERE FOUND: England

FOSSILS: Pelvis, some incomplete limb bones

LENGTH: 6.5 feet (2 meters); Small

Ceratosaurians

MINOTAURASAURUS

MEANING: "Man-bull reptile"

HOW TO SAY: MIN-oh-tar-ah-SORE-us

PERIOD: 70 million years ago, Late Cretaceous

WHERE FOUND: Unknown

FOSSILS: Complete skull

LENGTH: 10 feet (3 meters); Small

Anklyosaurs

MONKONOSAURUS

MEANING: "Monko lizard"

HOW TO SAY: mong-KON-uh-SORE-us

PERIOD: 112 to 100 million years ago, Middle Cretaceous

WHERE FOUND: China

FOSSILS: Partial skeleton

LENGTH: 16 feet (5 meters); Big

Stegosaurs

MIRAGAIA

MEANING: After area in Portugal where it was found

HOW TO SAY: MEER-ah-gai-ah

PERIOD: 150 million years ago, Late Jurassic

WHERE FOUND: Portugal

FOSSILS: Half of a skeleton and partial skull

LENGTH: 22 feet (6.7 meters); Big

Stegosaurs

MONOLOPHOSAURUS

MEANING: "One-crested lizard"

HOW TO SAY: MON-oh-LOAF-oh-SORE-us

PERIOD: 170 million years ago, Late Jurassic

WHERE FOUND: China

FOSSILS: Partial skeleton

LENGTH: 16 feet (5 meters); Big

Giant Meat Eaters

MONONYKUS

MEANING: "Single claw"

HOW TO SAY: mon-NO-nih-cuss

PERIOD: 72 million years ago, Late Cretaceous

WHERE FOUND: Mongolia

FOSSILS: Partial skeleton with very little skull material

LENGTH: 28 inches (0.7 meters); Small

Dromaeosaurs

MONTANOCERATOPS

MEANING: "Montana horned face"

HOW TO SAY: mon-TAN-oh-SER-ah-tops

PERIOD: 72 to 65 million years ago, Late Cretaceous

WHERE FOUND: U.S. (Montana)

FOSSILS: Two partial skeletons

LENGTH: 10 feet (3 meters); Small

Small Ceratopsians

MUSSAURUS

MEANING: "Mouse lizard"

HOW TO SAY: moo-SORE-us

PERIOD: 215 million years ago, Late Triassic

WHERE FOUND: Argentina

FOSSILS: Ten young individuals, four skulls, eggs

LENGTH: 10 feet (3 meters); Small

Prosauropods

MUTTABURRA–SAURUS

MEANING: "Muttaburra lizard"

HOW TO SAY: mutt-ah-BUHR-ah-SORE-us

PERIOD: 100 to 97.5 million years ago, Early Cretaceous

WHERE FOUND: Australia

FOSSILS: Two fragmentary skeletons, broken skull

LENGTH: 24 feet (7 meters); Big

Iguanodontians

MUYELENSAURUS

MEANING: "Colorado River lizard"

HOW TO SAY: moo-yay-len-SORE-us

PERIOD: 93 to 86 million years ago, Late Cretaceous

WHERE FOUND: Argentina

FOSSILS: braincase, several vertebrae, some leg bones

LENGTH: 26 to 30 feet (8 to 9 meters); Big

Sauropods

MYMOORAPELTA

MEANING: "Mygatt-Moore (Quarry) shield"

HOW TO SAY: my-MOOR-ah-PEL-tah

PERIOD: 155 to 145 million years ago, Late Jurassic

WHERE FOUND: U.S. (Colorado)

FOSSILS: Three incomplete skeletons, broken skull

LENGTH: 9 feet (2.7 meters); Small

Anklyosaurs

NANNINGOSAURUS

MEANING: "Nanning lizard"

HOW TO SAY: nan-ning-oh-SORE-us

PERIOD: 120 to 100 million years ago, Early Cretaceous

WHERE FOUND: China

FOSSILS: Partial skeleton

LENGTH: 42.5 feet (13 meters); Giant

Hadrosaurians

NANOSAURUS

MEANING: "Dwarf lizard"

HOW TO SAY: NAN-oh-SORE-us

PERIOD: 156 to 145 million years ago, Late Jurassic

WHERE FOUND: Western U.S.

FOSSILS: Jawbone

LENGTH: 4 feet (1.2 meters); Small

Pre-Iguanodontians

NANOTYRANNUS

MEANING: "Tiny tyrant"

HOW TO SAY: NAN-oh-tie-RAN-us

PERIOD: 68 to 65 million years ago, Late Cretaceous

WHERE FOUND: U.S. (Montana)

FOSSILS: Skull

LENGTH: 16 feet (5 meters); Big

Tyrannosaurs

NANSHIUNGO–SAURUS

MEANING: "Nanshiung lizard"

HOW TO SAY: nan-shee-UNG-uh-SORE-us

PERIOD: 130 to 125 million years ago, Early Cretaceous

WHERE FOUND: China

FOSSILS: Vertebrae, pelvis

LENGTH: 21 feet (6.5 meters); Big

Therizinosaurs

NEMEGTOMAIA

MEANING: "Nemegt good-mother"

HOW TO SAY: NEH-meg-toh-MA-ya

PERIOD: 100 to 65 million years ago, Cretaceous

WHERE FOUND: Mongolia

FOSSILS: Mostly complete skeleton and skull

LENGTH: 8 to 10 feet (2.5 to 3 meters); Small

Dromaeosaurs

NEOVENATOR

MEANING: "New hunter"

HOW TO SAY: NEE-oh-ven-AY-tor

PERIOD: 130 to 125 million years ago, Early Cretaceous

WHERE FOUND: England

FOSSILS: Partial skeleton

LENGTH: 24.5 to 26 feet (7.5 to 8 meters); Big

Giant Meat Eaters

NIOBRARASAURUS

MEANING: "Niobrara lizard"

HOW TO SAY: NEE-oh-BRAH-rah-SORE-us

PERIOD: 90 to 86 million years ago, Late Cretaceous

WHERE FOUND: U.S. (Kansas)

FOSSILS: Crushed skull, vertebrae, other bones

LENGTH: 18 feet (5.5 meters); Big

Anklyosaurs

NODOCEPHALO–SAURUS

MEANING: "Knob-headed lizard"

HOW TO SAY: no-doe-SEF-uh-lo-SORE-us

PERIOD: 83 to 70 million years ago, Late Cretaceous

WHERE FOUND: U.S. (New Mexico)

FOSSILS: Incomplete skull

LENGTH: 13 feet (4 meters); Small

Anklyosaurs

NEDCOLBERTIA

MEANING: After paleontologist Edwin "Ned" Colbert

HOW TO SAY: ned-kohl-BERT-ee-ah

PERIOD: 127 to 121 million years ago, Early Cretaceous

WHERE FOUND: U.S. (Utah)

FOSSILS: Three partial skeletons without skulls

LENGTH: 10 feet (3 meters); Small

Ceratosaurians

NEMEGTOSAURUS

MEANING: "Nemegt (Basin) lizard"

HOW TO SAY: NAY-meg-toe-SORE-us

PERIOD: 75 to 70 million years ago, Late Cretaceous

WHERE FOUND: Mongolia

FOSSILS: Skull

LENGTH: 69 feet (21 meters); Gigantic

Sauropods

NEUQUENSAURUS

MEANING: "Neuquen lizard"

HOW TO SAY: NOO-kwen-SORE-us

PERIOD: 85 to 83 million years ago, Late Cretaceous

WHERE FOUND: Argentina

FOSSILS: Vertebrae, right humerus, femur

LENGTH: 48 to 51 feet (14 to 15 meters); Giant

Sauropods

NIPPONOSAURUS

MEANING: "Japanese lizard"

HOW TO SAY: ni-PON-oh-SORE-us

PERIOD: 88 to 86 million years ago, Late Cretaceous

WHERE FOUND: Japan

FOSSILS: Partial skeleton with some skull material

LENGTH: 25 feet (7.6 meters); Big

Hadrosaurians

NODOSAURUS

MEANING: "Knobby or node lizard"

HOW TO SAY: NODE-oh-SORE-us

PERIOD: 113 to 98 million years ago, Early Cretaceous

WHERE FOUND: U.S. (Wyoming, Kansas)

FOSSILS: Three very incomplete skeletons without skulls

LENGTH: 13 to 20 feet (4 to 6 meters); Small

Anklyosaurs

NEIMONGOSAURUS

MEANING: "Nei Mongol lizard"

HOW TO SAY: NEH-ee-MON-go-SORE-us

PERIOD: 83 to 70 million years ago, Late Cretaceous

WHERE FOUND: China

FOSSILS: Almost complete skeleton

LENGTH: 8 feet (2.5 meters); Small

Therizinosaurs

NEOSODON

MEANING: "New tooth"

HOW TO SAY: NEE-oh-so-don

PERIOD: 150 to 145 million years ago, Late Jurassic

WHERE FOUND: France

FOSSILS: Teeth

LENGTH: Unknown, but large

Sauropods

NIGERSAURUS

MEANING: "Niger lizard"

HOW TO SAY: nee-ZHAER-SORE-us

PERIOD: 119 to 99 million years ago, Middle Cretaceous

WHERE FOUND: Niger

FOSSILS: Partial skeleton with skull

LENGTH: 30 feet (9 meters); Giant

Sauropods

NOASAURUS

MEANING: "Northwestern Argentina lizard"

HOW TO SAY: NOH-ah-SORE-us

PERIOD: 75 to 65 million years ago, Late Cretaceous

WHERE FOUND: Argentina

FOSSILS: Partial skeletons

LENGTH: 6 feet (1.8 meters); Small

Ceratosaurians

NOMINGIA

MEANING: After Nomingiin region of Mongolia

HOW TO SAY: no-MING-ee-a

PERIOD: 68 million years ago, Late Cretaceous

WHERE FOUND: Mongolia

FOSSILS: Vertebrae, hips

LENGTH: 3 feet (0.8 meters); Small

Dromaeosaurs

NOPSCASPONDYLUS

MEANING: "Transylvanian paleontologist Franz Nopsca's vertebra"

HOW TO SAY: NOP-sha-spon-DIE-luss

PERIOD: 90 to 85 million years ago, Late Cretaceous

WHERE FOUND: Argentina

FOSSILS: Vertebrae (now lost)

LENGTH: Unknown

Sauropods

NOTHRONYCHUS

MEANING: "Slothful claw"

HOW TO SAY: NOTH-row-NYE-cuss

PERIOD: 92 to 91 million years ago, Middle Cretaceous

WHERE FOUND: U.S. (New Mexico)

FOSSILS: Two nearly half-complete skeletons

LENGTH: 20 feet (6 meters); Big

Therizinosaurs

NOTOHYPSILO–PHODON

MEANING: "South high-ridge tooth"

HOW TO SAY: NO-toe-HIP-see-LO-fo-don

PERIOD: 100 to 93.5 million years ago, Late Cretaceous

WHERE FOUND: Argentina

FOSSILS: Young skeletons without skulls

LENGTH: 5 feet (1.5 meters); Small

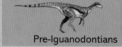
Pre-Iguanodontians

NQWEBASAURUS

MEANING: "Nqweba lizard"

HOW TO SAY: en-KWEB-ah-SORE-us

PERIOD: 135 to 130 million years ago, Early Cretaceous

WHERE FOUND: South Africa

FOSSILS: Nearly complete skeleton

LENGTH: 2.5 feet (0.8 meters); Small

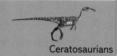
Ceratosaurians

NUTHETES

MEANING: "One who warns"

HOW TO SAY: NEW-thet-tees

PERIOD: 145 to 140 million years ago, Early Cretaceous

WHERE FOUND: England

FOSSILS: Teeth and jaw fragments

LENGTH: 6 feet (1.8 meters); Small

Dromaeosaurs

O

. . . .

OHMDENOSAURUS

MEANING: "Ohmden, Germany, lizard"

HOW TO SAY: OHM-den-oh-SORE-us

PERIOD: 191 million years ago, Early Jurassic

WHERE FOUND: Germany

FOSSILS: Tibia and tarsus bones

LENGTH: 13 feet (4 meters); Small

Sauropods

OLOROTITAN

MEANING: "Gigantic swan"

HOW TO SAY: ah-or-OH-titan

PERIOD: 70 to 65 million years ago, Late Cretaceous

WHERE FOUND: Russia

FOSSILS: Nearly complete skeleton

LENGTH: 30 feet (9 meters); Giant

Hadrosaurians

OMEISAURUS

MEANING: "Mount Emei [China] lizard"

HOW TO SAY: OH-may-SORE-us

PERIOD: 156 to 145 million years ago, Late Jurassic

WHERE FOUND: China

FOSSILS: Many complete skeletons

LENGTH: 68 feet (20 meters); Gigantic

Sauropods

OPISTHOCOELI–CAUDIA

MEANING: "Hollow-backed tail vertebrae"

HOW TO SAY: oh-PIS-tho-SEEL-ih-CAWD-ee-ah

PERIOD: 70 to 65 million years ago, Late Cretaceous

WHERE FOUND: Mongolia

FOSSILS: Nearly complete skeleton without neck vertebrae

LENGTH: 34 feet (10.5 meters); Giant

Sauropods

ORKORAPTOR

MEANING: "Toothed river thief"

HOW TO SAY: ork-oh-RAP-tore

PERIOD: 70 to 65 million years ago, Late Cretaceous

WHERE FOUND: Argentina

FOSSILS: Skull, teeth, tail vertebrae, partial tibia

LENGTH: 20 to 24 feet (6 to 7 meters); Big

Giant Meat Eaters

ORNITHODESMUS

MEANING: "Bird link"

HOW TO SAY: or-NITH-oh-dess-mus

PERIOD: 130 to 125 million years ago, Early Cretaceous

WHERE FOUND: England

FOSSILS: Incomplete skeleton

LENGTH: 4 to 6 feet (1.5 to 2 meters); Small

Dromaeosaurs

ORNITHOLESTES

MEANING: "Bird robber"

HOW TO SAY: or-NITH-oh-LES-teez

PERIOD: 156 to 145 million years ago, Late Jurassic

WHERE FOUND: U.S. (Wyoming, Utah)

FOSSILS: Partial skeleton

LENGTH: 6.5 feet (2 meters); Small

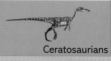
Ceratosaurians

ORNITHOMIMUS

MEANING: "Bird mimic"

HOW TO SAY: or-NITH-oh-MIME-us

PERIOD: 76 to 65 million years ago, Late Cretaceous

WHERE FOUND: Western U.S.; Canada; Mongolia

FOSSILS: Many specimens, including a mostly complete skeleton

LENGTH: 15 to 20 feet (4.5 to 6 meters); Big

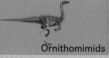
Ornithomimids

ORODROMEUS

MEANING: "Mountain runner"

HOW TO SAY: OR-oh-DROHM-ee-us

PERIOD: 77 to 73 million years ago, Late Cretaceous

WHERE FOUND: U.S. (Montana)

FOSSILS: Babies and juveniles

LENGTH: 8 feet (2.5 meters); Small

Pre-Iguanodontians

OTHNIELIA

MEANING: After 19th century paleontologist Charles Othniel Marsh

HOW TO SAY: OTH-ni-EE-lee-ah

PERIOD: 156 to 145 million years ago, Late Jurassic

WHERE FOUND: U.S. (Colorado, Utah)

FOSSILS: Two partial skeletons, teeth

LENGTH: 4.6 feet (1.4 meters); Small

Pre-Iguanodontians

PARASAUROLOPHUS
P. 172–173

P

OTHNIELOSAURUS

MEANING: After 19th-century paleontologist Charles Othniel Marsh

HOW TO SAY: oth-NEEL-o-SORE-us

PERIOD: 150 to 145 million years ago, Late Jurassic

WHERE FOUND: U.S. (Montana)

FOSSILS: Two skeletons, partial skeletal remains

LENGTH: 4 to 6.5 feet (1.5 to 2 meters); Small

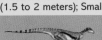

Pre-Iguanodontians

OVIRAPTOR

MEANING: "Egg thief"

HOW TO SAY: OH-vih-RAP-tore

PERIOD: 70 million years ago, Late Cretaceous

WHERE FOUND: Mongolia, China

FOSSILS: Several complete skeletons

LENGTH: 8 feet (2.4 meters); Small

Dromaeosaurs

PACHYCEPHALO–SAURUS

MEANING: "Thickheaded lizard"

HOW TO SAY: pack-ih-SEF-ah-low-SORE-us

PERIOD: 76 to 65 million years ago, Late Cretaceous

WHERE FOUND: U.S. (Montana, South Dakota, Wyoming)

FOSSILS: One nearly complete skull, some tops of skulls

LENGTH: 15 feet (4.6 meters); Small

Pachycephalosaurs

PAKISAURUS

MEANING: "Pakistan lizard"

HOW TO SAY: pack-ee-SORE-us

PERIOD: 70 million years ago, Late Cretaceous

WHERE FOUND: Pakistan

FOSSILS: Four tail vertebrae

LENGTH: 82 feet (25 meters); Gigantic

Sauropods

PALUXYSAURUS

MEANING: "Paluxy lizard"

HOW TO SAY: pal-ux-ee-SORE-us

PERIOD: 112 to 100 million years, Early Cretaceous

WHERE FOUND: U.S. (Texas)

FOSSILS: Fossil parts of four individuals

LENGTH: 30 feet (9 meters); Big

Sauropods

PANPHAGIA

MEANING: "All to eat"

HOW TO SAY: pan-FAY-gia

PERIOD: 228 million years ago, Late Triassic

WHERE FOUND: Argentina

FOSSILS: Skull, vertebrae, pelvic girdle, some limb bones

LENGTH: 4.3 feet (1.3 meters); Small

Prosauropods

PANTYDRACO

MEANING: "Panty (Quarry) dragon"

HOW TO SAY: PANT-uh-DRAY-co

PERIOD: 200 to 175 million years ago, Early Jurassic

WHERE FOUND: England

FOSSILS: Nearly complete skeleton, some partial skeletons

LENGTH: up to 6.5 feet (2 meters); Small

Prosauropods

OURANOSAURUS

MEANING: "Brave lizard"

HOW TO SAY: oo-RAHN-oh-SORE-us

PERIOD: 115 million years ago, Early Cretaceous

WHERE FOUND: Niger

FOSSILS: Two nearly complete skeletons

LENGTH: 24 feet (7 meters); Big

Iguanodontians

OZRAPTOR

MEANING: "Australian plunderer"

HOW TO SAY: oz-RAP-tore

PERIOD: 171 to 168 million years ago, Middle Jurassic

WHERE FOUND: Australia

FOSSILS: Part of a shinbone

LENGTH: 6.5 to 10 feet (2 to 3 meters); Small

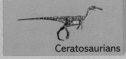

Ceratosaurians

PACHYRHINOSAURUS

MEANING: "Thick-nosed lizard"

HOW TO SAY: pack-ee-RINE-oh-SORE-us

PERIOD: 72 to 68 million years ago, Late Cretaceous

WHERE FOUND: U.S. (Alaska); Canada (Alberta)

FOSSILS: 12 partial skulls, some bones

LENGTH: 18 to 23 feet (5.5-7 meters); Big

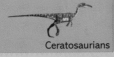

Ceratosaurians

PANOPLOSAURUS

MEANING: "Totally armored lizard"

HOW TO SAY: PAN-oh-ploh-SORE-us

PERIOD: 76 to 73 million years ago, Late Cretaceous

WHERE FOUND: Canada (Alberta); U.S. (Montana)

FOSSILS: Several partial skeletons and skulls

LENGTH: 23 feet (7 meters); Big

Sauropods

PARALITITAN

MEANING: "Tidal titan"

HOW TO SAY: pah-ral-e-TIE-tan

PERIOD: 100 million years ago, Early Cretaceous

WHERE FOUND: Egypt

FOSSILS: Upper arm bone, other skeletal parts from one individual

LENGTH: 78 to 100 feet (24 to 30 meters); Gigantic

Sauropods

PARANTHODON

MEANING: "Similar to Anthodon"

HOW TO SAY: par-AN-tho-don

PERIOD: 150 to 145 million years ago, Late Jurassic

WHERE FOUND: South Africa

FOSSILS: Partial skull

LENGTH: 16.5 feet (5 meters); Big

Stegosaurs

PARKSOSAURUS

MEANING: "Parks' lizard" after paleontologist William Parks

HOW TO SAY: PARK-soh-SORE-us

PERIOD: 68 to 65 million years ago, Late Cretaceous

WHERE FOUND: U.S. (Montana); Canada (Alberta)

FOSSILS: Partial skeletons and skulls

LENGTH: 7 feet (2 meters); Small

Pre-Iguanodontians

PARARHABDODON

MEANING: "Near Rhabdodon"

HOW TO SAY: PAR-a-RAB-do-don

PERIOD: 70 to 65 million years ago, Late Cretaceous

WHERE FOUND: Spain

FOSSILS: Partial skull, some vertebrae

LENGTH: 16.5 feet (5 meters); Big

Hadrosaurians

PARVICURSOR

MEANING: "Small runner"

HOW TO SAY: PAR-vi-KUHR-sore

PERIOD: 83 to 70 million years ago, Late Cretaceous

WHERE FOUND: Mongolia

FOSSILS: Pelvis, hind legs

LENGTH: 15 inches (29 cm); Small

Dromaeosaurs

PARASAUROLOPHUS

MEANING: "Like crested lizard"

HOW TO SAY: PAR-ah-saw-RAH-loh-fuss

PERIOD: 76 to 65 million years ago, Late Cretaceous

WHERE FOUND: U.S. (New Mexico, Utah); Canada (Alberta)

FOSSILS: Many skeletons and skulls

LENGTH: 33 feet (10 meters); Giant

Hadrosaurians

PATAGONYKUS

MEANING: "Patagonia claw"

HOW TO SAY: pat-ah-go-NYE-kus

PERIOD: 90 million years ago, Late Cretaceous

WHERE FOUND: Argentina

FOSSILS: Incomplete skeleton

LENGTH: 6.5 feet (2 meters); Small

Dromaeosaurs

PATAGOSAURUS

MEANING: "Patagonian lizard"

HOW TO SAY: PAT-a-go-SORE-us

PERIOD: 169 to 163 million years ago, Middle Jurassic

WHERE FOUND: Argentina

FOSSILS: 12 individuals

LENGTH: 65 feet (20 meters); Gigantic

Sauropods

PAWPAWSAURUS

MEANING: "Paw Paw (Formation) lizard"

HOW TO SAY: paw-paw-SORE-us

PERIOD: 97 million years ago, Late Cretaceous

WHERE FOUND: U.S. (Texas)

FOSSILS: Complete skull

LENGTH: 14.7 feet (4.5 meters); Small

Anklyosaurs

PEDOPENNA

MEANING: "Foot feather"

HOW TO SAY: ped-oh-PEN-ah

PERIOD: 154 million years ago, Late Jurassic

WHERE FOUND: China

FOSSILS: Hind legs

LENGTH: 3.3 feet (1 meter); Small

Dromaeosaurs

PELECANIMIMUS

MEANING: "Pelican mimic"

HOW TO SAY: PEL-uh-kan-uh-MIME-us

PERIOD: 132 to 121 million years ago, Early Cretaceous

WHERE FOUND: Spain

FOSSILS: Partial skull with some skin

LENGTH: 6.5 feet (2 meters); Small

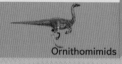
Ornithomimids

PELLEGRINISAURUS

MEANING: "Pellegrini lizard"

HOW TO SAY: pel-e-GREEN-ee-SORE-us

PERIOD: 83 to 70 million years ago, Late Cretaceous

WHERE FOUND: Argentina

FOSSILS: Vertebrae

LENGTH: 78 to 82 feet (24 to 25 meters); Gigantic

Sauropods

PELOROPLITES

MEANING: "Monster armored soldier"

HOW TO SAY: pell-or-oh-PLITE-ees

PERIOD: 116 to 109 million years ago, Early Cretaceous

WHERE FOUND: U.S. (Utah)

FOSSILS: Partial skull, some bones

LENGTH: 15 to 18 feet (5 to 5.5 meters); Big

Anklyosaurs

PELOROSAURUS

MEANING: "Monstrous lizard"

HOW TO SAY: pe-LOW-roh-SORE-us

PERIOD: 138 to 97 million years ago, Early Cretaceous

WHERE FOUND: England, Portugal

FOSSILS: Very incomplete skeleton, forelimb bone

LENGTH: 80 feet (24 meters); Gigantic

Sauropods

PENELOPOGNATHUS

MEANING: "Wild duck jaw"

HOW TO SAY: PEN-eh-LOPE-o-NAH-thus

PERIOD: 112 to 100 million years ago, Early Cretaceous

WHERE FOUND: China

FOSSILS: Part of right side of jaw

LENGTH: 13 feet (4 meters); Small

Iguanodontians

PENTACERATOPS

MEANING: "Five-horned face"

HOW TO SAY: PEN-ta-SER-ah-tops

PERIOD: 75 to 73 million years ago, Late Cretaceous

WHERE FOUND: U.S. (New Mexico)

FOSSILS: Nine skulls and some skeletons

LENGTH: 28 feet (8 meters); Big

Large Ceratopsians

PHAEDROLOSAURUS

MEANING: "Joyful little lizard"

HOW TO SAY: FEE-drol-o-SORE-us

PERIOD: 140 to 100 million years ago, Early Cretaceous

WHERE FOUND: China

FOSSILS: One tooth

LENGTH: Unknown

Giant Meat Eaters

PHUWIANGOSAURUS

MEANING: "Phu Wiang lizard"

HOW TO SAY: POO-WYAHNG-o-SORE-us

PERIOD: 136 to 130 million years ago, Early Cretaceous

WHERE FOUND: Thailand

FOSSILS: Upper leg bone

LENGTH: 49 to 65 feet (15 to 20 meters); Giant

Sauropods

PHYLLODON

MEANING: "Leaf tooth"

HOW TO SAY: FIL-o-don

PERIOD: 150 million years ago, Late Jurassic

WHERE FOUND: Portugal

FOSSILS: Teeth

LENGTH: Unknown, but small

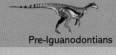
Pre-Iguanodontians

PIATNITZKYSAURUS

MEANING: After Argentine paleontologist Alejandro Piatnitzky

HOW TO SAY: piat-NYIT-skee-SORE-us

PERIOD: 169 to 163 million years ago, Middle Jurassic

WHERE FOUND: Argentina

FOSSILS: Two fragmentary skeletons

LENGTH: 14 feet (4.3 meters); Small

Giant Meat Eaters

PINACOSAURUS

MEANING: "Plank lizard"

HOW TO SAY: PIN-ah-co-SORE-us

PERIOD: 85 to 81 million years ago, Late Cretaceous

WHERE FOUND: Mongolia, China

FOSSILS: Over 35 incomplete skeletons

LENGTH: 18 feet (5.5 meters); Big

Large Ceratopsians

PISANOSAURUS

MEANING: "Pisano's lizard"

HOW TO SAY: pe-ZAHN-oh-SORE-us

PERIOD: 220 million years ago, Late Triassic

WHERE FOUND: Argentina

FOSSILS: Partial skeleton

LENGTH: 3 feet (1 meter); Small

Pre-Iguanodontians

PITEKUNSAURUS

MEANING: "To discover lizard"

HOW TO SAY: PIT-eh-kun-SORE-us

PERIOD: 83 million years ago, Late Cretaceous

WHERE FOUND: Argentina

FOSSILS: Isolated vertebrae and skull fragment

LENGTH: 66 feet

Sauropods

PIVETEAUSAURUS

MEANING: After French paleontologist Jean Piveteau

HOW TO SAY: peev-toh-SORE-us

PERIOD: 160 million years ago, Middle Jurassic

WHERE FOUND: France

FOSSILS: Very incomplete skeleton

LENGTH: 36 feet (11 meters); Giant

Giant Meat Eaters

PLANICOXA

MEANING: "Flat hipbone"

HOW TO SAY: plan-i-KOHK-suh

PERIOD: 120 million years ago, Early Cretaceous

WHERE FOUND: U.S. (Utah, South Dakota)

FOSSILS: Partial skeletons

LENGTH: 26 feet (8 meters); Big

Iguanodontians

PLATEOSAURUS

MEANING: "Flat lizard"

HOW TO SAY: PLAT-ee-oh-SORE-us

PERIOD: 222 to 200 million years ago, Late Triassic

WHERE FOUND: Northern and central Europe

FOSSILS: More than 100 skeletons

LENGTH: 23 feet (7 meters); Big

Prosauropods

PLATYCERATOPS

MEANING: "Flat horned face"

HOW TO SAY: plat-ee-SER-ah-tops

PERIOD: 75 to 72 million years ago, Late Cretaceous

WHERE FOUND: Mongolia

FOSSILS: Skull

LENGTH: 4 feet (1.2 meters); Small

Small Ceratopsians

PLEUROCOELUS

MEANING: "Hollow-sided vertebrae"

HOW TO SAY: PLOOR-oh-SEEL-us

PERIOD: 131 to 119 million years ago, Early Cretaceous

WHERE FOUND: U.S. (Maryland, Texas, Utah)

FOSSILS: Six individuals

LENGTH: 30 feet (8.8 meters); Big

Sauropods

POEKILOPLEURON

MEANING: "Varied rib or side"

HOW TO SAY: POH-key-loh-PLURE-on

PERIOD: 166 to 163 million years ago, Early to Middle Jurassic

WHERE FOUND: France

FOSSILS: partial skeleton

LENGTH: 26 feet (8 meters); Big

Giant Meat Eaters

POLACANTHUS

MEANING: "Many thorns"

HOW TO SAY: pol-ah-CAN-thuss

PERIOD: 135 to 119 million years ago, Early Cretaceous

WHERE FOUND: England

FOSSILS: Incomplete skeletons

LENGTH: 15 feet (4.6 meters); Small

Anklyosaurs

PRADHANIA

MEANING: After Sanskrit Pradhan for "lord"

HOW TO SAY: PRAD-ha-nee-a

PERIOD: 196 to 190 million years ago, Early Jurassic

WHERE FOUND: India

FOSSILS: Fragmentary skeleton

LENGTH: 13 feet (4 meters); Small

Sauropods

DINO DICTIONARY

PRENOCEPHALE

MEANING: "Sloping head"

HOW TO SAY: PREEN-o-SEFF-a-lee

PERIOD: 83.5 to 65 million years ago, Late Cretaceous

WHERE FOUND: U.S. (Montana); Canada (Alberta); Mongolia

FOSSILS: Skulls and a few bones

LENGTH: 7.5 feet (2.5 meters); Small

Pachycephalosaurs

PRENOCERATOPS

MEANING: "Bent horned face"

HOW TO SAY: pren-oh-SER-ah-tops

PERIOD: 83 to 74 million years ago, Late Cretaceous

WHERE FOUND: U.S. (Montana)

FOSSILS: Mostly complete skeleton

LENGTH: 6 feet (1.8 meters); Small

Small Ceratopsians

PROBACTROSAURUS

MEANING: "Before Bactrosaurus"

HOW TO SAY: pro-BACK-troh-SORE-us

PERIOD: 97.5 to 91 million years ago, Middle Cretaceous

WHERE FOUND: China

FOSSILS: Complete skeleton

LENGTH: 17 to 20 feet (5 to 6 meters); Big

Hadrosaurians

PROCERATOSAURUS

MEANING: "Before horned lizard"

HOW TO SAY: pro-ser-RAT-uh-SORE-us

PERIOD: 170 to 164 million years ago, Middle Jurassic

WHERE FOUND: England

FOSSILS: Partial skull

LENGTH: 10 feet (3 meters); Small

Dromaeosaurs

PROCOMPSO-GNATHUS

MEANING: "Before pretty jaw (from the Triassic Period)"

HOW TO SAY: pro-komp-SOG-nay-thus

PERIOD: 222 to 219 million years ago, Middle Triassic

WHERE FOUND: Germany

FOSSILS: Very incomplete skeleton

LENGTH: 3.8 feet (1.2 meters); Small

Dromaeosaurs

PROSAUROLOPHUS

MEANING: "Before Saurolophus"

HOW TO SAY: PROH-saw-ROL-oh-fuss

PERIOD: 77 to 73 million years ago, Late Cretaceous

WHERE FOUND: Canada (Alberta)

FOSSILS: Skulls and some skeletons from at least 25 individuals

LENGTH: 26 feet (8 meters); Big

Hadrosaurians

PROTARCHAEOP-TERYX

MEANING: "First ancient wing"

HOW TO SAY: PROH-tahr-kee-OP-ter-iks

PERIOD: 128 to 110 million years ago, Early Cretaceous

WHERE FOUND: China

FOSSILS: Partial skeleton in rock

LENGTH: 3.3 feet (1 meter); Small

Dromaeosaurs

PROTOAVIS

MEANING: "First bird"

HOW TO SAY: PROH-to-AY-vis

PERIOD: 215 million years ago, Late Triassic

WHERE FOUND: U.S. (Texas)

FOSSILS: skeleton

LENGTH: 3.3 to 6.6 feet (1 to 2 meters); Small

Dromaeosaurs

PROTOCERATOPS

MEANING: "First horned face"

HOW TO SAY: PRO-toh-SER-ah-tops

PERIOD: 86 to 71 million years ago, Late Cretaceous

WHERE FOUND: Mongolia

FOSSILS: Dozens of skeletons and eggs

LENGTH: 6 feet (1.8 meters); Small

Small Ceratopsians

PROTOGNATHO-SAURUS

MEANING: "Early jaw lizard"

HOW TO SAY: proh-tog-NAY-tho-SORE-us

PERIOD: 160 million years ago, Middle Jurassic

WHERE FOUND: China

FOSSILS: Incomplete jaw

LENGTH: 66 feet (20 meters)

Sauropods

PROTOHADROS

MEANING: "First hadrosaur"

HOW TO SAY: PRO-toe-HAD-ros

PERIOD: 95 million years ago, Late Cretaceous

WHERE FOUND: U.S. (Texas)

FOSSILS: Skull, some ribs and foot bones

LENGTH: 15 to 20 feet (4.6 to 6 meters); Big

Iguanodontians

PSITTACOSAURUS

MEANING: "Parrot lizard"

HOW TO SAY: SIT-ah-co-SORE-us

PERIOD: 119 to 97.5 million years ago, Early Cretaceous

WHERE FOUND: Mongolia, China, Thailand

FOSSILS: Many complete skeletons from over 400 individuals

LENGTH: 5.6 feet (2 meters); Small

Small Ceratopsians

PSITTACOSAURUS
P. 146–147

PUERTASAURUS

MEANING: After paleontologist Pablo Puerta

HOW TO SAY: POO-err-ta-SORE-us

PERIOD: 70 million years ago, Late Cretaceous

WHERE FOUND: Argentina

FOSSILS: Partial spine

LENGTH: possibly 115 to 131 feet (35 to 40 meters); Gigantic

Sauropods

PYRORAPTOR

MEANING: "Fire thief"

HOW TO SAY: PIE-row-RAP-tore

PERIOD: 70 to 65 million years ago, Late Cretaceous

WHERE FOUND: France

FOSSILS: A few bones

LENGTH: 5 to 8 feet (1.6 to 2.5 meters); Small

Dromaeosaurs

QINLINGOSAURUS

MEANING: "Qinling (mountain range) lizard"

HOW TO SAY: chin-ling-oh-SORE-us

PERIOD: 65 million years ago; Late Cretaceous

WHERE FOUND: China

FOSSILS: Three vertebrae and a few bones

LENGTH: 50 to 65 feet (15 to 20 meters); Giant

Sauropods

R

RAHONAVIS

MEANING: "Cloud-menace bird"

HOW TO SAY: rah-hoo-NAY-vis

PERIOD: 70 to 65 million years ago, Late Cretaceous

WHERE FOUND: Madagascar

FOSSILS: Partial skeleton

LENGTH: About 1 foot (0.3 meters); Small

Dromaeosaurs

RAPETOSAURUS

MEANING: "Mischievous giant lizard"

HOW TO SAY: RAH-peh-to-SORE-us

PERIOD: 70 to 65 million years ago, Late Cretaceous

WHERE FOUND: Madagascar

FOSSILS: Nearly complete skeleton with skull

LENGTH: 50 feet (15 meters); Giant

Sauropods

PUKYONGOSAURUS

MEANING: Lizard from Pukyong

HOW TO SAY: POOK-yong-o-SORE-us

PERIOD: 120 million years ago, Early Cretaceous

WHERE FOUND: South Korea

FOSSILS: Back and neck vertebrae

LENGTH: 66 feet (20 meters); Gigantic

Sauropods

Q

QANTASSAURUS

MEANING: "Lizard named for Qantas, the Australian airline"

HOW TO SAY: KWAN-tuh-SORE-us

PERIOD: 110 million years ago, Early Cretaceous

WHERE FOUND: Australia

FOSSILS: Skeleton and partial skull

LENGTH: 6 feet (1.8 meters); Small

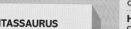
Pre-Iguanodontians

QUAESITOSAURUS

MEANING: "Abnormal or extraordinary lizard"

HOW TO SAY: kwee-SEE-toh-SORE-us

PERIOD: 85 to 80 million years ago, Late Cretaceous

WHERE FOUND: Mongolia

FOSSILS: Partial skull

LENGTH: 75 feet (23 meters); Gigantic

Sauropods

RAJASAURUS

MEANING: "Prince lizard"

HOW TO SAY: rah-jah-SORE-us

PERIOD: 70 to 65 million years ago, Late Cretaceous

WHERE FOUND: India

FOSSILS: Partial skeleton

LENGTH: 30 feet (9 meters); Big

Ceratosaurians

PYCNONEMOSAURUS

MEANING: "Thick forest lizard"

HOW TO SAY: PICK-no-NEM-o-SORE-us

PERIOD: 70 million years ago, Late Cretaceous

WHERE FOUND: Brazil

FOSSILS: Five incomplete teeth, seven partial vertebrae, right pubis, right tibia

LENGTH: 23 feet (7 meters); Big

Giant Meat Eaters

QINGXIUSAURUS

MEANING: "Reptile from Qingxiu"

HOW TO SAY: CHING-shoe-SORE-us

PERIOD: 65 million years ago, Late Cretaceous

WHERE FOUND: China

FOSSILS: Tail vertebrae and few other fossil parts

LENGTH: 49 feet (15 meters); Giant

Sauropods

QUILMESAURUS

MEANING: "Lizard of the Quilmes"

HOW TO SAY: keel-may-SORE-us

PERIOD: 84 to 70 million years ago, Late Cretaceous

WHERE FOUND: Argentina

FOSSILS: Hind limb

LENGTH: 16.5 to 20 feet (5 to 6 meters); Big

Ceratosaurians

PLATEOSAURUS
P. 180–181

RAPTOREX

MEANING: "Robber king"

HOW TO SAY: rap-TOR-ex

PERIOD: 125 million years ago, Early Cretaceous

WHERE FOUND: China

FOSSILS: One individual

LENGTH: 10 feet (3 meters); Small

Tyrannosaurs

RAYOSOSAURUS

MEANING: "Rayoso lizard"

HOW TO SAY: ray-YOH-so-SAWR-us

PERIOD: 99 million years ago, Early Cretaceous

WHERE FOUND: Argentina

FOSSILS: Scapula, femur, and partial fibula

LENGTH: 20 to 23 feet (6 to 7 meters); Big

Sauropods

REBBACHISAURUS

MEANING: "Rebbach-territory, Morocco lizard"

HOW TO SAY: re-BASH-eh-SORE-us

PERIOD: 113 to 97.5 million years ago, Late Cretaceous

WHERE FOUND: Morocco, Niger, Tunisia, Spain

FOSSILS: Vertebrae

LENGTH: 68 feet (20 meters); Gigantic

Sauropods

REGNOSAURUS

MEANING: "Sussex lizard"

HOW TO SAY: reg-NO-SORE-us

PERIOD: 140 to 136 million years ago, Early Cretaceous

WHERE FOUND: England

FOSSILS: Right lower jaw, pubic bone

LENGTH: 13 feet (4 meters); Small

Stegosaurs

RHABDODON

MEANING: "Rod or fluted tooth"

HOW TO SAY: RAB-doe-don

PERIOD: 83 to 65 million years ago, Late Cretaceous

WHERE FOUND: France, Austria, Hungary, Romania

FOSSILS: Femur and limb bone fragments, some vertebrae

LENGTH: 13 feet (4 meters); Small

Iguanodontians

RHOETOSAURUS

MEANING: "Rhoetos' lizard"

HOW TO SAY: REET-oh-SORE-us

PERIOD: 181 to 175 million years ago, Middle Jurassic

WHERE FOUND: Australia

FOSSILS: 22 vertebrae, some bones

LENGTH: 40 feet (12 meters); Giant

Sauropods

RICARDOESTESIA

MEANING: After paleontologist Richard Estes

HOW TO SAY: ri-KARD-o-es-TEE-zee-ah

PERIOD: 83 to 70 million years ago, Late Cretaceous

WHERE FOUND: U.S. (Montana, Wyoming); Canada (Alberta)

FOSSILS: Teeth and jaws

LENGTH: 6.5 feet (2 meters); Small

Dromaeosaurs

RINCHENIA

MEANING: After Mongolian paleontologist Rinchen Barsbold

HOW TO SAY: RIN-chen-ee-ah

PERIOD: 70 to 65 million years ago, Late Cretaceous

WHERE FOUND: Mongolia

FOSSILS: Complete skull and lower jaw, partial vertebrae, limbs, and some various bones

LENGTH: 5 feet (1.5 meters); Small

Dromaeosaurs

RINCONSAURUS

MEANING: "Reptile from Rincon"

HOW TO SAY: RIN-con-SORE-us

PERIOD: 80 million years ago, Late Cretaceous

WHERE FOUND: Argentina

FOSSILS: Three partial skeletons

LENGTH: 40 to 46 feet (12 to 14 meters); Giant

Sauropods

RIOJASAURUS

MEANING: "Reptile from La Rioja"

HOW TO SAY: REE-oh-hah-SORE-us

PERIOD: 225 million years ago, Late Triassic

WHERE FOUND: Argentina

FOSSILS: One partial skeleton and one skull

LENGTH: 36 feet (11 meters); Giant

Prosauropods

ROCASAURUS

MEANING: "Roca City lizard"

HOW TO SAY: ROH-kah-SORE-us

PERIOD: 80 million years ago, Late Cretaceous

WHERE FOUND: Argentina

FOSSILS: Partial skeleton

LENGTH: 27 feet (8 meters); Big

Sauropods

RUEHLEIA

MEANING: After paleontologist Hugo Ruehle von Lilienstern

HOW TO SAY: ROO-el-li-a

PERIOD: 216 to 203 million years ago, Late Triassic

WHERE FOUND: Germany

FOSSILS: Nearly complete skeleton

LENGTH: 27 feet (8 meters); Big

Prosauropods

RUGOPS

MEANING: "First wrinkled face"

HOW TO SAY: ROO-gops

PERIOD: 100 to 93 million years ago, Middle Cretaceous

WHERE FOUND: Niger

FOSSILS: Skull

LENGTH: 24 to 27 feet (7 to 8 meters); Big

Ceratosaurians

RUYANGOSAURUS

MEANING: "Lizard from Ruyang, China"

HOW TO SAY: ROO-yang-o-SORE-us

PERIOD: 95 to 80 million years ago, Late Cretaceous

WHERE FOUND: China

FOSSILS: Ribs, leg bones, and vertebrae

LENGTH: 98 feet (30 meters); Gigantic

Sauropods

S

SAHALIYANIA

MEANING: Literally "black," but refers to Amur/Heilongjiang River, where found

HOW TO SAY: sah-huh-lee-AH-nee-uh

PERIOD: 70 to 65 million years ago, Late Cretaceous

WHERE FOUND: China

FOSSILS: Partial skull

LENGTH: 30 to 33 feet (9 to 10 meters); Giant

Hadrosaurians

SCANSORIOPTERYX
P. 108–109

SANTANARAPTOR

MEANING: "Santana plunderer"

HOW TO SAY: san-TAN-a-RAP-tore

PERIOD: 112 to 99 million years ago, Early Cretaceous

WHERE FOUND: Brazil

FOSSILS: Partial skeleton and skin impressions

LENGTH: 6.5 feet (2 meters); Small

Dromaeosaurs

SATURNALIA

MEANING: After the Roman holiday Saturnalia

HOW TO SAY: sat-urn-ALE-ee-ah

PERIOD: 228 to 216 million years ago, Late Triassic

WHERE FOUND: Brazil

FOSSILS: Partial skeleton, jaw, teeth

LENGTH: 6.5 feet (2 meters); Small

Sauropods

SAUROPHAGANAX

MEANING: "King of the lizard eaters"

HOW TO SAY: SAWR-oh-FAG-ah-naks

PERIOD: 150 million years ago, Late Jurassic

WHERE FOUND: U.S. (Oklahoma)

FOSSILS: Incomplete skeleton

LENGTH: 45 feet (14 meters); Giant

Giant Meat Eaters

SAURORNITHO–LESTES

MEANING: "Lizard bird robber"

HOW TO SAY: SAWR-or-NITH-oh-LESS-tees

PERIOD: 76 to 73 million years ago, Late Cretaceous

WHERE FOUND: Canada (Alberta)

FOSSILS: Several partial skeletons, many isolated bones and teeth

LENGTH: 6 feet (1.8 meters); Small

Dromaeosaurs

SAICHANIA

MEANING: "Beautiful"

HOW TO SAY: siy-KAHN-ee-ah

PERIOD: 79 to 75 million years ago, Late Cretaceous

WHERE FOUND: Mongolia

FOSSILS: Nearly complete skeleton with skull and two other skulls and partial skeletons

LENGTH: 23 feet (7 meters); Big

Anklyosaurs

SARCOLESTES

MEANING: "Flesh robber"

HOW TO SAY: SAR-co-LESS-teez

PERIOD: 161 to 157 million years ago, Middle Jurassic

WHERE FOUND: England

FOSSILS: Partial lower jaw

LENGTH: 10 feet (3 meters); Small

Anklyosaurs

SAUROLOPHUS

MEANING: "Crested lizard"

HOW TO SAY: sawr-OHL-oh-fuss or SORE-oh-LOHF-us

PERIOD: 72 to 68 million years ago, Late Cretaceous

WHERE FOUND: Canada (Alberta); Mongolia

FOSSILS: Many nearly complete skeletons

LENGTH: 30 to 40 feet (9 to 12 meters); Giant

Hadrosaurians

SAUROPOSEIDON

MEANING: "Earthquake God lizard"

HOW TO SAY: SORE-oh-PO-sye-don

PERIOD: 112 million years ago, Early Cretaceous

WHERE FOUND: U.S. (Oklahoma)

FOSSILS: partial skeleton

LENGTH: 98 feet (30 meters); Giant

Sauropods

SCELIDOSAURUS

MEANING: "Limb lizard"

HOW TO SAY: SKEL-eye-doh-SORE-us

PERIOD: 200 to 195 million years ago, Early Jurassic

WHERE FOUND: U.S. (Arizona); England

FOSSILS: Two skeletons

LENGTH: 10 to 13 feet (3 to 4 meters); Small

Anklyosaurs

SALTASAURUS

MEANING: "Salta lizard"

HOW TO SAY: SALT-ah-SORE-us

PERIOD: 83 to 79 million years ago, Late Cretaceous

WHERE FOUND: Argentina, Uruguay

FOSSILS: Several incomplete skeletons and some plates

LENGTH: 40 feet (12 meters); Giant

Sauropods

SARCOSAURUS

MEANING: "Flesh lizard"

HOW TO SAY: SAHR-co-SORE-us

PERIOD: 206 to 200 million years ago, Early Jurassic

WHERE FOUND: England

FOSSILS: Partial hip and thigh bones, some vertebrae

LENGTH: 12 feet (3.5 meters); Small

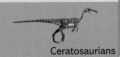
Ceratosaurians

SAUROPELTA

MEANING: "Lizard shield"

HOW TO SAY: SORE-oh-PEL-tah

PERIOD: 116 to 91 million years ago, Early/Middle Cretaceous

WHERE FOUND: U.S. (Montana, Wyoming, Utah)

FOSSILS: Partial skeletons

LENGTH: 25 feet (7.6 meters); Big

Anklyosaurs

SAURORNITHOIDES

MEANING: "Lizard bird form"

HOW TO SAY: SORE-or-nith-OY-dees

PERIOD: 85 to 77 million years ago, Late Cretaceous

WHERE FOUND: Mongolia

FOSSILS: Partial skull

LENGTH: 6.5 to 12.5 feet (2 to 3.5 meters); Small

Dromaeosaurs

SCIPIONYX

MEANING: "Scipio's claw"

HOW TO SAY: SKIP-ee-on-icks

PERIOD: 113 million years ago, Early Cretaceous

WHERE FOUND: Italy

FOSSILS: Complete hatchling

LENGTH: 6.5 feet (2 meters); Small

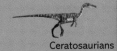
Ceratosaurians

SCUTELLOSAURUS

MEANING: "Little shield lizard"

HOW TO SAY: skoo-TELL-oh-SORE-us

PERIOD: 208 to 200 million years ago, Late Jurassic

WHERE FOUND: U.S. (Arizona)

FOSSILS: Two incomplete skeletons, hundreds of armor plates

LENGTH: 4 feet (1.2 meters); Small

Anklyosaurs

SEGNOSAURUS

MEANING: "Slow lizard"

HOW TO SAY: SEG-noh-SORE-us

PERIOD: 97.5 to 88.5 million years ago, Middle Cretaceous

WHERE FOUND: Mongolia

FOSSILS: Three partial skeletons

LENGTH: 13 to 30 feet (4 to 9 meters); Small

Therizinosaurs

SERENDIPACERATOPS

MEANING: "Pleasant surprise horned face"

HOW TO SAY: SER-end-dip-ah-SER-ah-tops

PERIOD: 125 to 112 million years ago, Early Cretaceous

WHERE FOUND: Australia

FOSSILS: 2 arm bones

LENGTH: 6.5 feet (2 meters); Small

Ceratosaurians

SHANTUNGOSAURUS

MEANING: "Shandong lizard"

HOW TO SAY: SHAHN-DUNG-oh-SORE-us

PERIOD: 83 to 73 million years ago, Late Cretaceous

WHERE FOUND: China

FOSSILS: Five incomplete skeletons

LENGTH: 38 to 48 feet (12 to 15 meters); Giant

Hadrosaurians

SHAOCHILONG

MEANING: "Shark-toothed dragon"

HOW TO SAY: SHA-ow-CHEE-long

PERIOD: 120 million years ago, Early Cretaceous

WHERE FOUND: China

FOSSILS: Parts of skull and vertebrae of one skeleton

LENGTH: 22 feet (7 meters); Big

Giant Meat Eaters

SECERNOSAURUS

MEANING: "Separated lizard"

HOW TO SAY: see-SIR-no-SORE-us

PERIOD: 73 to 65 million years ago, Late Cretaceous

WHERE FOUND: Argentina

FOSSILS: Some pelvic bones and partial skull

LENGTH: 10 feet (3 meters); Small

Hadrosaurians

SEISMOSAURUS

MEANING: "Earthquake lizard"

HOW TO SAY: SIZE-moh-SORE-us

PERIOD: 156 to 145 million years ago, Late Jurassic

WHERE FOUND: U.S. (New Mexico)

FOSSILS: Incomplete skeleton, including some ribs, vertebrae and partial hip

LENGTH: Up to 110 feet (34 meters); Gigantic

Likely invalid, *see Diplodocus, page 226*

Sauropods

SHAMOSAURUS

MEANING: "Desert lizard"

HOW TO SAY: SHAM-oh-SORE-us

PERIOD: 112 to 100 million years ago, Early Cretaceous

WHERE FOUND: Mongolia

FOSSILS: Three partial skeletons

LENGTH: 23 feet (7 meters); Big

Anklyosaurs

SHANXIA

MEANING: After Shanxi Province, China

HOW TO SAY: shan-SHEE-ah

PERIOD: 100 to 65 million years ago, Late Cretaceous

WHERE FOUND: China

FOSSILS: Partial skeleton

LENGTH: 11.5 feet (3.5 meters); Small

Anklyosaurs

SHENZHOUSAURUS

MEANING: "Reptile from Shenzhou"

HOW TO SAY: SHEN-zhoo-SORE-us

PERIOD: 130 to 125 million years ago, Early Cretaceous

WHERE FOUND: China

FOSSILS: Partial skeleton

LENGTH: 5 feet (1.5 meters); Small

Ornithomimids

SEGISAURUS

MEANING: "Segi canyon lizard"

HOW TO SAY: SEG-ee-SORE-us

PERIOD: 206 to 200 million years ago, Early Jurassic

WHERE FOUND: U.S. (Arizona)

FOSSILS: Partial skull

LENGTH: 3 feet (1 meter); Small

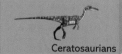
Ceratosaurians

SELLOSAURUS

MEANING: "Saddle lizard"

HOW TO SAY: SELL-oh-SORE-us

PERIOD: 219 to 208 million years ago, Late Triassic

WHERE FOUND: Germany

FOSSILS: 21 partial skeletons

LENGTH: 21 feet (6.5 meters); Big

Prosauropods

SHANAG

MEANING: After black-hatted dancers in Buddhist Tsam festival

HOW TO SAY: SHA-nag

PERIOD: 130 to 125 million years ago, Early Cretaceous

WHERE FOUND: Mongolia

FOSSILS: Partial jaw

LENGTH: Up to 6.5 feet (2 meters); Small

Dromaeosaurs

SHANYANGOSAURUS

MEANING: "South of the mountain lizard"

HOW TO SAY: shahn-yahng-o-SORE-us

PERIOD: 65 million years ago, Late Cretaceous

WHERE FOUND: China

FOSSILS: A few leg bones

LENGTH: 5 to 8 feet (1.5 to 2.5 meters); Small

Ceratosaurians

SHIDAISAURUS

MEANING: "Jin-Shidai lizard"

HOW TO SAY: she-day-SORE-us

PERIOD: 170 to 155 million years ago, Middle Jurassic

WHERE FOUND: China

FOSSILS: Partial skeleton

LENGTH: 26 feet (8 meters); Big

Giant Meat Eaters

SHIXINGGIA

MEANING: After Shixing, a county of Guadong Province, China

HOW TO SAY: SHE-jing-ee-ah

PERIOD: 70 to 65 million years ago, Late Cretaceous

WHERE FOUND: China

FOSSILS: Partial skeleton without skull

LENGTH: 4 to 6.5 feet (1.5 to 2 meters); Small

Dromaeosaurs

SHUANGMIAO–SAURUS

MEANING: "Shuangmiao lizard"

HOW TO SAY: SHOO-ang-ME-ow-SORE-us

PERIOD: 100 to 94 million years ago, Middle Cretaceous

WHERE FOUND: China

FOSSILS: Part of jaw

LENGTH: 26 feet (8 meters); Big

Iguanodontians

SHUNOSAURUS

MEANING: "Szechuan lizard"

HOW TO SAY: SHOO-noh-SORE-us

PERIOD: 175 to 163 million years ago, Middle Jurassic

WHERE FOUND: China

FOSSILS: 20 skeletons with 5 skulls

LENGTH: 40 feet (11 meters); Giant

Sauropods

SHUVUUIA

MEANING: "Bird"

HOW TO SAY: shu-VOO-ee-a

PERIOD: 85 to 75 million years ago, Late Cretaceous

WHERE FOUND: Mongolia

FOSSILS: Two skulls and some other bones

LENGTH: 3 feet (0.9 meters); Small

Dromaeosaurs

SIAMOSAURUS

MEANING: "Siamese lizard"

HOW TO SAY: si-AM-oh-SORE-us

PERIOD: 100 million years ago, Early Cretaceous

WHERE FOUND: Thailand

FOSSILS: Teeth

LENGTH: 30 feet (9.1 meters); Big

Giant Meat Eaters

SIAMOTYRANNUS

MEANING: "Siamese tyrant"

HOW TO SAY: sie-AM-oh-ti-RAN-us

PERIOD: 136 to 130 million years ago, Early Cretaceous

WHERE FOUND: Thailand

FOSSILS: Hip bones and vertebrae

LENGTH: 21 feet (6.5 meters); Big

Tyrannosaurs

SIGILMASSASAURUS

MEANING: "Sijilmassa lizard"

HOW TO SAY: see-jil-MAH-sah-SORE-us

PERIOD: 100 to 94 million years ago, Late Cretaceous

WHERE FOUND: Morocco

FOSSILS: One neck vertebra, possibly some other material

LENGTH: Unknown

Giant Meat Eaters

SILVISAURUS

MEANING: "Forest lizard"

HOW TO SAY: SILL-vih-SORE-us

PERIOD: 116 to 113 million years ago, Early Cretaceous

WHERE FOUND: U.S. (Kansas)

FOSSILS: Part of skeleton

LENGTH: 13 feet (4 meters); Small

Anklyosaurs

SIMILICAUDIPTERYX

MEANING: "Similar to Caudipteryx"

HOW TO SAY: SIM-ih-lih-CAW-dip-turr-icks

PERIOD: 120 million years ago, Early Cretaeous

WHERE FOUND: China

FOSSILS: Part of skeleton

LENGTH: 3 to 6 feet (0.8 to 1.8 meters); Small

Dromaeosaurs

SINOCALLIOPTERYX

MEANING: "Chinese beautiful feather"

HOW TO SAY: SINE-o-CAL-ee-AWP-ter-iks

PERIOD: 130 to 125 million years ago, Early Cretaceous

WHERE FOUND: China

FOSSILS: Nearly complete skeleton

LENGTH: Up to 7.5 feet (2.3 meters); Small

Dromaeosaurs

SINOCOELURUS

MEANING: "Chinese hollow tail"

HOW TO SAY: SINE-o-so-LOOR-us

PERIOD: 150 to 145 million years ago, Late Jurassic

WHERE FOUND: China

FOSSILS: Teeth

LENGTH: 4 to 7 feet (1.5 to 2.2 meters); Small

Dromaeosaurs

SINORNITHOIDES

MEANING: "Chinese bird-like"

HOW TO SAY: si-NOR-ni-THOI-deez

PERIOD: 110 to 100 million years ago, Middle Cretaceous

WHERE FOUND: Mongolia

FOSSILS: Nearly complete skeleton

LENGTH: 3.6 feet (1.1 meters); Small

Dromaeosaurs

SEISMOSAURUS
P. 194–195

SINORNITHOMIMUS

MEANING: "Chinese bird mimic"

HOW TO SAY: si-NOR-nith-o-MY-muss

PERIOD: 112 to 100 million years ago, Late Cretaceous

WHERE FOUND: China

FOSSILS: Several complete skeletons

LENGTH: About 6.5 feet (2 meters); Small

Ornithomimids

SINORNITHOSAURUS

MEANING: "Chinese bird lizard"

HOW TO SAY: SINE-or-nith-o-SORE-us

PERIOD: 124 million years ago, Early Cretaceous

WHERE FOUND: China

FOSSILS: Nearly complete skeleton with skull

LENGTH: 6.5 feet (2 meters); Small

Dromaeosaurs

SINOSAUROPTERYX

MEANING: "Chinese lizard with feathers"

HOW TO SAY: SINE-oh-sore-OP-ter-iks

PERIOD: 135 to 121 million years ago, Early Cretaceous

WHERE FOUND: China

FOSSILS: Two complete skeletons

LENGTH: 3.3 feet (1 meter); Small

Dromaeosaurs

SINOSAURUS

MEANING: "Chinese lizard"

HOW TO SAY: SINE-o-SORE-us

PERIOD: 200 to 180 million years ago, Early Jurassic

WHERE FOUND: China

FOSSILS: Upper jaw and teeth

LENGTH: 8 feet (2.4 meters); Small

Giant Meat Eaters

SINOVENATOR

MEANING: "Chinese hunter"

HOW TO SAY: sine-o-VEN-a-tore

PERIOD: 130 to 125 million years ago, Early Cretaceous

WHERE FOUND: China

FOSSILS: Incomplete skeletons and partial skull

LENGTH: 3.3 feet (1 meter); Small

Dromaeosaurs

SINRAPTOR

MEANING: "Chinese robber"

HOW TO SAY: sine-RAP-tore

PERIOD: 155 to 144 million years ago, Late Jurassic

WHERE FOUND: China

FOSSILS: Nearly complete skeleton

LENGTH: 26 feet (8 meters); Big

Giant Meat Eaters

SINUSONASUS

MEANING: "Big toothed curve nose"

HOW TO SAY: sien-ew-SON-ah-suss

PERIOD: 136 to 130 million years ago, Early Cretaceous

WHERE FOUND: China

FOSSILS: Mostly complete skeleton

LENGTH: 3.3 feet (1 meter); Small

Dromaeosaurs

SKORPIOVENATOR

MEANING: "Scorpion hunter"

HOW TO SAY: SCOR-pee-o-VEN-a-tor

PERIOD: 93 million years ago, Middle Cretaceous

WHERE FOUND: Argentina

FOSSILS: Nearly complete skeleton

LENGTH: 29 feet (9.5 meters); Big

Ceratosaurians

SONIDOSAURUS

MEANING: "Sonida lizard"

HOW TO SAY: SON-id-oh-SORE-us

PERIOD: 85 to 65 million years ago, Late Cretaceous

WHERE FOUND: China

FOSSILS: Some vertebrae and hip bones

LENGTH: Up to 30 feet (9 meters); Big

Sauropods

SONORASAURUS

MEANING: "Sonora lizard"

HOW TO SAY: son-OR-ah-SORE-us

PERIOD: 112 to 99 million years ago, Middle Cretaceous

WHERE FOUND: U.S. (Arizona)

FOSSILS: Incomplete skeleton

LENGTH: 45 to 55 feet (14 to 17 meters); Giant

Sauropods

SPINOSAURUS

MEANING: "Spiny lizard"

HOW TO SAY: SPINE-oh-SORE-us

PERIOD: 97.5 million years ago, Late Cretaceous

WHERE FOUND: Egypt, Morocco

FOSSILS: Several partial skeletons

LENGTH: 45 feet (13.7 meters); Giant

Giant Meat Eaters

SPINOSTROPHEUS

MEANING: "Spined vertebrae"

HOW TO SAY: SPY-no-STROH-fee-us

PERIOD: 112 to 100 million years ago, Early Cretaceous

WHERE FOUND: Niger

FOSSILS: Partial skeleton, no skull

LENGTH: 10 feet (3 meters); Small

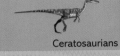
Ceratosaurians

STAURIKOSAURUS

MEANING: "Southern Cross lizard"

HOW TO SAY: STAWR-i-ko-SORE-us

PERIOD: 228 to 225 million years ago, Late Triassic

WHERE FOUND: Brazil

FOSSILS: Complete skeleton

LENGTH: 7 feet (2 meters); Small

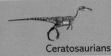
Ceratosaurians

STEGOCERAS

MEANING: "Roofed horn"

HOW TO SAY: STEG-oss-er-us

PERIOD: 76 to 65 million years ago, Late Cretaceous

WHERE FOUND: Canada (Alberta)

FOSSILS: Complete skeletons

LENGTH: 7 feet (2 meters); Small

Pachycephalosaurs

STEGOSAURUS

MEANING: "Roof lizard"

HOW TO SAY: STEG-oh-SORE-us

PERIOD: 156 to 140 million years ago, Late Jurassic

WHERE FOUND: U.S. (Colorado, Utah, Wyoming)

FOSSILS: Many partial and complete skeletons, various skulls

LENGTH: 26 to 30 feet (8 to 9 meters); Big

Stegosaurs

T

STENOPELIX

MEANING: "Narrow pelvis"

HOW TO SAY: ste-NOP-e-liks

PERIOD: 145 to 140 million years ago, Early Cretaceous

WHERE FOUND: Germany

FOSSILS: Partial skeleton without skull

LENGTH: 4.5 feet (1.5 meters); Small

Pachycephalosaurs

STOKESOSAURUS

MEANING: "Stokes's lizard"

HOW TO SAY: STOH-koh-SORE-us

PERIOD: 156 to 145 million years ago, Late Jurassic

WHERE FOUND: U.S. (Utah)

FOSSILS: Partial skeleton, hip bone some vertebrae

LENGTH: 13.5 feet (4 meters); Small

Tyrannosaurs

STORMBERGIA

MEANING: "Stormberg one"

HOW TO SAY: storm-BURG-ee-ah

PERIOD: 200 to 189 million years ago, Early Jurassic

WHERE FOUND: South Africa

FOSSILS: Partial skeletons

LENGTH: Up to 6.5 feet (2 meters); Small

Pre-Iguanodontians

STRUTHIOMIMUS

MEANING: "Ostrich mimic"

HOW TO SAY: strooth-ee-oh-MY-muss

PERIOD: 76 million years ago, Late Cretaceous

WHERE FOUND: U.S. (Wyoming, Utah); Canada (Alberta)

FOSSILS: Several skeletons

LENGTH: 14 feet (4.3 meters)

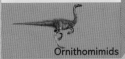

Ornithomimids

STRUTHIOSAURUS

MEANING: "Ostrich lizard"

HOW TO SAY: strooth-ee-oh-SORE-us

PERIOD: 83 to 65 million years ago, Late Cretaceous

WHERE FOUND: Austria, Romania

FOSSILS: Very incomplete skeletons

LENGTH: 7 feet (2 meters); Small

Dromaeosaurs

STYGIMOLOCH

MEANING: "Demon from the river Styx"

HOW TO SAY: STIG-ee-MOLL-uk

PERIOD: 68 to 65 million years ago, Late Cretaceous

WHERE FOUND: U.S. (Montana, Wyoming)

FOSSILS: Partial skulls

LENGTH: 7 to 10 feet (2 to 3 meters); Small

Pachycephalosaurs

STYRACOSAURUS

MEANING: "Spike lizard"

HOW TO SAY: sty-RACK-oh-SORE-us

PERIOD: 77 to 73 million years ago, Late Cretaceous

WHERE FOUND: U.S. (Montana); Canada (Alberta)

FOSSILS: Many complete skeletons

LENGTH: 18 feet (5.25 meters); Big

Large Ceratopsians

SUCHOMIMUS

MEANING: "Crocodile mimic"

HOW TO SAY: SOOK-oh-MIME-us

PERIOD: 100 million years ago, Early Cretaceous

WHERE FOUND: Niger

FOSSILS: Nearly complete skeleton

LENGTH: 36 feet (11 meters)

Giant Meat Eaters

SULAIMANISAURUS

MEANING: "Sulaiman lizard"

HOW TO SAY: SOOL-a-man-ee-SORE-us

PERIOD: 70 to 65 million years ago, Late Cretaceous

WHERE FOUND: Pakistan

FOSSILS: 11 tail vertebrae

LENGTH: 82 feet (25 meters); Giant

Sauropods

SUPERSAURUS

MEANING: "Super lizard"

HOW TO SAY: SOUP-er-SORE-us

PERIOD: 155 to 145 million years ago, Late Jurassic

WHERE FOUND: U.S. (Colorado)

FOSSILS: Incomplete skeleton, including ribs, shoulder blades, pelvis, and vertebrae

LENGTH: 138 feet (42 meters); Gigantic

Sauropods

SUUWASSEA

MEANING: "Ancient thunder"

HOW TO SAY: SOO-woss-ee-ah

PERIOD: 150 million years ago, Late Jurassic

WHERE FOUND: U.S. (Montana)

FOSSILS: Partial skeleton

LENGTH: 46 to 49 feet (14 to 15 meters); Giant

Sauropods

SUZHOUSAURUS

MEANING: "Suzhou lizard"

HOW TO SAY: soo-joe-SORE-us

PERIOD: 125 to 100 million years ago, Early Cretaceous

WHERE FOUND: China

FOSSILS: Partial skeleton

LENGTH: 15 to 20 feet (4.5 to 6 meters); Big

Therizinosaurs

TALARURUS

MEANING: "Wicker basket tail"

HOW TO SAY: TAL-a-RU-rus

PERIOD: 80 million years ago, Late Cretaceous

WHERE FOUND: Mongolia

FOSSILS: One nearly complete skeleton, two incomplete skulls, and some other material

LENGTH: 20 feet (6 meters); Big

Anklyosaurs

TALENKAUEN

MEANING: "Small head"

HOW TO SAY: TAL-en-con

PERIOD: 70 to 65 million years ago, Late Cretaceous

WHERE FOUND: Argentina

FOSSILS: Partial skeleton

LENGTH: 13 feet (4 meters); Small

Pre-Iguanodontians

TANGVAYOSAURUS

MEANING: "Tang Vay lizard"

HOW TO SAY: tahng-VIE-o-SORE-us

PERIOD: 112 to 100 million years ago, Early Cretaceous

WHERE FOUND: Thailand, Laos

FOSSILS: Two partial skeletons without skulls

LENGTH: 50 feet (15 meters); Giant

Sauropods

TANIUS

MEANING: "Of the Tan"

HOW TO SAY: TAN-ee-us

PERIOD: 88.5 to 65 million years ago, Late Cretaceous

WHERE FOUND: China

FOSSILS: Jawbones with teeth

LENGTH: 27 to 30 feet (8 to 9 meters); Big

Hadrosaurians

TARBOSAURUS

MEANING: "Alarming reptile"

HOW TO SAY: Tar-bow-SORE-us

PERIOD: 70 to 65 million years ago, Late Cretaceous

WHERE FOUND: Mongolia, China

FOSSILS: Several complete and partial skeletons

LENGTH: Large

Tyrannosaurs

TATANKACEPHALUS

MEANING: "Buffalo head" (in honor of Buffalo, N.Y., home city of discoverer William Parsons)

HOW TO SAY: TAH-tank-a-SEFF-a-luss

PERIOD: 125 to 100 million years ago, Early Cretaceous

WHERE FOUND: U.S. (Montana)

FOSSILS: Partial skull, some ribs, a tooth

LENGTH: 15 to 20 feet (4.5 to 6 meters); Big

Anklyosaurs

TAWA

MEANING: "Big hollow"

HOW TO SAY: TAH-WAH

PERIOD: 215 million years ago, Late Triassic

WHERE FOUND: U.S. (New Mexico)

FOSSILS: Complete skeleton

LENGTH: 13 feet (4 meters); Small

Early Dinosaurs

TAZOUDASAURUS

MEANING: "Tazouda lizard"

HOW TO SAY: TAH-ou-da-SORE-us

PERIOD: 175 to 171 million years ago, Middle Jurassic

WHERE FOUND: Morocco

FOSSILS: Two partial skeletons

LENGTH: 30 feet (9 meters)

Sauropods

TANYCOLAGREUS

MEANING: "Long limb hunter"

HOW TO SAY: TAN-ee-co-LA-gree-us

PERIOD: 150 to 145 million years ago, Late Jurassic

WHERE FOUND: U.S. (Wyoming)

FOSSILS: Partial skeleton including incomplete skull

LENGTH: Up to 16.5 feet (5 meters)

Dromaeosaurs

TARCHIA

MEANING: "Brainy one"

HOW TO SAY: TAHR-key-ah

PERIOD: 78 to 69 million years ago, Late Cretaceous

WHERE FOUND: Mongolia

FOSSILS: One nearly complete skeleton without skull, two complete skulls

LENGTH: 26 to 28 feet (8 to 8.5 meters); Big

Anklyosaurs

TATISAURUS

MEANING: "Ta-Ti lizard"

HOW TO SAY: tah-TEE-SORE-us

PERIOD: 205 to 189 million years ago, Early Jurassic

WHERE FOUND: China

FOSSILS: Partial jaw

LENGTH: 4 feet (1.2 meters); Small

Anklyosaurs

TEHUELCHESAURUS

MEANING: "Tehuelche lizard"

HOW TO SAY: tay-WAYL-chay-SORE-us

PERIOD: 164 to 161 million years ago, Late Jurassic

WHERE FOUND: Argentina

FOSSILS: Incomplete skeleton

LENGTH: 49 feet (15 meters); Giant

Sauropods

TARASCOSAURUS

MEANING: "Tarsque (Spanish dragon) lizard"

HOW TO SAY: TA-rass-co-SORE-us

PERIOD: 83 to 70 million years ago, Late Cretaceous

WHERE FOUND: France

FOSSILS: A few bones, including a femur

LENGTH: 20 feet (6 meters); Big

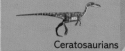
Ceratosaurians

TASTAVINSAURUS

MEANING: After Rio Tastavins

HOW TO SAY: Tass-TA-vin-SORE-us

PERIOD: 120 million years ago, Early Cretaceous

WHERE FOUND: Spain

FOSSILS: Well-preserved skeleton

LENGTH: 82 feet (25 meters)

Sauropods

TAVEIROSAURUS

MEANING: "Taveiro lizard"

HOW TO SAY: tah-VAY-roo-SORE-us

PERIOD: 70 million years ago, Late Cretaceous

WHERE FOUND: Portugal

FOSSILS: Teeth

LENGTH: unknown

Pachycephalosaurs

SEISMOSAURUS
P. 174–175

TELMATOSAURUS

MEANING: "Marsh lizard"

HOW TO SAY: tell-MAT-oh-SORE-us

PERIOD: 83 to 65 million years ago, Late Cretaceous

WHERE FOUND: France, Netherlands, Romania

FOSSILS: Some vertebrae

LENGTH: 16 feet (5 meters); Big

Hadrosaurians

TEXASETES

MEANING: "Texas resident"

HOW TO SAY: Tek-sa-SEE-teez

PERIOD: 112 to 99 million years ago, Middle Cretaceous

WHERE FOUND: U.S. (Texas)

FOSSILS: Skull fragment, some limbs, vertebrae, a tooth, and hip bones

LENGTH: 8 to 10 feet (2.5 to 3 meters); Small

Anklyosaurs

THERIZINOSAURUS

MEANING: "Cut off reptile"

HOW TO SAY: THERE-ih-ZIN-oh-SORE-us

PERIOD: 70 million years ago, Late Cretaceous

WHERE FOUND: Mongolia, China

FOSSILS: Several limb bones, including huge claws

LENGTH: 36 feet (11 meters); Giant

Therizinosaurs

TIANYULONG

MEANING: "Dragon of Tianyu," after Shandong Tianyu Museum of Nature

HOW TO SAY: tea-ahn-YOU-long

PERIOD: 130 million years ago, Early Cretaceous

WHERE FOUND: China

FOSSILS: Incomplete skeleton with partial skull

LENGTH: 2 feet (0.7 meters); Small

Pre-Iguanodontians

TIENSHANOSAURUS

MEANING: "Heaven mountain lizard"

HOW TO SAY: TIEN-SHAHN-o-SORE-us

PERIOD: 156 million years ago, Late Jurassic

WHERE FOUND: China

FOSSILS: Partial skeleton

LENGTH: 33 feet (10.1 meters); Giant

Sauropods

TENDAGURIA

MEANING: After Tendaguru beds in Tanzania

HOW TO SAY: TEN-duh-GOO-ree-uh

PERIOD: 150 million years ago, Late Jurassic

WHERE FOUND: Tanzania

FOSSILS: Two vertebrae

LENGTH: 66 feet (20 meters); Gigantic

Sauropods

THECODONTO–SAURUS

MEANING: "Socket-toothed lizard"

HOW TO SAY: THEE-co-DONT-oh-SORE-us

PERIOD: 216 to 200 million years ago, Late Triassic

WHERE FOUND: England, Wales

FOSSILS: Partial skeleton in rock

LENGTH: 7 feet (2.1 meters); Small

Sauropods

THESCELOSAURUS

MEANING: "Marvelous lizard"

HOW TO SAY: THES-ke-loh-SORE-us

PERIOD: 77 to 65 million years ago, Late Cretaceous

WHERE FOUND: U.S. (Wyoming, Montana, South Dakota); Canada (Alberta, Saskatchewan)

FOSSILS: One complete skeleton and eight incomplete skeletons, skin impressions

LENGTH: 12 feet (3.5 meters); Small

Pre-Iguanodontians

TIANYURAPTOR

MEANING: "Thief of Tianyu," after Shandong Tianyu Museum of Nature

HOW TO SAY: tea-ahn-you-RAP-tore

PERIOD: 155 million years ago, Late Jurassic

WHERE FOUND: China

FOSSILS: Nearly complete skeleton

LENGTH: 7 feet (2.1 meters); Small

Dromaeosaurs

TIMIMUS

MEANING: "Tim [Rich and Tim Flannery]'s mimic"

HOW TO SAY: TIM-I-muss

PERIOD: 106 million years ago, Early Cretaceous

WHERE FOUND: Australia

FOSSILS: Two leg bones

LENGTH: 10 feet (3 meters); Small

Ornithomimids

TENONTOSAURUS

MEANING: "Sinew lizard"

HOW TO SAY: ten-ONT-oh-SORE-us

PERIOD: 116 to 113 million years ago, Early Cretaceous

WHERE FOUND: U.S. (Montana, Wyoming, Oklahoma, Texas)

FOSSILS: Many complete skeletons

LENGTH: 24 feet (7 meters); Big

Pre-Iguanodontians

THEIOPHYTALIA

MEANING: "Garden belonging to the gods"

HOW TO SAY: THEY-o-fye-TAH-lee-a

PERIOD: 112 to 100 million years ago, Early Cretaceous

WHERE FOUND: U.S. (Colorado)

FOSSILS: Fragmentary skull

LENGTH: 20 to 27 feet (6 to 8 meters); Big

Iguanodontians

TIANCHISAURUS

MEANING: "Heavenly pool lizard"

HOW TO SAY: TYAN-CHU-a-SORE-us

PERIOD: 171 to 164 million years ago, Middle Jurassic

WHERE FOUND: China

FOSSILS: Skull and limb bone fragments, some vertebrae

LENGTH: 10 feet (3 meters); Small

Anklyosaurs

TIANZHENOSAURUS

MEANING: "Tianzhen lizard"

HOW TO SAY: TIEN-shen-o-SORE-us

PERIOD: 90 million years ago, Middle Cretaceous

WHERE FOUND: China

FOSSILS: Nearly complete skeleton without skull, nearly complete skull, partial jaw

LENGTH: 14 feet (4 meters); Small

Anklyosaurs

TOCHISAURUS

MEANING: "Ostrich reptile"

HOW TO SAY: TOHK-i-SORE-us

PERIOD: 70 to 65 million years ago, Late Cretaceous

WHERE FOUND: Mongolia

FOSSILS: Partial foot bones

LENGTH: 8.2 feet (2.5 meters); Small

Dromaeosaurs

TORVOSAURUS

MEANING: "Savage lizard"

HOW TO SAY: TOR-voh-SORE-us

PERIOD: 156 to 145 million years ago, Late Jurassic

WHERE FOUND: U.S. (Colorado)

FOSSILS: Partial skull, back, hip, hand, and arm bones

LENGTH: 40 feet (12 meters); Giant

Giant Meat Eaters

TRIMUCRODON

MEANING: "Triply-pointed tooth"

HOW TO SAY: trie-MOO-kro-don

PERIOD: 150 million years ago, Late Jurassic

WHERE FOUND: Portugal

FOSSILS: One tooth

LENGTH: Unknown

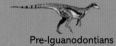
Pre-Iguanodontians

TSAGANTEGIA

MEANING: "Tsagan-Teg animal"

HOW TO SAY: TSAA-gan-teg-ee-ah

PERIOD: 100 to 93 million years ago, Middle Cretaceous

WHERE FOUND: Mongolia

FOSSILS: Complete skull

LENGTH: 21 feet (6.5 meters); Big

Anklyosaurs

TUOJIANGOSAURUS

MEANING: "Tuo River lizard"

HOW TO SAY: Too-oh-gee-ANG-oh-SORE-us

PERIOD: 163 to 150 million years ago, Late Jurassic

WHERE FOUND: China

FOSSILS: Half-complete skeleton and very incomplete skeleton

LENGTH: 23 feet (7 meters); Big

Stegosaurs

TYLOCEPHALE

MEANING: "Swollen head"

HOW TO SAY: TY-low-SEF-ah-lee

PERIOD: 80 to 75 million years ago, Late Cretaceous

WHERE FOUND: Mongolia

FOSSILS: Incomplete skull

LENGTH: 7 feet (2.5 meters); Small

Pachycephalosaurs

TRICERATOPS

MEANING: "Three-horned face"

HOW TO SAY: tri-SERR-uh-tops

PERIOD: 72 to 65 million years ago, Late Cretaceous

WHERE FOUND: Western Canada and western U.S.

FOSSILS: About 50 skulls and some partial skeletons

LENGTH: 25 feet (8 meters); Big

Large Ceratopsians

TROODON

MEANING: "Wound tooth"

HOW TO SAY: TRO-oh-don

PERIOD: 76 million years ago, Late Cretaceous

WHERE FOUND: U.S. (Montana, Wyoming, Alaska); Canada (Alberta)

FOSSILS: 20 skeletons, many teeth, and eggs

LENGTH: 6.5 feet (2 meters); Small

Dromaeosaurs

TSINTAOSAURUS

MEANING: "Lizard from Tsintao"

HOW TO SAY: sin-tau-SORE-us

PERIOD: 70 million years ago, Late Cretaceous

WHERE FOUND: China

FOSSILS: Complete skeleton

LENGTH: 33 feet (10 meters); Giant

Hadrosaurians

TURANOCERATOPS

MEANING: "Turan horn face"

HOW TO SAY: too-RAHN-o-SER-a-tops

PERIOD: 90 million years ago, Late Cretaceous

WHERE FOUND: Uzbekistan

FOSSILS: Parts of skull, teeth, shoulder bone

LENGTH: 22 feet (7 meters)

Large Ceratopsians

TYRANNOSAURUS REX

MEANING: "Tyrant lizard king"

HOW TO SAY: tye-RAN-oh-SORE-us

PERIOD: 65 million years ago, Late Cretaceous

WHERE FOUND: U.S. (Colorado, Montana, New Mexico, South Dakota, Wyoming); Canada (Alberta, Saskatchewan); Mongolia

FOSSILS: More than 20 skeletons up to 90% complete

LENGTH: 40 feet (12 meters); Giant

Tyrannosaurs

TRIGONOSAURUS

MEANING: "Triangulo Mineiro lizard"

HOW TO SAY: TRY-gon-oh-SORE-us

PERIOD: 70 to 65 million years ago, Late Cretaceous

WHERE FOUND: Brazil

FOSSILS: Some vertebrae

LENGTH: Up to 31.5 feet (9.5 meters); Big

Sauropods

TSAAGAN

MEANING: "White"

HOW TO SAY: SAA-gan

PERIOD: 83 to 70 million years ago, Late Cretaceous

WHERE FOUND: China

FOSSILS: Skull and some vertebrae

LENGTH: Up to 10 feet (3 meters); Small

Dromaeosaurs

TUGULUSAURUS

MEANING: "Tugulu group lizard"

HOW TO SAY: too-GOO-loo-SORE-us

PERIOD: 140 to 136 million years ago, Early Cretaceous

WHERE FOUND: China

FOSSILS: Very incomplete skeleton

LENGTH: 10 feet (3 meters); Small

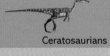
Ceratosaurians

TURIASAURUS

MEANING: "Turia lizard"

HOW TO SAY: tur-ee-ah-SAWR-us

PERIOD: 145 million years ago, Late Jurassic

WHERE FOUND: Spain

FOSSILS: Skull fragments, left forelimb, teeth, vertebrae, and ribs

LENGTH: 98 feet (30 meters); Gigantic

Sauropods

TYRANNOTITAN

MEANING: "Tyrant giant"

HOW TO SAY: tie-RAN-oh-TIE-tan

PERIOD: 118 million years ago, Early Cretaceous

WHERE FOUND: Argentina

FOSSILS: Partial jaw, teeth, vertebrae, ribs and some other various bones

LENGTH: 39 to 42 feet (12 to 13 meters); Giant

Giant Meat Eaters

U

UBERABATITAN

MEANING: "Uberaba titan"

HOW TO SAY: oo-BEAR-a-ba-TIE-tan

PERIOD: 71 to 65 million years ago, Late Cretaceous

WHERE FOUND: Brazil

FOSSILS: Incomplete skeleton

LENGTH: 30 feet (9 meters); Big

Sauropods

UDANOCERATOPS

MEANING: "Horn face from Udan-Sayr"

HOW TO SAY: oo-DAHN-o-SERR-a-tops

PERIOD: 85 to 83 million years ago, Late Cretaceous

WHERE FOUND: Mongolia

FOSSILS: Skull

LENGTH: 10 feet (3 meters); Small

Small Ceratopsians

UNAYSAURUS

MEANING: "Black water lizard"

HOW TO SAY: oo-NAH-ee-SORE-us

PERIOD: 216 to 203 million years ago, Late Triassic

WHERE FOUND: Brazil

FOSSILS: Nearly complete skull, complete lower jaw, partial skeleton

LENGTH: Up to 8 feet (2.5 meters); Small

Prosauropods

UNENLAGIA

MEANING: "Almost bird"

HOW TO SAY: oon-en-LAHG-ee-ah

PERIOD: 80 million years ago, Late Cretaceous

WHERE FOUND: Argentina

FOSSILS: Incomplete skeleton

LENGTH: 7.5 feet (2.2 meters); Small

Dromaeosaurs

UNQUILLOSAURUS

MEANING: "Unquillo lizard"

HOW TO SAY: oong-KEE-yo-SORE-us

PERIOD: 83 to 70 million years ago, Late Cretaceous

WHERE FOUND: Argentina

FOSSILS: Pubis bone

LENGTH: 10 feet (3 meters); Small

Dromaeosaurs

URBACODON

MEANING: "Urbac tooth"

HOW TO SAY: er-BACK-o-don

PERIOD: 93 to 89 million years ago, Late Cretaceous

WHERE FOUND: Uzbekistan

FOSSILS: Dentary with teeth

LENGTH: 3 to 5 feet (1 to 1.5 meters); Small

Dromaeosaurs

UTAHRAPTOR

MEANING: "Utah thief"

HOW TO SAY: YOO-tah-RAP-tore

PERIOD: 125 million years ago, Early Cretaceous

WHERE FOUND: U.S. (Utah)

FOSSILS: One half-complete skeleton

LENGTH: 19.5 feet (5.9 meters); Big

Dromaeosaurs

V

VALDORAPTOR

MEANING: "Weald robber"

HOW TO SAY: VAHL-doh-RAP-tor

PERIOD: 120 million years ago, Early Cretaceous

WHERE FOUND: England

FOSSILS: upper foot bones

LENGTH: 16 feet (5 meters); Big

Dromaeosaurs

VALDOSAURUS

MEANING: "Weald lizard"

HOW TO SAY: VAL-do-SORE-us

PERIOD: 145 to 125 million years ago, Early Cretaceous

WHERE FOUND: England, Romania

FOSSILS: Thighbones, partial jaw, teeth

LENGTH: 10 feet (3 meters); Small

Pre-Iguanodontians

VARIRAPTOR

MEANING: "Var [River] robber"

HOW TO SAY: vahr-ee-RAP-tore

PERIOD: 70 million years ago, Late Cretaceous

WHERE FOUND: France

FOSSILS: Skull fragments, some vertebrae, arm bone, femur, claw, and some teeth

LENGTH: 5 to 6 feet (1.5 to 1.8 meters); Small

Dromaeosaurs

VELAFRONS

MEANING: "Sailed forehead"

HOW TO SAY: VEL-uh-frons

PERIOD: 83 to 70 million years ago, Late Cretaceous

WHERE FOUND: Mexico

FOSSILS: Nearly complete skull, partial skeleton

LENGTH: 30 to 33 feet (9 to 10 meters); Giant

Hadrosaurians

VELOCIRAPTOR

MEANING: "Speed thief"

HOW TO SAY: veh-LOSS-ih-RAP-tore

PERIOD: 80 million years ago, Late Cretaceous

WHERE FOUND: Mongolia

FOSSILS: Skeletons

LENGTH: 6.5 feet (2 meters); Small

Dromaeosaurs

VELOCISAURUS

MEANING: "Speedy lizard"

HOW TO SAY: veh-LOSS-ee-SORE-us

PERIOD: 85 to 83 million years ago, Late Cretaceous

WHERE FOUND: Argentina

FOSSILS: Partial hind limb bone

LENGTH: 3.3 feet (1 meter); Small

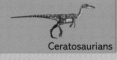
Ceratosaurians

VENENOSAURUS

MEANING: "Poison lizard"

HOW TO SAY: ve-NEE-no-SORE-us

PERIOD: 136 to 130 million years ago, Early Cretaceous

WHERE FOUND: U.S. (Utah)

FOSSILS: Two incomplete skeletons

LENGTH: 27 feet (8 meters); Big

Sauropods

VOLKHEIMERIA

MEANING: After W. Volkheimer

HOW TO SAY: VOLK-hie-MEER-ee-a

PERIOD: 164 to 161 million years ago, Middle Jurassic

WHERE FOUND: Argentina

FOSSILS: Partial skeleton

LENGTH: 33 feet (10 meters); Giant

Sauropods

VULCANODON

MEANING: "Vulcan (Roman god of fire) tooth"

HOW TO SAY: vul-KAN-uh-don

PERIOD: 200 to 219 million years ago, Early Jurassic

WHERE FOUND: Zimbabwe

FOSSILS: Partial skeleton

LENGTH: 20 feet (6.5 meters); Big

Sauropods

WUERHOSAURUS

MEANING: "Lizard from Wuerho, China"

HOW TO SAY: woo-AYR-hoh-SORE-us

PERIOD: 135 to 120 million years ago, Early Cretaceous

WHERE FOUND: Mongolia

FOSSILS: Partial skeleton without complete skull

LENGTH: 27 feet (8 meters); Big

Stegosaurs

XENOTARSOSAURUS

MEANING: "Strange-ankle lizard"

HOW TO SAY: zeen-oh-TAR-soh-SORE-us

PERIOD: 83 to 73 million years ago, Late Cretaceous

WHERE FOUND: Argentina

FOSSILS: A few vertebrae and leg bone

LENGTH: 24 to 27 feet (7 to 8 meters); Big

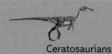
Ceratosaurians

XIONGGUANLONG

MEANING: "Grand Pass Dragon"

HOW TO SAY: SHEE-yong-GUAN-long

PERIOD: 125 to 100 million years ago, Early Cretaceous

WHERE FOUND: China

FOSSILS: Skulls, vertebrae

LENGTH: 12 feet (3.5 meters); Small

Tyrannosaurs

Y

YAMACERATOPS

MEANING: "Yama (lord of death) horned face"

HOW TO SAY: YAHM-ah-SERR-a-tops

PERIOD: 125 to 100 million years ago, Early Cretaceous

WHERE FOUND: Mongolia

FOSSILS: Two partial skulls and some other bones

LENGTH: Up to 3.3 feet (1 meter); Small

Small Ceratopsians

W

WANNANOSAURUS

MEANING: After the Chinese province

HOW TO SAY: wah-NAN-oh-SORE-us

PERIOD: 83 to 73 million years ago, Late Cretaceous

WHERE FOUND: China

FOSSILS: Incomplete skeleton

LENGTH: 2 feet (0.6 meters); Small

Pachycephalosaurs

WULAGASAURUS

MEANING: "Wulaga lizard"

HOW TO SAY: woo-LAH-guh-SORE-us

PERIOD: 70 to 65 million years ago, Late Cretaceous

WHERE FOUND: China

FOSSILS: Partial lower jaw

LENGTH: 30 to 33 feet (9 to 10 meters); Big

Hadrosaurians

XIAOSAURUS

MEANING: "Little lizard"

HOW TO SAY: sheow-SORE-us

PERIOD: 169 to 163 million years ago, Middle Jurassic

WHERE FOUND: China

FOSSILS: Teeth and a few isolated bones

LENGTH: 3 feet (1 meter); Small

Pre-Iguanodontians

XUANHANOSAURUS

MEANING: "Xuanhan [County] lizard"

HOW TO SAY: SHWAN-han-oh-SORE-us

PERIOD: 167 to 164 million years ago, Middle Jurassic

WHERE FOUND: China

FOSSILS: Very incomplete remains

LENGTH: 20 feet (6 meters); Big

Dromaeosaurs

YANDUSAURUS

MEANING: "Yandu (salt capital of Szechuan Province, China) lizard"

HOW TO SAY: YAN-doo-SORE-us

PERIOD: 175 to 163 million years ago, Middle Jurassic

WHERE FOUND: China

FOSSILS: Two nearly complete skeletons

LENGTH: 5 feet (1.5 meters); Small

Pre-Iguanodontians

X

WINTONOTITAN

MEANING: "Winton's giant" from Winton, Australia

HOW TO SAY: WIN-ton-o-TIE-tan

PERIOD: 100 mllion years ago, Middle Cretaceous

WHERE FOUND: Australia

FOSSILS: Front leg, back vertebrae, parts of hip, and tail vertebrae

LENGTH: 50 feet (16 meters); Giant

Sauropods

XENOPOSEIDON

MEANING: "Strange god of the sea"

HOW TO SAY: zen-OH-pos-SI-don

PERIOD: 145 to 136 million years ago, Early Cretaceous

WHERE FOUND: England

FOSSILS: One partial vertebra

LENGTH: 49 to 65 feet (15 to 20 meters); Giant

Sauropods

XINJIANGOVENATOR

MEANING: "Xinjiang hunter"

HOW TO SAY: shin-CHANG-oh-VEN-a-tore

PERIOD: 112 to 100 million years ago, Early Cretaceous

WHERE FOUND: China

FOSSILS: Right leg bone

LENGTH: 8.2 to 14.8 feet (2.5 to 4.5 meters); Small

Dromaeosaurs

XUANHUACERATOPS

MEANING: "Xuanhua horned face"

HOW TO SAY: sh-WON-hwa-SERR-a-tops

PERIOD: 161 to 145 million years ago, Late Jurassic

WHERE FOUND: China

FOSSILS: Vertebra, front limbs

LENGTH: up to 3.3 feet (1 meter); Small

Small Ceratopsians

YANGCHUANO–SAURUS

MEANING: "Reptile from Yangchuan"

HOW TO SAY: YANG-chew-an-oh-SORE-us

PERIOD: 163 million years ago, Late Jurassic

WHERE FOUND: China

FOSSILS: Several nearly complete skeletons

LENGTH: 36 feet (11 meters); Giant

Giant Meat Eaters

YAVERLANDIA

MEANING: "Yaverland (Point) one"

HOW TO SAY: ya-vuhr-LAN-dee-a

PERIOD: 126 to 121 million years ago, Early Cretaceous

WHERE FOUND: England

FOSSILS: Partial skull

LENGTH: 3 feet (1 meter); Small

Pachycephalosaurs

YIXIANOSAURUS

MEANING: "Yixian lizard"

HOW TO SAY: YEE-shee-an-o-SORE-us

PERIOD: 130 to 125 million years ago, Early Cretaceous

WHERE FOUND: China

FOSSILS: Partial skeleton

LENGTH: About 1.2 feet (0.4 meters); Small

Dromaeosaurs

ZANABAZAR

MEANING: After Mongolian ruler and artist

HOW TO SAY: ZAN-ah-BAH-zarr

PERIOD: 80 million years ago, Late Cretaceous

WHERE FOUND: Mongolia

FOSSILS: Skull, vertebrae, part of hips, and hind leg

LENGTH: 9 feet (2.7 meters); Small

Dromaeosaurs

ZHEJIANGOSAURUS

MEANING: "Zhejiang lizard"

HOW TO SAY: Je-JEE-yang-o-SORE-us

PERIOD: 100 to 93 million years ago, Middle Cretaceous

WHERE FOUND: China

FOSSILS: Partial skeleton

LENGTH: 20 feet (6 meters); Big

Anklyosaurs

ZIZHONGOSAURUS

MEANING: "Zizhong lizard"

HOW TO SAY: ZIH-JUNG-oh-SORE-us

PERIOD: 180 million years ago, Early Jurassic

WHERE FOUND: China

FOSSILS: Back vertebrae, hip bone, and leg bone

LENGTH: 30 feet (9 meters); Big

Sauropods

YIMENOSAURUS

MEANING: "Yimen lizard"

HOW TO SAY: yee-MUHN-o-SORE-us

PERIOD: 200 to 196 million years ago, Early Jurassic

WHERE FOUND: China

FOSSILS: Two partial skeletons

LENGTH: 27 to 30 feet (8 to 9 meters); Big

Prosauropods

YUNNANOSAURUS

MEANING: "Yunnan (Province) lizard"

HOW TO SAY: YOU-NAN-oh-SORE-us

PERIOD: 208 to 194 million years ago, Early Jurassic

WHERE FOUND: China

FOSSILS: About 20 skeletons

LENGTH: 23 feet (7 meters); Big

Prosauropods

ZAPALASAURUS

MEANING: "Zapala lizard"

HOW TO SAY: za-PAL-ah-SORE-us

PERIOD: 130 to 112 million years ago, Early Cretaceous

WHERE FOUND: Argentina

FOSSILS: Vertebrae and some limb bones

LENGTH: 66 feet (20 meters)

Sauropods

ZHONGYUANSAURUS

MEANING: "Zhongyuan [District] lizard"

HOW TO SAY: jong-YOU-an-SORE-us

PERIOD: 100 to 65 million years ago, Cretaceous

WHERE FOUND: China

FOSSILS: Skull, arm, hip, and tailbones

LENGTH: 10 feet (3 meters); Small

Anklyosaurs

ZUNICERATOPS

MEANING: "Zuni horned face"

HOW TO SAY: ZOO-nee-SERR-ah-tops

PERIOD: 90 million years ago, Middle Cretaceous

WHERE FOUND: U.S. (New Mexico)

FOSSILS: Skull and a few bones

LENGTH: 10 to 12 feet (3 to 3.7 meters); Small

Small Ceratopsians

YINLONG

MEANING: "Crouching dragon"

HOW TO SAY: yin-LONG

PERIOD: 161 to 155 million years ago, Late Jurassic

WHERE FOUND: China

FOSSILS: Nearly complete skeleton

LENGTH: Up to 3.3 feet (1 meter); Small

Ceratosaurians

Z

ZALMOXES

MEANING: After the god Zalmoxes

HOW TO SAY: ZAL-mock-zees

PERIOD: 70 to 65 million years ago, Late Cretaceous

WHERE FOUND: Romania, Austria

FOSSILS: Partial skull

LENGTH: About 6.5 feet (2 meters); Small

Iguanodontians

ZEPHYROSAURUS

MEANING: "Zephyr's (god of the west wind) lizard"

HOW TO SAY: ZEF-eye-roh-SORE-us

PERIOD: 119 to 113 million years ago, Early Cretaceous

WHERE FOUND: U.S. (Montana)

FOSSILS: Partial skull and some vertebrae

LENGTH: 6 feet (1.8 meters); Small

Pre-Iguanodontians

ZHUCHENGOSAURUS

MEANING: "Zhucheng lizard"

HOW TO SAY: zoo-SHENG-o-SORE-us

PERIOD: 100 to 93 million years ago, Middle Cretaceous

WHERE FOUND: China

FOSSILS: Skulls, limbs, and vertebrae

LENGTH: 54 feet (16.6 meters); Giant

Hadrosaurians

ZUPAYSAURUS

MEANING: "Devil lizard"

HOW TO SAY: zoo-pay-SORE-us

PERIOD: 220 million years ago, Late Triassic

WHERE FOUND: Argentina

FOSSILS: Complete skull and isolated bones

LENGTH: 16.5 feet (5 meters); Big

Giant Meat Eaters

GLOSSARY

AMMONITE – a mollusk in a coiled shell with chambers that lived in the Mesozoic Era

AMPHIBIAN – animal that is able to live both on land and in water

ASTEROID – any of a number of small planetary rocks that are mainly found in the asteroid belt that lies between Mars and Jupiter

AWL – a pointed hand tool used to make small holes

BADLANDS – an area of land where little vegetation grows and natural forces have worn away the soft rocks into different shapes

CAMBRIAN PERIOD – the earliest period of the Paleozoic Era of geologic time, 545 to 505 million years ago, when nearly every major invertebrate animal group and fish appeared on Earth

CARBONIFEROUS PERIOD – the fifth period of the Paleozoic Era of geologic time, 355 to 280 million years ago, represented by extensive fossil swamps and forests found in Europe

CARNIVORE – a meat eater. Nearly all dinosaur meat eaters had sharp teeth. Often those teeth had grooves like a steak knife to help slice through flesh and muscle.

CENOZOIC ERA – a period of geologic time when mammals, birds, flowering plants, and grasses rapidly evolved. This is the geologic era that the Earth is currently in.

CLIMATE – the weather conditions of a particular area, including moisture, winds, and temperature

CONIFER – a group of many kinds of evergreen trees. Their leaves are usually needle–shaped. These types of trees do not lose their leaves in the fall.

COURTSHIP – the act of giving special attention or engaging in a social relationship that leads to mating

CRETACEOUS PERIOD – the third and last period of the Mesozoic Era of geologic time, 145 to 65 million years ago. Most dinosaurs became extinct at the end of the Cretaceous Period.

DEVONIAN PERIOD – the fourth period of the Paleozoic Era of geologic time, 410 to 355 million years ago, when ferns, insects, and amphibians dominated land and the first ammonites appeared in seas

DINOSAUR – extinct carnivorous or herbivorous reptiles that existed in the Mesozoic Era

DISEASE – an abnormal bodily condition that gets in the way of proper body functions

EARTHQUAKE – a sudden movement of the Earth that happens when energy is released in the Earth's crust

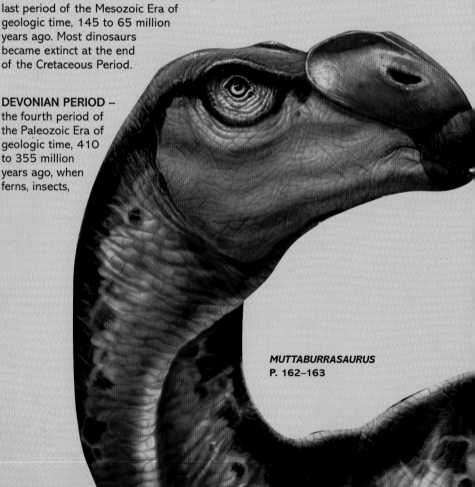

MUTTABURRASAURUS
P. 162–163

EQUATOR – an imaginary circle around the middle of the Earth that is an equal distance from the north and south poles

EXCAVATE – to remove or make hollow by digging out material

EXPLORATION – to travel for the purpose of investigating, examining, and discovering

EXTINCTION – an end to one or more forms of life

FOSSIL – a preserved body part, track, or trace of an ancient animal, insect, or plant. Most dead animals do not form fossils. It takes special conditions such as a covering of mud or sand to allow minerals to enter the fossil, which hardens and is then preserved.

GEOLOGIC TIME – the eras and periods of Earth's history

GEOLOGY – the area of science that deals with Earth's physical history

HABITAT – a particular environment of plants and animals

HERBIVORE – a plant eater. Most dinosaurs were herbivores. Their teeth were designed to grind or snip plants, and their stomachs were built to process plants.

HYPOTHESIS – an explanation that is assumed but not known to be true because it needs more investigation

IRIDIUM – a hard, whitish-yellow, metallic element that is found mostly in asteroids or volcanic rock

JURASSIC PERIOD – the second period of the Mesozoic Era of geologic time, 200 to 145 million years ago, when dinosaurs lived and birds first appeared on Earth

KERATIN – the bony sheath that makes up some dinosaur horns and the covering of their claws. Keratin also makes up your fingernails and toenails.

MAMMAL – warm-blooded vertebrates that include humans and other animals that are covered with hair and produce milk to feed their young

MANGROVE – a long-rooted tree native to tropical coastlines. A mangrove sits as on stilts above its exposed roots set under the water. The mangrove roots form shelter for fish and a rich environment for the growth of many marine creatures.

MATE – male and female animals coming together to produce young

MESOZOIC ERA – the era of geologic time that includes Triassic, Jurassic, and Cretaceous Periods. During this time flying reptiles, birds, and flowering plants appeared on Earth.

MIGRATE – to change locations regularly. Many dinosaurs may have migrated in spring and fall in search of better food or weather.

NEOGENE PERIOD – a period of geologic time from 23 million years ago to the present when the Earth became cooler and drier. This period is in the Cenozoic era.

NORTHERN HEMISPHERE – the half of the Earth that lies north of the Equator

ORDOVICIAN PERIOD – the second period of the Paleozoic Era of geologic time, 505 to 438 million years ago, when fish first appeared on Earth

OVERBURDEN – rock and soil that are lying over mineral deposits such as bone beds where fossils are found

PALEOCENE PERIOD – the earliest part of the Cenozoic Era of geologic time, 65 to 23 million years ago, when mammals evolved from small and simple forms into many diverse animals

PALEONTOLOGIST – a scientist who studies extinct animals and their environments

PALEOZOIC ERA – the era of Earth's history when vertebrates and land plants first appeared on Earth

PANGAEA – a land area that is believed to have once connected the Northern and Southern Hemispheres 235 to 200 million years ago

PERMIAN PERIOD – the sixth and last period of the Paleozoic Era of geologic time, 280 to 250 million years ago, when most of the animals and plants became extinct and reptiles began to dominate the land

PREDATOR – an animal that hunts for food. Most meat eaters are both scavengers and predators.

PREY – an animal that is hunted and killed by another animal (a predator) for food

PTEROSAUR – extinct flying reptile of the Mesozoic Era

SCAVENGER – an animal that eats dead creatures

SILURIAN PERIOD – the third period in the Paleozoic Era of geologic time, 438 to 410 million years ago, when fish diversified

SKELETON – a firm and supportive structure of an animal made of bone or cartilage that supports the soft tissues and organs of the body

SOUTHERN HEMISPHERE – the half of the Earth that lies south of the Equator

THEORY – the general ideas or principles of science that explain facts or events of the natural world

TRIASSIC PERIOD – the first period of the Mesozoic Era of geologic time, 250 to 200 million years ago,, when dinosaurs and mammals first appeared on Earth

VEGETATION – plant life. The plants alive in a particular environment are referred to as its vegetation.

VERTEBRATE – refers to animals that have backbones or spinal columns

RECOMMENDED
BOOKS, WEBSITES, VIDEOS

BOOKS

Barrett, Paul. *National Geographic Dinosaurs.* Washington, D.C.: National Geographic Children's Books, 2001.

Bishop, Nic. *Digging for Bird-Dinosaurs: An Expedition to Madagascar.* Logan, IA: Perfection Learning, 2002.

Lessem, Don. *Dinosaurs A to Z: The Ultimate Dinosaur Encyclopedia.* New York: Scholastic, 2003.

Lowell, Dingus and Mark A. Norell. *Searching for Velociraptor.* New York: Harper Collins Children's Books, 1996.

Manning, Phillip. *Dinomummy.* New York: Kingfisher, 2007.

Relf, Pat. *A Dinosaur Named Sue: The Story of the Colossal Fossil, The World's Most Complete T. Rex.* New York: Cartwheel, 2000.

Sabuda, Robert and Matthew Reinhart. *Encyclopedia Prehistorica Dinosaurs: The Definitive Pop-Up.* Somerville, MA: Candlewick, 2005.

Sloan, Christopher. *Bizarre Dinosaurs: Some Very Strange Creatures and Why We Think They Got That Way.* Washington, D.C.: National Geographic Children's Books, 2008.

Sloan, Christopher. *How Dinosaurs Took Flight: Fossils, Science, What We Think We Know, and Mysteries Yet Unsolved.* Washington, D.C.: National Geographic Children's Books, 2005.

The Dinosaur Museum: An Unforgettable, Interactive Virtual Tour Through Dinosaur History. Washington, D.C.: National Geographic Children's Books, 2008.

WEBSITES

To test your knowledge of dinosaur discoveries, visit the National Geographic Kids website:
http://kids.nationalgeographic.com/Games/PuzzlesQuizzes/Brainteaserdinosaurs

For tons of information about the prehistoric world, visit National Geographic's website:
http://science.nationalgeographic.com/science/prehistoric-world.html

STEGOSAURUS
P. 128–129

PLACES TO VISIT

Dinosaur National Monument and Dinosaur Land Region

Field Museum of Natural History

Cleveland Museum of Natural History

Carnegie Museum of Natural History

Royal Ontario Museum

Canadian Museum of Nature

Harvard University Museum of Comparative Zoology

Dinosaur Isle

Natural History Museum

Yale Peabody Museum of Natural History

American Museum of Natural History

Academy of Natural Sciences

National Museum of Natural History

North Carolina Museum of Natural Sciences

Denver Museum of Natural History & Denver Museum of Nature and Science

Dallas Museum of Natural History & Fort Worth Museum of Science and History

Houston Museum of Natural Science

Oxford University Museum of Natural History

Sedgwick Museum of Earth Sciences, Cambridge University

The Natural History Museum

Royal Institute of Natural Sciences

Senckenberg Nature Museum

Natural History Museum, Humboldt University

Paleobiology Institute, Academy of Sciences

Paleontological Institute of the Russian Academy of Sciences

National Museum of Natural History

National Museum of Natural History

Natural History Museum

The Museum of Dinosaurs Esp eraza

Natural Science Museum

Museum of Earth Sciences

Geology Museum, Indian Statistical Institute

Beijing Museum of Natural History & The Institute of Vertebrate Paleontology and Paleoanthropology

National Science Museum

Gunma Museum of Natural History

Osaka Museum of Natural History

Dalian Museum of Natural History

Royal Tyrrell Museum

Museum of the Rockies

Utah Museum of Natural History

Thanksgiving Point: The Museum of Ancient Life

California Academy of Sciences & Museum of Paleontology, University of California

Natural History Museum of Los Angeles

New Mexico Museum of Natural History and Science

Mexico City Natural History Museum

NORTH AMERICA

SOUTH AMERICA

San Miguel de Tucum an Museum

Argentine Museum of Natural Sciences

Rio de Janeiro National Museum

Museum of La Plata University

EUROPE

ASIA

AFRICA

Bernard Price Institute for Palaeontological Research, University of Witwatersrand

AUSTRALIA

Western Australian Museum

South Australian Museum

Monash Science Centre

Queensland Museum

Australian Museum

• Dinosaur museum

For great information about paleontology, visit the American Museum of Natural History's Website:
http://www.amnh.org/ology/index.php?channel=paleontology

For facts, trivia, videos, and more, visit Don Lessem's Website:
http://www.dinodon.com/

For information about some of the best known dinosaurs, check out Dino Russ's Lair:
http://www.dinoruss.com/

For dinosaur jokes, quizzes, and much, much more, visit Enchanted Learning:
http://www.enchantedlearning.com/subjects/dinosaurs/

To learn all about *T. rex* Sue and many other dinosaurs, visit The Field Museum's website:
http://www.fieldmuseum.org/

For information about dinosaurs and paleontology, check out:
http://www.giftedkids.ie/dinosaurs.html

Read all about dinosaurs and play dinosaur games at the Dinosaurs for Kids Web site:
http://www.kidsdinos.com/

For links to lots of great kid-friendly dinosaur information, visit these sites:
http://www.kidsites.com/sites-edu/dinosaurs.htm

For a tour of geologic time, state-by-state fossil records, and much more, visit the University of California Museum of Paleontology:
http://www.ucmp.berkeley.edu/

MOVIES

NATIONAL GEOGRAPHIC

Bizarre Dinosaurs

Dinosaur Hunters: Secrets of the Gobi Desert

I Love Dinosaurs

Really Wild Animals: Dinosaurs and Other Creature Features

Sky Monsters

BBC

Allosaurus: A Walking with Dinosaurs Special

Chased by Dinosaurs

Walking with Dinosaurs

DISCOVERY

Clash of the Dinosaurs

Dinosaur Planet

Dinosaurs: Inside and Out

JANSON MEDIA

Dinosaur: Eggs & Babies

INDEX

Published by the National Geographic Society

John M. Fahey, Jr., *President and Chief Executive Officer*
Gilbert M. Grosvenor, *Chairman of the Board*
Tim T. Kelly, *President, Global Media Group*
John Q. Griffin, *Executive Vice President;*
  President, Publishing
Nina D. Hoffman, *Executive Vice President; President,*
  Book Publishing Group
Melina Gerosa Bellows, *Executive Vice President, Children's Publishing*

Prepared by the Book Division

Nancy Laties Feresten, *Vice President, Editor in Chief,*
  Children's Books
Jonathan Halling, *Design Director, Children's Publishing*
Jennifer Emmett, *Executive Editor, Reference and Solo,*
  Children's Books
Carl Mehler, *Director of Maps*
R. Gary Colbert, *Production Director*
Jennifer A. Thornton, *Managing Editor*

Staff for This Book

Priyanka Lamichhane, *Project Editor*
Eva Absher, *Art Director*
Lori Epstein, Annette Kiesow, *Illustrations Editors*
Eva Absher & Rachael Hamm Plett, *Designers*
Ruthie Thompson, *Production Designer*
Kate Olesin, *Editorial Assistant*
XNR Productions, *Map Research and Production*
Grace Hill, *Associate Managing Editor*
Lisa A. Walker, *Production Manager*
Susan Borke, *Legal and Business Affairs*

Manufacturing and Quality Management

Christopher A. Liedel, *Chief Financial Officer*
Phillip L. Schlosser, *Vice President*
Chris Brown, *Technical Director*
Nicole Elliott, *Manager*
Rachel Faulise, *Manager*

The National Geographic Society is one of the world's largest nonprofit scientific and educational organizations. Founded in 1888 to "increase and diffuse geographic knowledge," the Society works to inspire people to care about the planet. National Geographic reflects the world through its magazines, television programs, films, music and radio, books, DVDs, maps, exhibitions, live events, school publishing programs, interactive media and merchandise. *National Geographic* magazine, the Society's official journal, published in English and 32 local-language editions, is read by more than 35 million people each month. The National Geographic Channel reaches 310 million households in 34 languages in 165 countries. National Geographic Digital Media receives more than 13 million visitors a month. National Geographic has funded more than 9,200 scientific research, conservation and exploration projects and supports an education program promoting geography literacy. For more information, visit nationalgeographic.com.

For more information, please call 1-800-NGS LINE (647-5463) or write to the following address: National Geographic Society, 1145 17th Street N.W. Washington, D.C. 20036-4688 U.S.A.

Visit us online at www.nationalgeographic.com/books

For librarians and teachers: www.ngchildrensbooks.org

More for kids from National Geographic: kids.nationalgeographic.com

For information about special discounts for bulk purchases, please contact National Geographic Books Special Sales: ngspecsales@ngs.org

For rights or permissions inquiries, please contact National Geographic Books Subsidiary Rights: ngbookrights@ngs.org

Library of Congress Cataloging-in-Publication Data

Lessem, Don.
 National Geographic kids ultimate dinopedia : the most complete dinosaur reference ever / by Don Lessem ; illustrated by Franco Tempesta.
   p. cm.
 Includes bibliographical references and index.
 ISBN 978-1-4263-0164-3 (hardcover : alk. paper) -- ISBN 978-1-4263-0165-0 (lib. bdg. : alk. paper)
 1. Dinosaurs--Pictorial works--Juvenile literature. I. Tempesta, Franco, ill. II. National Geographic Society (U.S.) III. Title. IV. Title: Kids ultimate dinopedia.
 QE861.5.L4946 2010
 567.9--dc22
                                        2010007146

Printed in China

10/RRDS/1